D0375086

RESEARCH AND INFORMATION GUIDES
IN BUSINESS, INDUSTRY,
AND ECONOMIC INSTITUTIONS

THE AMERICAN STOCK EXCHANGE

GARLAND REFERENCE LIBRARY
OF SOCIAL SCIENCE
VOL. 768

RESEARCH AND INFORMATION GUIDES IN BUSINESS, INDUSTRY, AND ECONOMIC INSTITUTIONS

WAHIB NASRALLAH
General Editor

FRANCHISING BUSINESS
A Guide to Information Sources
by Lucy Heckman

THE INFORMAL ECONOMY
A Research Guide
by Abol Hassan Danesh

STAFF TRAINING
An Annotated Review of the Literature
by William Crimando and T.F. Riggar

THE WORLD BANK GROUP
A Guide to Information Sources
by Carol R. Wilson

GLOBAL COUNTERTRADE
An Annotated Bibliography
by Leon Zurawicki
and Louis Suichmezian

THE NEW YORK STOCK EXCHANGE
A Guide to Information Sources
by Lucy Heckman

THE AMERICAN STOCK EXCHANGE
A Guide to Information Resources
by Carol Z. Womack
and Alice C. Littlejohn

U.S. SECURITIES AND EXCHANGE COMMISSION
A Research and Information Guide
by John W. Graham

THE INTERNATIONAL MONETARY FUND, 1944–1992
A Research Guide
by Mary Elizabeth Johnson

To Tiffany + Bob.

Health, wealth + happiness!

THE AMERICAN STOCK EXCHANGE

A Guide to Information Resources

Carol Z. Womack

Carol Z. Womack
Alice C. Littlejohn

Alice C. Littlejohn

GARLAND PUBLISHING, Inc.
New York & London / 1995

Library of Congress Cataloging-in-Publication Data

Womack, Carol Z., 1946–
    The American Stock Exchange : a guide to informa-
tion resources / by Carol Z. Womack and Alice C.
Littlejohn.
        p.   cm. — (Research and information guides in
business, industry, and economic institutions ; v. 7)
(Garland reference library of social science ; vol. 768)
    Includes indexes.
    ISBN 0-8153-0223-1
    1. American Stock Exchange—Bibliography.
2. Stock exchanges—New York (N.Y.)—Bibliography.
I. Littlejohn, Alice C.   II. Title.   III. Series.
IV. Series: Garland reference library of social science ;
v. 768.
Z7164.F5W86   1995
[HG4575.2]
332.64'273—dc20   94-42750
                                                               CIP

Printed on acid-free, 250-year-life paper
Manufactured in the United States of America

SERIES FOREWORD

The new information society has exceeded everyone's expectations in providing new and exciting media for the collection and dissemination of data. Such proliferation has been matched by a similar increase in the number of providers of business literature. Furthermore, many emerging technologies, financial fields, and management processes have amassed an amazing body of knowledge in a short period of time. Indicators are that packaging of information will continue its trend of diversification, confounding even the experienced researcher. How then will information seekers identify and assess the adequacy and relevancy of various packages to their research needs?

It is my hope that Garland's *Research and Information Guides in Business, Industry, and Economic Institutions* series will bridge the gap between classical forms of literature and new alternative formats. Each guide will be devoted to an industry, a profession, a managerial process, or a field of study. Organization of the guides will emphasize subject access to formats such as bibliographic and numeric databases on-line, distributed databases, CD-Rom products, loose-leaf services, government publications and books, and periodical articles. Although most of the guides will serve as locators and bridges to bodies of knowledge, some may be reference books with self-contained information.

Since compiling such guides requires substantial knowledge in the organization of information or the field of study, authors are selected on the basis of their expertise as information professionals or subject specialists. Inquiries about the series and its content should be addressed to the Series Editor.

Wahib Nasrallah
Langsam Library
University of Cincinnati

TABLE OF CONTENTS

PREFACE

This guide to information resources on the American Stock Exchange is not intended to be a detailed history of the Amex. It does cover the literature of the Exchange from 1900 through 1993. Research methodology included searching of major cataloging systems, reviewing of print and electronic indexes, and summarizing of publications in the American Stock Exchange library. All publications identified were read and summarized.

The guide is arranged into numbered, annotated records. Three indices provide references to the numbered records by titles, personal names and subjects. Organization of the seven chapters is:

Chapter 1. An introduction and brief history of the Exchange.

Chapters 2-4. Chronological histories of the Exchange.

Chapters 5-7. Special subjects: "non-stock" products of the Exchange, governance and surveillance by outside agencies, and seat price as an economic indicator. In table format, this final chapter includes nearly 700 articles from the *New York Times* and *Wall Street Journal* reporting changes in membership prices.

Three appendices contain highlights of annual reports of the Exchange; a select list of publications by and about the Exchange which includes serials, media, and software; and, a glossary of terms used in the book.

A special effort was made not to include general materials on stock exchanges or the stock market. To expand the picture of American exchanges and trading provided by publications summarized in this guide, we recommend Lucy Heckman's *The New York Stock Exchange: a Guide to Information Resources* (New York: Garland Publishing, Inc., 1992).

Thanks are due to a number of persons whose assistance made this work possible. At the American Stock Exchange, the staffs of the library and public relations offices were especially helpful. Our greatest debt is to the interlibrary loan staffs of our respective institutions: at the University of California, Irvine, Pam LaZarr, Lynn Long, Mimi Upton, and Pat Staump, and student assistants Kevin Larson and Eric Merkt; at California State University, Long Beach, Cathrine Lewis Ida, Sharlene LaForge and Victoria Lima.

Carol Z. Womack
Alice C. Littlejohn
1994

Chapter 1

INTRODUCTION AND HISTORY

The American stock exchanges trace their roots to the birth of the nation and the presidency of George Washington. The first exchange activities included the selling of lottery tickets, insurance, and commodities. Washington's first government office was established in New York, close to the activities of Wall Street. When the United States Treasury first issued bonds, the Wall Street brokers sold them, along with commercial paper issued by banks and insurance companies. As exchanges began to organize, a group of merchants joined to form the New York Stock Exchange and to buy and sell shares in companies. Other trading remained outdoors; these outdoor traders were known as "curbstone brokers" as early as the 1830s. They traded in new and small companies, establishing a trend maintained throughout development of the American Stock Exchange.

The late 1800s and Gold Rush constituted a key era in the history of the American Stock Exchange. Mining and railroad companies emerged to take advantage of activity in the West. Considered too speculative to be traded on the New York Stock Exhange, many found a home on the street. The curb market grew and traders developed an elaborate system of communication--hand signals representing price and volume information. In addition to the American Stock Exchange, the curb market generated the New York Gold Exchange, the Open Board of Stock Brokers, the Mining Exchange, and the Petroleum and Stock Board, along with small securities boards and organizations trading commodities futures and securities.

The Early Years

In 1908, formal organization of the Exchange began. Curbstone broker Emanuel S. Mendels, Jr., developed the Curb Market Agency with trading rules which proved ineffectual. In 1911, a group led by Mendels formed the New York Curb Association and drafted a constitution. The brokers moved indoors to Trinity Place in June 1921.

The bull market of the 1920s concluded in the crash of 1929. While the media reported record trading followed by a market crash and hysterical selling, the annual report of the New York Curb Exchange (NYCE) recognized only record trading volumes and a high peak of prosperity. The NYCE traded a record 7,096,000 shares in one day, October 19, 1929. Memberships sold at a high of $254,000. In 1930, the Exchange finally noted that a sharp industrial recession had occurred in the second half of 1929. Memberships sold at a low $70,000.

In 1931, only one-third of the Exchange's stocks paid dividends, but recovery was in progress. The Exchange began introducing new products, a strategy which became its continuing response to competition from the New York Stock Exchange and the emerging over-the-counter market. The introduction of American Depositary Receipts enabled Americans to trade in the shares of foreign stocks.

The federal government established the Securities and Exchange Commission in 1934 and new rules were drafted in an attempt to prevent another crash.

The end of World War II ushered in a new bull market. The Amex continued to create new instruments which were rapidly copied by the other exchanges. The Amex was first to look into automation of routine trading functions. It was during this new "golden age" that the Amex was able to attract growing numbers of young entrepreneurial companies.

In 1946, the Amex celebrated 25 years of indoor trading and finally noted signs of growth in the economy and in the securities market. Business continued to improve in the aftermath of the war; market value and volume of securities traded continued to grow. The ticker system expanded across the United States and into Canada, and members established offices in eight foreign countries.

The Fifties and Sixties

The title American Stock Exchange was adopted in 1953. During the Fifties, the public became more interested in investing in securities, and technology began to play a role, providing instantaneous price quotes. The Exchange defined its future in technology and derivative products.

The year 1960, one of the three most active in the history of the Exchange, was followed, in 1961, by one of the most difficult years in the history of the Exchange. The largest scandal in the Exchange's history, involving the Res, resulted in a major investigation of the Exchange by the Securities and Exchange Commisssion and the resignation of Exchange Chairman Edward T. McCormick.

Automation

In 1964, Am-Quote was introduced, featuring an electronic voice which gave subscribers trade information on all Amex stocks, handling 72,000 inquiries per hour. As the volume of paperwork increased and operational problems multiplied, the Amex continually sought electronic solutions. As the Exchange provided the leadership, many advances led to partnerships.

In 1971, the Amex announced plans to consolidate its communications, clearing and automation facilities with the New York Stock Exchange into a jointly owned subsidiary, the Securities Industry Automation Corporation (SIAC). In 1973, SIAC announced plans for a computer system called Centaur, which would automate communications, trading, reporting and clearing operations. SIAC merged with the National Clearing Corporation and began clearing for NASD in 1975; clearing costs for the industry were reduced by several million dollars per year. In January 1977, the SEC approved the merger of the NASD's National Clearing Corporation, the NYSE's Stock Clearing Corporation, and the Amex's Exchange Clearing Corporation into a single entity, the National Securities Clearing Corporation (NSCC). By 1980, the Amex and SIAC were looking at network design; the Amex adopted AMNET to reduce the floor space required by hardware and wiring needs.

The Exchange joined the Committee on Uniform Security Identification Procedures (CUSIP) in 1972 to require the use of unique alpha-numeric codes to provide electronic identification of stock certificates for quick processing. By 1974, a consolidated transaction-reporting tape had been introduced. In 1978, the major exchanges moved toward a Congressionally mandated national market system with the Intermarket Trading System, a composite quotation system which electronically displayed bid and asked prices and allowed traders at any of the five exchanges to determine the best available price.

By the Eighties, the Amex continued to establish "firsts" in automation. AUTOPER, a touch sensitive screen display, allowed traders to interact with the Exchange floor in buying and selling stocks. In 1986, the Amex converted from its Digital Equipment Corporation (DEC) machines to Tandem and Stratus computers to provide fault-tolerant architecture. By 1990, DEC was back as the need for fault tolerance was less obvious and flexibility was in.

AMOS (Amex Options Switching System), developed in 1978, was extended by AUTO-EX to provide automatic and instant execution of market orders in the Major Market Index. Quick-Quote continued to allow specialists to update a number of options quotes simultaneously.

An alliance with Reuters Holdings PLC and its subsidiary, Instinet, which provided an electronic order-execution system, opened immediate two-way access to the Amex floor for foreign investors. Building on Reuters technology, the Amex built SITUS, a system for trading privately placed stocks and bonds through Reuters' worldwide electronic trading system.

Products

Aggressive marketing became a major theme for the Amex. The Market Value Index was introduced in 1973 and a plan to trade options was developed. Further expansion included markets in gold and silver commodities, mortgage futures, U.S. government securities, and bonds of foreign companies. In 1976, the Amex Board of Governors approved dual trading of stock, opening the doors to direct competition with the NYSE.

Internationalization became key. In 1977, foreign issues constituted one of every 20 stock issues traded. The Amex extablished a trading link with the Toronto Stock Exchange in 1984. The offering of Major Market Index options on the floor of the European Options Exchange in Amsterdam marked the first time that a U.S. index option was available for trading before the opening of markets in New York. The Exchange also filed an application with the SEC to trade an International Market Index which would create the first broad worldwide index with real time pricing of the component securities during the U.S. trading day. As 1989 turned into 1990, the last and first stock listings were for foreign companies. The Exchange listed a truly international product, put warrants issued by the Kingdom of Denmark, underwritten by America's Goldman Sachs, and based on the Nikkei Stock Average of leading Japanese companies. In the 1990s, the Amex continued its drive toward globalization through alliances with Reuters Holdings PLC and through the advent of warrant trading on the London Financial Times-Stock Exchange 100 Share Index and on France's CAC 40. In 1991, an alliance with both Reuters and the Chicago Board Options Exchange established an after-hours trading market for equities, options and derivatives. In 1992, strategic alliances were formed with the stock exchanges in Argentina, Chile, Brazil, Spain, Hong Kong, and Malaysia.

The Amex Commodities Exchange (ACE) began trading GNMA futures in 1978. In 1981, the Amex listed the highest number of new issues in nine years. The American Gold Coin Exchange, a new subsidiary, began trading in the Canadian Maple Leaf and later added four other gold bullion coins. A year later, the Amex began trading in interest rate options on U.S. Treasury notes and bills. In 1983, four new index options were initiated: the Major Market Index (XMI), Market Value Index (XAM), Computer Technology Index (XCI), and the Oil and Gas Index (XOI).

In 1989, the Amex celebrated 15 consecutive years of profitability with a net income of over $4 million and filed with the SEC to begin trading in two new products: options based on an index of 50 foreign stocks and options on a Japanese index. The Amex answered the need for trading in emerging growth companies in 1992 by establishing the Emerging Company Marketplace, the first new marketplace in 20 years. Beleaguered in its early days by the quality of listings, the marketplace survives. In 1993, it lists 22 companies and trades over 66 million shares; 12 companies graduated to the primary list, two were delisted, and two transferred back to NASDAQ. Several new products were on the way--basket instruments, international products and futures in areas such as fixed-income securities.

People

The history of the Exchange is not just dollars, paper, and environmental impact. It is also, and perhaps primarily, about people--the traders, the administrators, the investors. They cannot all be mentioned here, but some are far more frequently cited in this work than others.

Notable in a negative sense are the Res--Gerard A. and his son, Gerard F., specialists who made more than $10 million illegally over a six year period in the 1950s by rigging prices of stocks for which they served as specialists. They were expelled from the Exchange in 1961. This scandal also ended the tenure of the Exchange's longest serving chief executive officer. Edward T. McCormick assumed the presidency of the New York Curb Exchange in 1951, served as the first president of the American Stock Exchange when the new title was adopted in 1953, and ended his ten-year tenure through resignation because of his involvement in the Re scandal.

Also frequently mentioned in the literature are the succeeding chief executive officers of the Exchange. In 1962, in the wake of the Re scandal, the Exchange selected 37-year-old Edwin Deacon Etherington to lead reorganization. He moved the Exchange from a committee system toward professional staffing and automation. Standards were raised and 63 stocks were delisted; these losses were more than offset by new arrivals from the over-the-counter market. He was succeeded, in 1966, by Ralph Southey Saul, who had headed the Securities and Exchange Commission probe of the Amex four years earlier. Saul became noteworthy for modernization of the trading floor, establishment of surveillance procedures, and upgrade of listing standards and disclosure requirements for corporate developments. Arthur Levitt, Jr., assumed the chairmanship in 1978, establishing himself as the head of the people's exchange by championing small business. The Exchange excelled in public relations; broker clubs were formed. Levitt was replaced, in 1989, by a Washington insider, James R. Jones. Jones led a customer-driven strategy and the internationalization of trading. To keep the Exchange competitive, he encouraged new trading instruments such as warrants for trading puts and calls on foreign market instruments and the Emerging Marketplace, designed to serve as an incubator market for small companies.

The Seventies and Eighties

As the Exchange matured, trading share and dollar volume continually reached record levels. The Amex began trading stock options in January 1975.

In the 1980s, the Amex was an aggressive, innovative force in the world market; its mix of equities and options made it the nation's best balanced market. The year 1983 was extremely successful. For the first time, the Amex traded over two billion shares, surpassing previous weekly, monthly, and annual highs. The Amex Market Value Index gained 31 percent, outperforming all other leading indicators. Nearly one third of Amex stocks appreciated by 50 percent or more. The Amex, in 1984, became the first stock exchange to transmit live television broadcasts via satellite across the country through the Cable News Network (CNN).

On October 19, 1987, a tidal wave of trading started in the Far East, swept across Europe, and crashed onto the U.S. markets. On October 19th and 20th, volume soared three times higher than the year's previous average until specialists intervened. The big loser on Black Monday was the small investor.

Conclusion

As this history closes, the Exchange thrives as both an equities market and leading trader of derivative securities in a high-speed trading arena based on leading edge technology.

Records continued to be established. The year 1993 ranked first in annual share volume with 4,582,013,270 shares traded. Share volume for three days in 1993 ranked among the top ten days in history; the all-time record is 43,432,760 shares traded on October 20, 1987. Trading in foreign issues reached an all-time high: 894,859,370 shares for 90 issues, 19.5 percent of Amex trading volume.

The price of membership, a seat, on the Amex has ranged from a low of $650 in 1942 to a high of $420,000 on October 9, 1987 and again on October 16th of the same year. The Amex has 661 full members and 193 options principal members. It lists 868 companies and 1,005 issues. It also lists 58 individual stock options including four broad-based index options and a number of stock index options: the Major Market Index, the XMI LEAPS Index, Standard & Poor's MidCap 400 Index, the Institutional Index, the Japan Index, the Eurotop 100 Index, the Biotechnology Index, the Computer Technology Index, the North American Telecommunications Index, the Morgan Stanley Consumer and Cyclical Indexes, the Oil Index, and the Pharmaceutical Index. Introduced in 1993 were LEAPS (Long-Term Equity AnticiPation Securities) on the Biotechnology, Pharmaceutical and MidCap Indexes and FLEX (FLEXible Exchange Index Options) on the Institutional, Major Market and MidCap Indexes.

As this chronology concludes at the end of 1993, a search was in progress for a new chairman of the Exchange. Richard F. Syron, president of the Boston Federal Reserve Bank, was named chairman on February 10, 1994. (See: "New Amex Chairman," *New York Times*, 11 February 1994, Section D, p. 2 and "Amex Names Boston Fed's Syron Its New Chairman," *Wall Street Journal*, 11 February 1994, Section B, p. 3.)

The "last" publication cited in this record of the American Stock Exchange is most appropriate. On December 31, 1993, the *Wall Street Journal* reported the imminent release of the Securities and Exchange Commission's Market 2000 report, focusing on issues of technology and competition. Its publication early in 1994 provided not an end to this chronology of literature on the Exchange, but a new beginning with a look toward the emerging era of electronic trading systems. (United States. Securities and Exchange Commission. Division of Market Regulation. *Market 2000: an examination of current equity market developments.* Washington: The Commission. For sale by the Superintendent of Documents, USGPO, 1994.)

Chapter 2

CURB EXCHANGE: EARLY HISTORY
(1900-1953)

The early half century of the Exchange includes its most colorful period. It begins as the Curb operates outdoors at the corners of William and Beaver Streets and at Broad Street and Exchange Place and includes the move indoors to Trinity Place. The designation of the Exchange progresses through five variations: the Outdoor Curb, the New York Curb Agency (1908), the New York Curb Market Association (1911), the New York Curb Market (1921), and the New York Curb Exchange (1929). Trading in foreign stock issues is inaugurated and American Depositary Receipts (ADR) are born. Early history ends as the Exchange becomes the American Stock Exchange in 1953.

BOOKS, DOCUMENTS, & REPORTS

1. New York Curb Exchange, Committee on Public Relations. *New York Curb Exchange*. New York: Curb Exchange, 1937.

> The Curb Exchange, predecessor of the American Stock Exchange, had its origins out of doors. During the Civil War, trading ran from 8 a.m. to 6 p.m. In 1908, the New York Curb Agency was founded by a group of "Curb" brokers. It became the New York Curb Market in 1911 and was organized as a voluntary association. Offices were located at 6 Wall Street and a Listing Department was created. Trading hours were 10 a.m. to 3 p.m. during the week and 10 a.m. to noon on Saturdays. Soon business increased substantially and the outdoor market became inadequate. The original building was officially opened on June 27, 1921; an addition was built in 1931. In 1929, the market officially became the New York Curb Exchange. This book describes the then "current" operations of the Exchange: the stock and bond trading floors, the quotation system, the hand signalling system developed by the traders, the clearing system. The Exchange was composed of a Board of Governors and several standing committees: Arbitration, Agreements, Business Conduct, Commissions, Constitution, Finance, Law, Listing, Membership, Public Relations, Quotations, Securities, and a General Committee. The many photographs are particularly interesting.

2. Sterling, Dorothy. *Wall Street: the Story of the Stock Exchange*. Garden City, N. Y.: Doubleday, 1955.

> A popular history of the American stock exchange system, beginning with the indoor and outdoor markets which became the New York and American exchanges.

Information is dated, but the pictures are interesting: traders "hand signalling" the alphabet and number systems; telephone clerks in the "grandstand" facing the brokers; and, the "curb market" in its heyday.

3. Sobel, Robert. *The Curbstone Brokers: the Origins of the American Stock Exchange.* New York: Macmillan, 1970.

Sobel tells the story of the outdoor markets of Manhattan from the late eighteenth century to 1921, when the last of them went indoors. The focus is not on the markets, but on the brokers themselves. Whether they were at the corner of William and Beaver Streets or at Broad Street near Exchange Place, the Curb brokers provided the "most picturesque, exciting, and incomprehensible segment of American business." While the Big Board members frequented the North Shore of Long Island and Park Avenue, the Curb brokers came from middle class homes in Nutley, New Jersey, or Brooklyn Heights. From McCormack to McCormick, from Mendels to Morgan, the book abounds with names. In "An Essay on Sources and Methodology," Sobel notes the absolute lack of primary sources and the importance of interviews with surviving members of the Curb. An interesting appendix provides excerpts from *The Curb News*, 1909-1911, a weekly newsletter with an annual subscription rate of two dollars.

ARTICLES

1904

4. "The Curb and the Men Who Compose It," *New York Times*, 23 October 1904, sec. IV, p. 5.

A literary sketch of the few hundred "pushing and shouting men" who work the outdoor market. They have one rule only--all contracts are binding.

1905

5. "Asks Police To Stop Curb Brokers' Racket," *New York Times*, 14 June 1905, p. 16.

Police Commissioner William McAdoo is more concerned with the food and drink peddlers on the curb than he is with the noise of the traders.

6. "Curb Market Escapes Command To Move On," *New York Times*, 17 June 1905, p. 2.

Police Commissioner McAdoo works out a compromise that keeps the traders within bounds on the street and chases away loiterers; this gives the Curb Market official recognition.

1911

7. "Curb Ready for War on Swindling Stocks," *New York Times*, 9 February 1911, p. 9.

> A new constitution is sent out for members' signatures. The organization is modeled after the New York Stock Exchange and is designed to eliminate irresponsible brokers and worthless stocks from the outside market. The market's new name will be the New York Curb Market.

8. "Curb Organized Now," *New York Times*, 18 March 1911, p. 15.

> The Curb Association will control the outside market; officers are elected. A Board of Representatives made up of 15 outside brokers will govern the association; major functions will be exercised through subcommittees, as with the Stock Exchange.

1919

9. "Curb Brokers Form a Realty Company," *New York Times*, 12 June 1919, p. 5.

> This is the first step in regulating the market. The company's job is to lease property in the financial district, to move the market indoors and to construct a building for the market.

10. "Seek a Building for Curb Market," *New York Times*, 22 June 1919, sec. II, p. 1.

> The Board of Representatives limits future membership in the market to 500.

11. "Exit the Curb Market," *Independent and Weekly Review* 99 (July 26, 1919): 112-114.

> District Attorney's office prosecutes based on alleged offerings of fraudulent companies. Reforms include moving the market inside depriving New York sightseers a view of what is perhaps the "most picturesque part of Wall Street."

12. "Curb Market's New Plans," *New York Times*, 21 December 1919, sec. I, p. 23.

> Chairman Edward R. McCormick announces two classes of membership: present active membership, including those who may be elected to membership by the Board of Representatives; and associate membership. Active members will pay an initiation fee of $250 and a membership fee of $500. Associate members will have no floor privileges and will pay nominal initiation fees and dues for transactions. Nearly 100 checks have already been received.

13. "Curb Moving Will Relieve Wall St," *New York Times*, 21 December 1919, sec. I, p. 23.

The purchase of the building formerly occupied by American Bond Note Co. in Trinity Place will provide indoor quarters for the Curb Market and offices for some of its members. Office space is now at a premium in the financial district. Almost without exception, new buildings are fully rented before completion. Lack of office space is causing brokers to relocate client services uptown while maintaining a clearing office in the financial district.

1920

14. "Curb Market To Leave the Curb," *Literary Digest* 64 (March 20, 1920): 152.

The Curb Market Association pays one million dollars for a plot of land running along Trinity Church Yard. A real estate board is working with architects. Association officers are concerned about health of members who have spent working hours out of doors in all weather and now will be shut up within four walls.

15. "New Curb Market Building at Greenwich Street and Trinity Place To Cost About $1,300,000," *New York Times*, 5 December 1920, sec. IX, p. 9.

Article provides description and illustrations of the Curb Market's new building. Ground is broken on property that cost $1,000,000. The second floor will house the Board Room; the third floor will have executive offices for the Association. The four functions of the Curb Market include: the sale of issues of companies during organization or reorganization; a market for stocks of companies in the process of development; a market for mining, oil and industrial stocks not listed on the Stock Exchange; a market for Standard Oil stock. Trading on the street will be unauthorized.

16. "Confessions of a Curb Broker," *Collier's* 50 (December 18, 1920): 8-9.

A Curb broker explains the language, listings, dealings and financing of trading. He remains anonymous to avoid "being boycotted and ostracized by every broker and employee inside the Curb Association and out." As he begins his tale, he notes: "One minute after ten o'clock on the first Monday morning in December 1912, I stole fifty dollars. . . . my victims were a trusting pair of properous gamblers. . . . I am a reputable broker and trader on the New York Curb . . . daily I operate in stocks worth many thousands by a mere nod of the head, sometimes with an almost imperceptible wink."

1921

17. "Curb Market Goes Indoors Tomorrow," *New York Times*, 26 June 1921, sec. II, p. 9.

>   In 1909, E. S. Mendels set up a committee to draw up rules and regulations for the Curb exchange. During the war the Stock Exchange closed and the Curb Market expanded. It traded its own stocks and those of the Exchange. The move indoors is designed primarily for the purpose of controlling the traders.

18. "Curb Market Deserts the Curb," *Literary Digest* LXX:2 (July 9, 1921): 42-44.

>   The Curb moves inside. Gone is the "holiday crowd, the mob scene from 'Julius Caesar'." Speculation predicts that a new association will spring up on Broad Street.

1922

19. "Find Curb Market Useful to Business," *New York Times*, 11 July 1922, p. 24.

>   In response to a questionnaire of the Bureau of Business Research of New York University, members of the American Economic Association express their belief in the economic necessity of both the Curb Market and the Stock Exchange. Of the 203 responses, only four say the Market should not continue. A majority of the members state that to abolish either would be disastrous or would lead to the setting up of substitutes. They further state that if the Curb were abolished, it would injure business in general and retard industrial development and the mobility of capital.

1923

20. "Clearing House for Curb," *New York Times*, 21 February 1923, p. 28.

>   Plans are made for the establishment of a clearing house for securities trades by the Curb Market at 51 Exchange Place. All regular members and associates of their New York offices will be members of the organization.

1926

21. "Curb Leases New Clearing House," *New York Times*, 16 February 1926, p. 34.

>   With a total of 300 issues now being cleared, new quarters are leased at 30 Broad Street.

22. "New Tickers for the Curb," *New York Times*, 30 September 1926, p. 36.

> New York Stock Exchange quotations will be projected on the floor of the Curb by "movie tickers" installed by Trans-Lux Daylight Picture Screen Corp. This is only the second time in history that the NYSE has allowed projection of its quotations on the floor of another exchange; the first was at the Chicago Stock Exchange in January 1926.

23. "Curb Seeks Margin Data," *New York Times*, 10 December 1926, p. 44.

> Members who carry margin accounts for customers must furnish to the Business Conduct Committee statements on their financial condition. A certified accountant of the Exchange will determine whether additional information or capital must be supplied. The accountant will not know the identity of the customer in question and strict confidence will be maintained.

1927

24. "More Office Space for Curb," *New York Times*, 17 May 1927, p. 48.

> The Curb's listing department moves to larger quarters in the Trinity Court Building. The offices are accessible to the Curb Exchange via a connection between Trinity Court and the Curb Exchange Building.

1928

25. "2 Exchanges Here Will Close Tomorrow," *New York Times*, 4 May 1928, p. 37.

> Trading will be suspended for a day to permit members to catch up on their books. All other business will be transacted as usual. The excited trading of the last eight weeks has overtaxed brokerage personnel, who are not now returning phone calls or answering questions about trades. The close will make it possible to return to work "with the same good temper and courtesy as in the past."

1929

26. "Curb Substitutes 'Exchange' for 'Market' in Its Name," *New York Times*, 27 June 1929, p. 41.

> Members vote to use "exchange" in the Curb's title.

27. "Worst Stock Crash Stemmed By Banks; 12,894,650-Share Day Swamps Market," *New York Times*, 25 October 1929, pp. 1, 2.

Bankers say the market crash was caused by technical rather than fundamental considerations. Total sales for the Curb were 6,337,415, compared with the record of 3,715,499 set Monday. Bonds were strong, reaching a volume of $23,233,000, the biggest day since 1926.

28. "6,337,400 Share Day Sets a New Curb Record," *New York Times*, 25 October 1929, p. 2.

Prices decline 10-75 points and the ticker lags three hours in a severe wave of selling.

29. "Exchanges Defer Action for Closing," *New York Times*, 26 October 1929, p. 23.

The exchanges decide not to suspend trading because it might create suspicion in the minds of some and bring further hysterical selling. The market will be open Sunday to catch up on clerical work.

30. "Stocks Mount in Strong All-Day Rally," *New York Times*, 31 October 1929, pp. 1, 2.

The Exchange closes on Friday and Saturday due to the exhaustion of brokerage staff. Turnover at the Curb was only 3,809,200 shares. The ticker was just an hour late all day. Suspension of trading meets with approval in the financial district.

31. "5 Hour Day Monday on Stock Market," *New York Times*, 23 November 1929, p. 2.

The regular schedule resumes, but the Exchange will close on Thursday (Thanksgiving), Friday, and Saturday. The Exchange has been open three hours daily since November 6th.

32. "Curb, with Bull as Emblem, Adopts Optimistic Slogans," *New York Times*, 7 December 1929, p. 32.

"For Better Business Be Bullish" and "Prepare for Prosperity" are printed on lapel buttons being distributed to reporters, pages and telephone clerks on the floor of the Exchange. The buttons are part of a campaign stimulated by President Hoover's policy of inspiring confidence in the business world. The buttons are red, white and blue, the size of a half dollar, with the head of a bull in the center.

1931

33. "Curb Open for Inspection Next Week," *New York Times*, 9 September 1931, p. 43.

    Governors of the New York Curb Exchange send out invitations to inspect the new building at 86 Trinity Place.

34. "New Home Dedicated by Curb Exchange," *New York Times*, 15 September 1931, p. 37.

    The new building is regarded as the most modern securities exchange in the country. The trading floor has specially designed trading posts and telephone booths.

1933

35. "Curb Curbed," *Business Week* (July 19, 1933): 17-18.

    The New York Curb Exchange puts into effect new rules on trading in unlisted stocks and bonds. By decree of the governors, symbols on the ticker must separate listed from unlisted issues, companies must have been operating for not less than two years and show "satisfactory earnings," and companies must furnish stockholders financial statements certified by independent accountants at least once a year. The new regulations are the Exchange's promise of reform to New York's Attorney General, who was investigating unlisted practices on the Exchange.

1934

36. "Exchange Advisers Get Work Outlined," *New York Times*, 13 December 1934, p. 35.

    The Advisory Council of the New York Stock Exchange delivers for the first time suggestions on which decisions will later be made, including the feasibility of merging the New York and Curb Exchanges. The Council has discussed virtually every major policy area.

1935

37. "Curb To Enlarge Bond Section," *New York Times*, 3 February 1935, sec. II, p. 12.

    The trading floor has been rearranged for increased bond business. The new department will occupy an area three times its current size.

38. Adams, Mildred, "Expectant Wall Street," *New York Times*, 23 June 1935, sec. VII, pp. 5, 17.

> Having accepted reform, the Curb now watches and waits for another boom. The Curb is brighter and more modern than its big brother, the NYSE; it never filled the space it planned for itself in the booming days of 1929. The floor is neither dull nor hectic, sad nor cheerful. The investors who created the bull market of 1928-29 are now "scared stiff."

1936

39. "Second Firm Asks Stock for Counter," *New York Times*, 1 September 1936, p. 29.

> Bristol and Willett, a large over-the-counter house in New York, asks to trade preferred American District Telegraph Co. stock because of insufficient public trading on the Curb Exchange. The first request was by Tweedy and Co. to take over trading for Piedmont and Northern Railway Co. and Suburban Homes Co. from the Curb.

1938

40. "Curb's Plan Calls for Paid Executives," *New York Times*, 8 July 1938, p. 21.

> The Curb's new constitution, if approved, will create a smaller board of governors and a reduction in the number and size of committees. An executive vice president will be paid $20,000 to $25,000 per year. This reorganization is an attempt to adapt the recommendations of the New York Stock Exchange's Carl C. Conway Committee to the special needs of the Curb. The paid executive will correspond to the paid president of the Stock Exchange, will have direct charge of the technical staffs, and cannot be a member of the Curb Exchange. A president will be elected by the membership and will be a member; currently the president is elected by the Board of Governors. Committee duties will be advisory rather than administrative. Current president Fred Moffatt sees this as a more efficient operation.

41. "Curb Reform Plan," *Newsweek* 12 (September 12, 1938): 35.

> The New York Curb, the nation's second largest exchange with eight percent of dollar volume of sales (compared to the Big Board's 88 percent), follows the New York Stock Exchange toward reorganization. A special committee reporting to the Curb's Board of Governers recommends: no paid head, greater responsibility for salaried employees, a smaller board, and establishment of four administrative departments.

42. "Curb's New Constitution Approved by 353-2 Vote," *New York Times*, 13 December 1938, p. 37.

> The new constitution passes almost unanimously. A previous vote for reorganization taken in October passed 416 to 1.

1939

43. "General Clearings Proposed for Curb," *New York Times*, 15 June 1939, pp. 35, 40.

> The Board of Governors passes and submits to membership an amendment to the constitution which authorizes the New York Curb Exchange Securities Clearing Corporation to act as clearinghouse for the nation. Its facilities would be made available to all over-the-counter firms. It would take effect June 29th and would grant the clearing corporation the authority to settle transactions made off the floor. The Curb Exchange would receive additional revenues for the service from the clearing corporation and OTC firms would have an important new convenience, cutting down on paperwork and expense.

1940

44. "Officers of Corporations, For First Time, Become Associate Members of the Curb," *New York Times*, 10 July 1940, p. 27.

> Under a new rule regarding corporate memberships, the Curb Board of Governors approves the applications of Joseph J. Bodell, John S. Young, and Fred L. Clarke to become associate members of the Curb. Bodell was formerly senior partner of Bodell & Co., formed in 1909. The firm became a corporation on June 26th, with Bodell as president. Young and Clarke were associate members of the Curb as Young, Clarke & Co., which recently dissolved. They joined Durk-Harbison Co., Inc., of Los Angeles, as officers and directors. The new rule took effect on December 21, 1938.

45. "Curb Exchange Hunts Business," *Business Week* (October 19, 1940): 55-57.

> Faced with decimated volume, exchanges begin aggressively seeking business. The New York Curb encourages newspapers across the country to print figures for local investors (the South and West are found "woefully deficient") and arranges broadcast of daily activities with 300 radio stations.

1941

46. "Curb Seeks To Rent Part of Building," *New York Times*, 12 June 1941, p. 35.

   Because of declining business volume resulting from Wall Street's continuing deflation, the Curb is making available 20-25,000 square feet of space on five floors of its main building on Trinity Place and an additional 7,500 square feet in the Hamilton Building at 22 Thames.

47. "Seeking Volume," *Business Week* (September 13, 1941): 74-75.

   The New York Curb proposes dealer trading to the Securities and Exchange Commission to increase sales volume. Members of the Exchange and of the National Association of Securities Dealers would record bids as "price less a stated amount of discount."

1942

48. "Wall Street Woes," *Business Week* (March 7, 1942): 78-79.

   Yearly results for 1941 are in the red. The Curb's losses include an $18,000 write-off representing loss on investment in the New York World's Fair. Solution boosts transaction cost by one cent for stocks selling between 50 cents and $10 a share and a minimum commission of 35 cents for stocks selling for $90 a share or more.

1946

49. "Curb To Pay 15.2% Bonus," *New York Times*, 9 April 1946, p. 38.

   A 15.2 percent bonus is granted to employees for the first quarter of 1946 under the Exchange's incentive compensation plan. The bonus was based on the ratio of employees (327) to the average reported volume of trading in stocks.

50. Williams, Warren, "Curb Market, Growing Pains Over, Aiming at Bigger Financial Role," *New York Times*, 30 June 1946, sec. III, pp. 1, 2.

   In celebration of its 25th anniversary indoors, the Curb Exchange hosts a gathering of financial leaders at the Waldorf-Astoria. The Curb, traditionally the incubator for new issues that later graduate to the Big Board, is determined to make its list and the services it offers to corporations a better investment.

51. "Trading: Whether To Curb the Curb Exchange," *Newsweek* 28 (July 15, 1946): 70, 72.

> Having celebrated their 25th anniversary indoors, the Curb is attacked by the Ohio state securities commission for listing securities without earnings and "misleading the general investing public." The company in question is the Kaiser-Frazer Corporation, whose stock price doubled in a year.

52. Williams, Warren, "New Listings Rate Priority on Curb," *New York Times*, 18 November 1946, p. 40.

> The Curb leads American exchanges in providing stock and bond issues from other parts of the world. Today more than 140 foreign issues have unlisted trading privileges on the Curb. Acting in conjunction with Guaranty Trust Co. of New York, the Curb pioneered the system of American Depositary Receipts now commonly used for trading in foreign shares in this country. The future rebuilding in Europe will bring new European issues and revive activity; additional future financial expansion and industrial development opportunities lie across the Pacific in the Far East and south in Central and South America.

1947

53. "Indoors," *Business Week* (March 15, 1947): 44, 46-49.

> Francis Adams Truslow assumes the presidency of the Curb at a time when things are looking up. The Curb's greatest advantages are a "seasoning" market and a cheap method of advertising for new stock issues. The market didn't lose its eccentricities when it moved out of Broad Street. "Finger talk" and "high pitched whoops" continue.

1951

54. Crane, Burton, "New York Curb Leading Market in Nation for Trading in Foreign Concerns' Shares," *New York Times*, 2 December 1951, sec. III, pp. 1, 8.

> The Curb Exchange now trades 111 foreign stock issues, almost five times as many as the New York Stock Exchange. The reason can be traced back to the boom years of the Twenties when shares by two British companies were sold to the general public. Investors quickly realize how greatly the British stock market practices differ from ours. Investors need to employ British agents, provide witnessed signatures of both buyer and seller, and pay an ad valorem tax of one percent. The Curb, seeing the great interest in foreign stocks, tackles the problem. In cooperation with the Guaranty Trust Co. of New York, the Curb works out a system of American Depositary

easily as an ordinary American issue.

1952

55. "Times Will Publish Weekly Stock, Bond Tables Every Sunday," *New York Times*, 5 September 1952, p. 1.

Starting on September 7th, the *New York Times* will publish complete weekly tables for the Curb and New York Stock Exchange. Information will include weekly high, low, and last prices, net change, high and low for the year, and weekly volume for each stock and bond traded.

1953

56. "'Curb' Disappears as a Market Here," *New York Times*, 6 January 1953, pp. 33, 36.

On January 5th, the Curb becomes the American Stock Exchange, abbreviated "Amex." From the mid-1800s to 1908 the "outdoor Curb" had no formal organization. In 1908, it became the "New York Curb Agency". In 1911, it changed its name to the New York Curb Market Association. In 1921, it moved indoors and became the New York Curb Market. Since 1929, it has been the New York Curb Exchange (NYCE).

Chapter 3

AMERICAN STOCK EXCHANGE: RECENT HISTORY
(1953 - 1972)

With its title established as the American Stock Exchange, the Exchange enters a period of innovation through automation and internationalization. A long line of chief executives includes Edward T. McCormick, Edwin Posner, Edwin D. Etherington, and Ralph Saul. The Exchange is rocked by scandal involving the Res.

BOOKS, DOCUMENTS & REPORTS

57. American Stock Exchange. *Statement on Floor Trading Submitted by the American Stock Exchange to the Securities and Exchange Commission.* March 1964.

> This statement comes in response to an SEC Special Study recommendation that floor trading on the New York and American Stock Exchanges be eliminated except for transactions made by specialists and odd lot dealers and those effected to offset errors. Studies done by the American Stock Exchange show that floor traders add substantial liquidity to markets that need liquidity and on balance their transactions have provided a stabilizing force. Further, they state that the elimination of floor trading at the American Stock Exchange would be injurious to the public; new standards designed to direct floor trading into consistently useful channels, essentially through the cumulative impact of stabilizing transactions, would be timely and feasible.   A simplification of regulations backed by increasingly effective surveillance techniques is possible.

58. North American Rockwell Information Systems Company. *Securities Industry Overview Study, Final Report.* September 1969.

> The American Stock Exchange, "believing that a fresh, systematic appraisal of the operations of the securities industry was needed, retained North American Rockwell Corporation to study the industry's operating systems and to make recommendations for improvements."   The study, which was conducted between February and August 1969, studied each of the processes in the total securities transaction system: the investor and his registered representative; entering an order into the system; the transmission and editing of the order; executing the order on the floor of an exchange or through the over-the-counter trading system; reporting back to the brokerage firm; confirmation to the customer; settlement of both certificates and dollars; and, associated actions such as dividend handling and transfer operations. The four key recommendations were: automation and editing of customer orders, as they enter the system, and automation of customer files to reduce errors and improve service; a trade reporting system to "lock in" the trade and make many of "today's overlapping

operations" unnecessary; development of back office and transfer agent systems using machine readable documents to achieve faster processing, better control and reduced manpower needs; and, a settlement system built around bank-transfer agent depositories to minimize certificate movement and increase industry capacity.

59. Petruschell, R. L., D. J. Dreyfuss, L. E Knollmeyer and J. Y. Lu. *Reducing Costs of Stock Transactions: a Study of Alternative Trade Completion Systems: a Report Prepared for American Stock Exchange, National Association of Securities Dealers, New York Stock Exchange.* Santa Monica, CA: The Rand Corporation, December 1970.

Reacting to "unforeseen and unprecedented" trading levels in 1968, the major exchanges invite The Rand Corporation to discuss industry problems and use Rand research techniques to identify the most promising solutions. Rand develops a simulation model to represent the entire trade completion system. Results are presented in a four-part report: Volume I, a summary of the study and results; Volume II, a description of the model in general terms, the cost methods, the alternatives examined, and the savings that could be realized under alternative configurations; Volume III, a detailed description of the model, the computer program, and the data collected; and, in a supplement to Volume III, the computer program.

60. Tymieniecka, Maria. *American Stock Exchange Terminology.* (Amerykanska terminologia gieldowa.) Warszawa, Poland: Wydawnictwa Uniwersytetu Warszawskiego, 1970.

Tymieniecka provides 73 pages of English to Polish translation of terminology for all American stock exchanges. Terms range from "account" through "jiggle back and forth" and from "remain stable" to "zero-plus."

61. Sobel, Robert. *Amex: a History of the American Stock Exchange, 1921-1972.* New York: Weybright and Talley, 1972.

Sobel continues his history of the Exchange published in 1970. He begins as the curbstone brokers conduct their last outdoor session on June 25, 1921. The Curb community continues to prosper; by 1928, a pattern of upward surge followed by minor decline has been established. In 1929, stock volume rises to 476 million shares, a level not again reached until 1961. The 1930s are described as the "dismal years." There were no million share days; seat prices declined from a high of $254,000 in 1929 to a low of $7,000 in 1939. Prosperity brings abuses and the Amex administration of the 1940s and 1950s does little to correct them; in fact, Edward T. McCormick, president from 1951 to 1961, participates in questionable activities. In the aftermath of the Re scandal, Edwin Posner leads a reform movement. The Etherington years (1962-1966) see more changes than any other period; in 1965, the Board unveils a long-term plan for automation. In 1961, the Amex has its first five-million share day and passes the ten-million mark in 1968.

ARTICLES

1953

62. "Names and Faces: Little Mac's Big Job," *Business Week*, (March 28, 1953): 118-128.

     A profile of Edward Theodore McCormick, "one of the bright young men who came to the nation's money Mecca to make his fortune only to wind up disillusioned." McCormick feels his challenge is to interest a great many more people in taking a much more active part in free enterprise through ownership of shares in American industry.

63. "By Another Name," *New Yorker* (June 20, 1953): 18.

     The Exchange is accused of name dropping for the past 100 years--through the Outdoor Curb, the New York Curb Agency, and the New York Curb Market Association, to the New York Curb Market and the New York Curb Exchange. And they've done it again adopting a new name, the American Stock Exchange. A visit with Edward T. McCormick provides a brief biography and description of a typical day. Facts reported about the exchange include that more than 50 percent of common stocks have paid dividends for ten or more consecutive years while two have paid for more than a hundred consecutive years--Providence Gas, for 104 years, and Pepperell Manufacturing, for 101 years.

1954

64. "Business Abroad Briefs: Dutch Stock Listed," *Business Week* (January 30, 1954): 123.

     The American Stock Exchange approves for trading the U.S. shares of Algemene Kunstzidje Unie--AKU, for short. The rayon company, one of the world's largest producers, will be the first Dutch company to have its securities traded on a U.S. exchange since 1936. AKU's offering of shares is the first from Europe to be registered with the Securities and Exchange Commission. AKU never sought a listing on the New York Stock Exchange.

1955

65. Brooks, John, "Profiles: the True Nobility," *New Yorker* 31 (October 1, 1955): 41-72.

     A Wall Street specialist is profiled. "As he goes about fulfilling his socially beneficent function, the scrupulous specialist not only must turn his back daily on juicy opportunities to make an illegitimate killing but must frequently, in the line of duty, take the risk of personally losing as much as a hundred thousand dollars in a matter of a few hours, or even minutes." An example of this "breed of cat" is David Sidney Jackson, a "small, thin, sharp-faced, seemingly excitable but actually steel-nerved bespectacled man." Jackson has been a specialist since 1925. His trading in Pantepec stock is detailed.

66. Pryde, Thomas M., "Film Tells Story of Stock Market," *New York Times*, 23 December 1955, p. 30.

Behind the Ticker Tape is a 22-minute color movie made for the American Stock Exchange by United World Films, a subsidiary of Universal. It tells the Amex story from its founding as the Curb Exchange in 1849 and is performed by professional actors. It will be made available for theater showings and distributed to nontheater sources for promotional purposes. President Edward T. McCormick and two assistants observed the filming process to safeguard against inaccuracies in the portrayal of the organization's history and operations.

1956

67. White, Peter F., "Hand Talk," *New York Times Magazine* (May 20, 1956): 25.

The *Invest in America Week* column presents pictures of "finger-wagging unmatched in the pulpit, the schoolroom or the home." Photographs picture signs for demand and supply, an order for 700 shares, a 3/8 bid, and a stock with the letter "x" in its ticker designation. Signals range through the alphabet and provide fractions down to 1/64.

68. Weymuller, Fred, "What's the Quote on the Big Board?" *Wall Street Journal*, 10 October 1956, p. 1.

During the World Series, trading is down at the Amex. There are three TV sets strategically placed on the trading floor. In one corner is a big screen and five rows of seats. The "tiny portable transistor radio" has been a boon for traders following the series. Of course, if something got hot on the floor, "the boys would put away their radios darned fast."

1958

69. "Quality Issues on the Little Board," *Financial World* 110 (September 24, 1958): 21.

The American Stock Exchange has long been considered a "farm system" for the Big Board, but the smaller market has some major companies. Reasons for its popularity include: standards concerning size of companies are less rigid; rules on the number of shares that must be public before trading is permitted are more flexible; non-voting stocks are admitted to trading; and, the cost of securing an original listing is relatively low. Many of the oldest names in corporate history are found on the Amex. More than 45 percent of listings have paid dividends without interruption for ten to over 100 years. Some of the top names are the Singer Manufacturing Company (uninterrupted dividend distributions since 1863), Sherwin-Williams (a 72-year string of unbroken dividend payments), and Chesebrough-Pond's, makers of Vaseline and Pond's products (dividend checks distributed for 75 consecutive years).

70. "Mrs. Mary G. Roebling Named to Board of American Exchange," *Wall Street Journal*, 29 October 1958, p. 26.

Head of the Trenton (N.J.) Trust, Mrs. Roebling is the first woman governor of any exchange. She joins two other women in setting precedent: Mrs. Charles Ulrick Bay, chairman and president of A. M. Kidder & Co., is the first woman to head a New York Stock Exchange member firm; and Mrs. Margaret E. Kennedy, partner in Lubetkin, Regan & Kennedy is the first to have her name in the title of a stock exchange member firm. Edward T. McCormick, president of the American Stock Exchange, states that Mrs. Roebling has been selected for two main reasons: because of her executive ability and because she is a woman. "We welcome the opportunity to give proper recognition to the vital role that women shareowners are playing in the economy," says McCormick. A majority of shareholders are women. Mrs. Roebling holds directorates and trusteeships in a number of corporate, educational, and cultural institutions. She is the mother of two children.

1959

71. "Furor on the Amex," *Forbes* 83 (February 1, 1959): 17.

Over the first half of January, volume on the Amex approaches an all-time high. On one trading day, the Amex trades a record-breaking 2.6 million shares, their highest since November 1929. What accounts for the sudden current trading furor is the growing dearth of low-priced stocks for small traders on the NYSE.

72. "Wall Street: the Other Exchange," *Time* 73 (March 30, 1959): 81.

In a frenetic trading week, the Amex is unable to keep pace with its popularity among novice investors. The Amex tickers, which transmit prices to 215 cities, print only 300 characters a minute and often run from five to 25 minutes behind. Among new listings, Desilu Productions, Inc. of TV's Desi Arnaz and Lucille Ball joins the Amex ranks.

73. "Pandemonium at Amex," *Forbes* 83 (April 15, 1959): 46.

Volumes on the Amex reach their highest levels since the 1929 crash. Paperwork becomes so overwhelming that the Exchange enlists help from the NYSE in its clearing operation. According to President Edward McCormick, the volume is not necessarily healthy; it's the result of America's get rich quick small investors bypassing the higher priced blue chips on the NYSE and taking chances on the more speculative, cheaper stocks on the Amex. Seat prices also escalate; in March, a seat on the Exchange sold for $44,000, the highest price since 1930. The Chairman of the NYSE joins with the Amex in advising member firms to conduct their business soundly and conservatively in order to prevent "reckless speculation by the uninformed."

1960

74. "New American Board Ticker," *New York Times*, 1 January 1960, p. 32.

The new ticker tape system will be able to print 500 characters per minute, compared to 300 per minute at present.

75. "American Board Listings," *New York Times*, 7 January 1960, p. 46.

A 23-page booklet, *Industrial Classification of Securities Traded on the American Stock Exchange* has been printed. It lists nearly 800 companies and almost 900 issues traded on the Exchange under 29 major industrial classifications and sixty subclasses. It shows ticker symbols, par values and price ranges for 1958 and 1959, and shares outstanding. It is available free from the Exchange.

76. "Ten Blue Chips on the Little Board," *Financial World* 114 (July 6, 1960): 5.

Quality issues are not the exclusive territory of the New York Stock Exchange. The Amex, often considered a seasoning ground for the Big Board, has its share. A number of old veterans include ten issues which vie for quality with almost any of the blue chip equities found on the larger exchange. A diversity of industries is represented, ranging from cosmetics to insurance. Three of the firms operate in Canada.

77. "The Markets: the Pros and Cons of Being Listed," *Business Week* (December 10, 1960): 125-126.

In previous years, when stock prices were generally rising, smart investors on Wall Street felt they had a sure-fire formula for success by investing in companies newly listed on the major exchanges. In 1960, this practice didn't work. There were more new listings than ever before--54 on the NYSE and 105 on the Amex. Yet, prices dropped sharply after shares were listed. One major factor may be that companies are listing earlier in their corporate life or when their stocks are selling at extremely high prices. Performance of new listings is shown in tabular format.

1961

78. Bedingfield, Robert E., "Exchange Here Second Largest," *New York Times*, 16 May 1961, p. 57.

> The Amex has never achieved the status of the New York Stock Exchange, but it is more popular with speculators because its stocks are cheaper and move faster. Its requirements are also easier to meet; the NYSE listing fee is $5,000, compared with the Amex's $1,000. The Amex has no annual fee while the NYSE's annual fees range from $500 up. The average price of stock on the Amex is $16; on the NYSE, $48. The article describes the purpose of the exchanges and how trades are done--including the use of hand signals.

79. "High Times on the Curb," *Forbes* 87 (June 1, 1961): 33-4.

> The NYSE has always been the stock exchange in terms of volume of shares traded, number of companies listed, and value of shares. The Amex has always been a distant second, even though it is by far the largest of the eleven other U.S. exchanges. Volume on the Amex has been building recently; in March, trading almost equalled the NYSE. Three days after Amex volume hit a 32-year high, the SEC began a probe into members' activities. This followed the recent disclosures that partners in member firm Re, Re and Sagarese had rigged the prices of some stocks they traded as specialists on the Exchange. Over a six year period, Gerard A. and Gerard F. Re allegedly made millions illegally. Volume on the Exchange has since recovered, but Amex brokers are wondering how long such activity can last.

80. "Scholar of Wall Street; Edward Theodore McCormick," *New York Times*, 12 December 1961, p. 64.

> McCormick left academic life for the frenzy of Wall Street. His doctoral thesis dealt with aspects of the Securities Act of 1933 aimed at correcting speculative practices. He joined the newly created SEC as an analyst and was named a commissioner in 1949. He was elected, in February 1951, as president of the New York Curb Exchange and became the first president of the American Stock Exchange. He was President during the time when attention was directed toward the increasingly glamorous issues in the electronics and aerospace industries. He has been active in elevating the status of the Amex and in grooming many American corporations for their debut on Wall Street. Yesterday he resigned as president of the Amex.

81. "Sudden Shift at ASE Means Reform Ahead," *Business Week* (December 16, 1961): 31-2.

> The forced resignation of American Stock Exchange president Edward T. McCormick heralds a transformation of the Exchange with a tougher staff and stiffer rules and

regulations. McCormick's downfall is a result of the scandal involving Gerard A. and Gerard F. Re, a father and son firm of Amex specialists charged by the SEC with fraud and stock manipulation. McCormick had been involved in personal stock transactions with the Res. Under McCormick, the Amex enjoyed a period of prosperity, both because of a bull market and because of McCormick's talent as a salesman and promoter for the Exchange.

82. "Wall Street: Little Mac's Exit," *Time* 78 (December 22, 1961): 46.

In the wood-paneled splendor of their boardroom, 26 governors of the American Stock Exchange face an unpleasant task. Within an hour, the deed is done. Out of his $75,000 a year job as president of Amex goes "genial, silver-haired" Edward T. McCormick, 50. Amex members grumble that Little Mac liked the Stork Club and the excitement of bringing new companies to the board much better than the tedium of tending to the administrative problems of the growing exchange he was creating.

83. "McCormick's Hasty Exit from Amex," *Newsweek* 58 (December 25, 1961): 61.

Amex governors announce the immediate resignation of Edward T. McCormick from his $75,000 a year job as president of the Exchange. Also quitting is Amex general counsel Michael Mooney. *The Wall Street Journal* reports that, when the governors learned that McCormick had allegedly allowed financier Alexander Guterma to pay off a gambling debt that McCormick ran up in a Havana casino in 1956, it was "a last straw heaped on a heavy weight of anti-McCormick sentiment." There was nothing illegal about the transaction, but the governors considered it improper. Guterma is serving time in a Federal penitentiary for stock fraud.

1962

84. "The Market Pattern: No Free Lunch," *Business Week* (January 13, 1962): 88.

Release of an SEC report provides "a black eye for Wall Street as a whole." The Amex's "shoddy ethical standards were known to a great many responsible people in Wall Street who, until recently, preferred to turn a blind eye and do nothing." The reluctance stems from the club like atmosphere which pervades Wall Street. It can also be argued that the SEC, which has ultimate responsibility for policing the markets, should share in the blame because of their slowness in deciding Wall Street would not do its own policing.

85. "Stock Exchanges: Next for Amex?" *Newsweek* 59 (January 22, 1962): 66.

Trading and prices run strong as the Amex closes the week with a roar. However, behind the bustling scenes, radical changes are taking place. Two of the Amex's top reform leaders--Gustave Levy of Goldman, Sachs and Edwin Posner, a veteran broker and the official exchange nominee for chairman--head for Washington for a conference with SEC officials. There seems no doubt that the SEC has issued an ultimatum. Unless there is a clean sweep, the government will step in to enforce the rules. While two governors up for re-election show no signs of stepping down, it is rumored that James Dyer and chairman Edward Reilly are "on the way out." It seems probable that just about everyone who has held authority on the Amex in recent years will have to go.

86. "After the Storm," *Forbes* 69 (February 1, 1962): 16.

After a seven month investigation by the SEC, the Amex is trying to return to normal. Its president, Edward McCormick, has resigned and public confidence has suffered. Companies listed on the Exchange are considering delisting and switching to the NYSE or over-the-counter market. *Forbes* concludes that the Amex is likely to emerge reformed and substantially as important as before.

87. "ASE Starts To Clean House To Show It Can Do the Job Itself," *Business Week* (February 3, 1962): 78.

The American Stock Exchange expels the specialist firm of Gilligan, Will & Co., which is accused by the SEC of "manifold and prolonged abuses" on the Amex. The Exchange's own committee of reformers headed by Gustave L. Levy of Goldman, Sachs presents their report on new standards, including the issuing of quarterly--rather than annual--earnings statements to shareholders.

88. "Counter-Reformation?" *Forbes* 89 (March 15, 1962): 18.

New Chairman and President Pro Tem Posner has 53 years of experience in the securities business. He has inherited the mess left after the SEC investigation that resulted in the resignation of the Amex's president and the censuring of several of its members. Posner was the choice of a reform group of Amex members headed by Gustave Levy of Goldman, Sachs. At his first press conference, Posner announces that the Amex plans to find a permanent president, adopt new rules to discipline wayward members, and tighten listing requirements.

89. "Members' Fees Up on American Board," *New York Times*, 20 March 1962, p. 56.

The Amex Board of Governors approves a schedule of increased member charges and fees to provide an annual increase in income of $330,000 to pay the costs incurred as a result of the investigatory work of the Exchange's Levy Committee. Dues will increase from $500 to $750 a year; specialists' fees will rise from $300 to $400.

90. "Edwin Etherington Named ASE President in Victory for Reform Movement," *Business Week* (March 31, 1962): 98.

Edwin D. Etherington, 37, a partner in Pershing & Co., an NYSE firm, is named new president of the Amex. Despite his age, Etherington has an extensive background in securities regulation and stock law. He succeeds Edward T. McCormick, who was fired by the Amex in December 1961.

91. "Executives: New Man for Amex," *Newsweek* (April 9, 1962): 86-88.

A special committee of the Amex seeking a successor to Edward T. McCormick interviewed 70 candidates from the worlds of finance, law, politics, and education. Although the names remain a secret, it is unlikely that any belong to a younger or less-known person than Edwin D. (for Deacon) Etherington--the man chosen for the job. Etherington knows the Amex and its problems; he served as a special consultant to the blue ribbon Wall Street committee that began cleaning house after an SEC investigation. Born in Bayonne, New Jersey, Etherington won his Phi Beta Kappa key at Wesleyan in 1948. He stayed on for a year as an English instructor, received a law degree from Yale in 1952, and joined a firm handling legal matters for the New York Stock Exchange. He was soon named the Big Board's secretary and became a vice president in 1958, doing liaison work with the SEC. Early in 1961, he became a partner in Pershing and Co., a brokerage house. Etherington, who hopes to scrap the committee system, has stated, "I'm going to lead" and adds that, as long as the Exchange is well run, its reputation "will take care of itself."

92. "In the Markets: ASE Governors O.K. New Constitution, Push Housecleaning Job," *Business Week* (June 9, 1962): 104.

The Board of Governors of the American Stock Exchange approves a final draft of a new constitution; it should be approved by the membership within weeks. Insiders say that the draft follows the recommendations of the Levy committee, which was set up in Fall 1961 to study Amex organization and rules.

93. "Gyrations on the Amex," *Financial World* 118 (September 26, 1962): 6, 28.

Rumors of take-over attempts have resulted in heavy trading of secondary oil stocks on the American Stock Exchange. The trend toward consolidation has been found to be more profitable for small independent oil companies. At the same time, the major oil companies are constantly looking for suitable merger partners as a cheap way to build their reserves.

94. "Exchange Arrays Stocks," *New York Times*, 30 October 1962, p. 56.

> The Amex has begun distribution of a 24-page booklet listing by industry the more
> than 1,000 stocks of 922 companies traded on the Amex. Titled *Industrial
> Classification of Securities Traded on the American Stock Exchange*, it shows high and
> low stock prices for 1961 and for the first half of 1962. The booklet is available free
> from the Amex and member firms.

1963

95. "American Exchange: Fire Brigade," *Newsweek* 61 (March 11, 1963): 75-76.

> Following a scandal, a blue-ribbon Wall Street committee moved into the Amex,
> carved out a set of stiff reforms, and drafted Edwin Posner, 72, a partner in Andrews,
> Posner, and Rothschild, as chairman and interim president. Then, from about 100
> candidates, it chose Edwin D. Etherington as the new Amex president. In just six
> months, Etherington's reorganization has restored the confidence of Wall Street's most
> exacting professionals. Some Amex members refer to Etherington, Posner, and
> company as the "hook and ladder brigade" because they have ordered the bell on the
> trading floor rung four times in five months to announce member suspensions for rules
> violations. They also delisted 31 companies that could not meet Amex's required
> standards.

96. "American Exchange To Help Clear Stocks Sold Over the Counters," *Wall Street
Journal*, 3 April 1963, p. 16.

> Clearing facilities for 1,200 over-the-counter stocks will be furnished by the Amex for
> the National OTC Clearing Corp. under plans announced by the two organizations.
> The National OTC Clearing Corp. was formed in 1961 to provide members of the
> NASD, banks, and others that deal in unlisted stocks with clearing facilities similar to
> those of the Amex. Currently, a physical delivery of securities certificates must be
> made; with the new program, transactions would be validated at the clearing center,
> where all receipts of securities sold would be matched against those bought and only
> a net delivery would be made to respective firms. This would reduce physical
> handling of securities and would speed settlements and lower back office
> costs. The Amex will be reimbursed for space, equipment, personnel, and
> out-of-pocket expenses.

97. "Amex: a New Face and Form," *Business Week* (June 8, 1963): 91-2.

> Nine months have passed since Edwin D. Etherington assumed the job as president of
> the American Stock Exchange and began his program of reforms. The Exchange is
> now stronger than it ever was, its standards are higher, and administration is more
> competent. The recent Amex scandal resulted in the first full-fledged investigation

into the securities industry since the 1930s. If the Exchange is successful in reforming itself, it will be a strong argument in favor of self-policing of the securities business. The important changes brought forth by Etherington include a shift in operating authority from committees of members to a professional executive staff; tightening of listing requirements; accelerating the move toward automation of the Exchange; revising the way associate members are treated; and, changing the way stocks are allocated to specialists.

98. Allan, John H., "Etherington Says Worst Is Over," *New York Times*, 3 September 1963, pp. 45, 48.

Etherington states that last month's SEC study reported that the accomplishment of reform appears to be an excellent demonstration of effectiveness of self-regulation under responsible leadership. The Amex now has six staff divisions to manage daily activities, including 51 supervisors and executive personnel hired to bolster staff operations.

99. "Mistaken Identity? Shenanigans Last Month in Data-Control Were Quite an Embarrassment to the Recently Reformed American Stock Exchange," *Forbes* 92 (September 15, 1963): 35.

Wall Street analysts believe that thousands of investors have bought stock in a small Danbury, Connecticut, aircraft and space vehicle component maker named Data-Control, thinking they were buying giant Control Data, which trades on the NYSE. Data-Control's stock began trading on the Amex in June at $13 and quickly moved up to over $30. The company has a net income of 70 cents per share. In 30 days, 1.2 million shares were traded, even though there were only about 100,000 shares available. The available shares had turned over eight times in two months, with changes in price of only 1/8 of a point or no changes at all. Even with new controls in place, the Amex has demonstrated that wild swings in price are still possible.

100. Lee, John M., "Financial and Commodities Markets Shaken; Federal Reserve Acts To Avert Panic," *New York Times*, 23 November 1963, p. 7.

The assassination of President John F. Kennedy has an immediate and crushing impact on the markets, which closed soon after 2 p.m. when news of the shooting was circulated. The Federal Reserve issues a statement that there is no need for special action to thwart any speculation against the dollar on foreign exchange markets. The New York and American Stock Exchanges plan to open as usual on Monday, unless the funeral is held then.

101. "American Stock Exchange: Does Honesty Pay?," *Forbes* 92 (December 15, 1963): 31-2.

Ted Etherington became president of the Amex in September, 1962, after a long and costly SEC investigation revealed "manifold and prolonged abuses." Under Etherington, the Amex has made a quick recovery: standards for listing have been raised, resulting in the delisting of 63 stocks. Many of the active glamour stocks are gone, bringing trading volume down. New minimums for listing include a net worth of $1 million, earnings of $150,000, market value of $2 million, and a total of 750 shareholders, at least 500 of whom must own 100 shares or more.

1964

102. "Electronic Clerk Quotes Stock Prices," *Business Week* (May 16, 1964): 166.

"Spoken" messages assembled from pre-recorded words, letters, and numbers are now available to brokers over leased telephone lines to the American Stock Exchange's quotation service. The NYSE is scheduled to install a similar system in early 1965. The system can accommodate calls from all subscribers at once. A caller dials the code number assigned to a particular stock and is given eight pieces of information, all in less than half the time it would take a clerk to look up the last bid/ask prices.

103. Rolland, Louis J., "The 'Amex' Automates," *Financial World* 121 (May 20, 1964): 20.

The American Stock Exchange inaugurates its automated telephone quotation system. Am-Quote is designed to furnish market data at speeds up to 72,000 responses per hour, with no busy signal. Designed and constructed by the Teleregister Corporation, Am-Quote will begin reporting on any one of approximately 1,100 stocks within one second after a broker calls. It will furnish the ticker symbol, bid, ask, last sale, net change from previous close, volume to the moment, and open, high, and low prices. Am-Quote has a current capacity of up to 750 telephone lines and can be expanded to 1,000. The NYSE is also in the process of streamlining the recording and transmitting of its trading data by way of a system linked to IBM computers.

104. Etherington, E. D., "Second Largest Exchange Looks Confidently Ahead," *Commercial and Financial Chronicle* 200 (September 24, 1964): 57, 77-79.

Edwin D. Etherington, Amex president, provides a 25-year review of Exchange affairs which stresses the past three years. Cited are growth in membership, listings and dividend payments, changes in quotation systems, geographic coverage--both in the U.S. and internationally, and self-regulation.

1965

105. Wise, T. A., "Young Ted Etherington's AMEX," *Fortune* 71 (January 1965):
166-70, 216.

Since Ted Etherington took over as president, the Amex has better quality stocks and
more stable markets. The turnaround since the SEC investigation has been economic
as well as moral. Issues lost due to a tightening of the listing criteria have been more
than offset by new arrivals from the over-the-counter market. The Exchange's
revenues are at an all time high of $8.5 million. Where previously the Amex was
considered a training ground, major brokerage houses are now sending over trained,
high caliber traders. Etherington's contributions thus far have given the Amex better
quality stocks and more stable markets, and jokes made about the Exchange have
almost stopped.

106. "Stock Markets: Retreat from Wall St.," *Newsweek* 66 (August 16, 1965): 68.

Wolverine Aluminum Corporation's Don Smith asks the Amex to delist the stock of
his Lincoln Park, Michigan, aluminum fabricating company one trading day after the
symbol WVA first flashed across the Amex's ticker tape. Smith roasted Exchange
procedure as "a shockingly antique and unsanitary way of doing business." He
compared floor activity to a "bunch of grownups playing cowboys and Indians with
their shouting and waving and sending signals."

1966

107. "They're Up; They're Down," *Forbes* 97 (February 15, 1966): 15-18, 64.

Even with all the changes that have taken place recently on the Amex, one thing that
has not changed is the appeal of low-priced stocks to the small investor. The average
price on the Amex is about $18 per share, compared to $50 on the NYSE. In
addition, fewer shares are available to be traded. The result is that supply cannot keep
up with demand, and prices go up dramatically. Although the Amex's policing of
trading has been greatly stepped up, the wide price swings and frequent trading halts
are a direct result of the scarcity of stocks. Specialists are unable to keep an issue
moving at small, fractional price changes between trades. A company with as few as
250,000 shares is eligible for trading on the Amex, while the minimum on the NYSE
is 700,000 shares. It takes a lot more money to move a stock on the Big Board. The
greed of the small speculator is once more blamed for these price fluctuations and the
result can only be heavy losses when the process turns around.

108. "High Flyers on the Amex," *Financial World* 125 (February 16, 1966): 14, 23.

A growing interest in the American Stock Exchange is evidenced by swelling trading volume. The Exchange is second only to the New York Stock Exchange and has a preponderance of low-priced, speculative stocks, making it particularly attractive to traders seeking quick profits with little capital. The upward price momentum has shown a blatant disregard for the fundamentals--the price-earnings ratios, yields, and other measures of a stock's worth. These "high flyers" have price swings of five to 15 points in a single session and a general market decline could be disastrous.

109. Smith, William D., "New Securities Numbers Would Reduce Confusion," *New York Times*, 13 March 1966, sec. III, pp. 1, 7.

In the near future every security will have its own unique alpha-numeric designation that will be recognized by humans and machines. Currently a stock like General Motors might have an NYSE ID number, a bank trust department number, a bank security pricing service number, and a brokerage house number. The CUSIP (Committee on Uniform Security Identification Procedures) is developing a system for alphabetically and numerically identifying securities to speed their handling. The CUSIP number will consist of a base number of six digits to be known as the issuer number, with a two-character suffix to be known as the issue number. The committee is also working on developing an alphabetic standard security description, which along with the CUSIP number, could be printed on individual security certificates.

110. Hammer, Alexander R., "Volume on Amex Near 1929 Record," *New York Times*, 15 April 1966, p. 51.

On April 14, 1966, 6.56 million shares trade; this is the second busiest day in Amex history. On October 29, 1929, 7.09 million shares traded.

111. "Listing Procedure Amended by Amex," *New York Times*, 23 May 1966, p. 58.

The Amex announces that it is amending its listing application to include a requirement that the company disclose conflicts of interest between companies and officers, directors or large stockholders. Each case will be reviewed on an individual basis.

112. Morgello, Clem, "Wall Street: Lessons of the Amex," *Newsweek* 68 (July 4, 1966): 73.

News of a big order of jet liners and an optimistic outlook for the aerospace industry sparks a stock market rally. Unconfirmed rumors of White House meetings on the economy and on Vietnam touch off heavy selling. However, overall volume on the Amex is down sharply, a solid indication that much of the speculative frenzy seen earlier in the year has died. The Amex still has its high-flying action stocks, but there aren't as many as there were. A few months earlier, Robert Stovall of E. F. Hutton called them the "unexplored moose pasture stocks"--mining companies, small makers of electronics parts and the like. Market experts feel better about their ability to measure and analyze price trends on the Amex, thanks to the Exchange's new price index, which covers all 1,040 common stocks and warrants listed.

113. Proctor, James W., Jr., "The Voice Response System," *Datamation* 12 (August 1966): 43-44.

An enhancement to the Am-Quote system enables stockbrokers to dial four-digit codes on their regular office phones and receive stock quotations in the form of an electronically controlled human voice. The codes correspond to the securities traded on the Amex. The response includes the stock symbol, the bid and ask prices, number of shares traded, and the open, high and low prices for the day. The system can answer 1,200 inquiries per minute and up to 72,000 per hour, totalling over a half million during an average day.

114. "Amex Hires Its Critic: Choice of Ralph Saul, Who Worked on SEC Probes, Raises Some Members' Eyebrows," *Business Week* (August 20, 1966): 36.

Ralph Saul is selected as the new president of the American Stock Exchange. Saul headed an SEC probe of the Amex which led to a reorganization of the Exchange and a revision of its rules. Saul is a native of New York who joined the SEC staff in 1958 and rose to become head of the Trading and Markets Division. His election as president of the Amex is expected to be a surprise to its members.

115. "Shades of Horatio Alger: a Note on the New Head of the American Stock Exchange (R. S. Saul)," *Barron's National Business and Financial Weekly* 46 (August 22, 1966): 1.

Ralph Saul's success story is in the tradition of Horatio Alger. His rise in the last year from the Securities and Exchange Commission to vice president of the huge midwestern financial company, Investors Diversified Services, and now to president of the American Stock Exchange has some members of the financial community wondering. They are especially concerned about his move from bureaucracy to one of the highest posts on Wall Street. *Barron's* stand is that regulators should not work for those they regulate.

116. "Hiring the Harasser: New President," *Time* 88 (August 26, 1966): 68.

Article cites "an old Wall St. gag" that the Mafia once turned down a seat on the American Stock Exchange for fear of picking up a bad reputation. The Amex, which dates from the California gold-rush days, prospered for decades as a place where speculative stock buyers could find action that was unavailable on the relatively staid

Big Board of the New York Stock Exchange. In naming a new president, the Amex chooses Ralph S. Saul, the "ex-SEC man who was largely responsible for Amex's reformation." Saul, after WWII service as a naval gunnery officer, earned degrees from the University of Chicago and Yale Law School, was a legal assistant to New York governor Thomas E. Dewey, and a corporate lawyer for RCA Victor. In 1958, he joined the SEC in a $12,770 a year position and headed the investigation that led to Amex reforms.

117. "New Man at Amex," *Newsweek* 68 (August 29, 1966): 56.

In the world of high finance, reformers rarely land lush executive jobs. But the American Stock Exchange bestows such an honor on ex-critic Ralph Southey Saul by electing him to the $80,000-a-year Amex presidency. It was only four years earlier that Saul, supervising an SEC investigation, accused the Exchange of "manifold and prolonged abuse by specialists and floor traders." Saul replaces Edwin D. Etherington who leaves to be president of Connecticut's Wesleyan University.

118. "Can He Trade Up Amex's Image?" *Business Week* (October 19, 1966): 150, 152-3.

Ralph Saul, former SEC official, sees the SEC and the Exchange as partners in the regulation of trading. He spent seven years with the SEC, during which time he became a recognized expert on the workings of Wall Street. Saul has the administrative savvy and the integrity to inspire new public confidence in the Exchange. Besides his famous investigation into the activities of the Amex, Saul was also associate director of the SEC's special study of the securities market. That study, which was published in 1963, called for changes in the way securities are traded and the way stock exchanges and brokerage houses operate. It brought attention to the conflict of interest that sometimes exists when a member trades, for his own account, securities that he is also buying and selling for the public. Despite the open dislike by some brokers, Saul is in general regarded as open-minded and reasonable.

119. "Tamer Than the Image," *Time* 88 (November 11, 1966): 101.

The Amex sheds its reputation as "scandal-tainted" and "where speculators seek action." A survey of a week's trading in 8,000 stocks has several revelations. Banks, insurance companies and pension funds account for 11 percent of trading, individuals for 63 percent (compared to 49 percent on the NYSE), and members, 26 percent. Nearly 40 percent of shares bought are for long-term investment. Eighty-six percent of Amex buyers have incomes of $10,000 or more while 84 percent of NYSE buyers fall in that bracket.

1967

120. Merjos, Anna, "Up on the Curb: on the Amex, an Application Often Does More for a Stock Than a Listing," *Barron's National Business and Financial Weekly* 47 (May 1, 1967): 9-10, 15.

Hundreds of over-the-counter companies decide to list their stocks on a major exchange. The reason is the 1964 amendment to the Securities Exchange Act of 1934, which extends to OTC securities the same registration, reporting, proxy solicitation and insider reporting and trading regulations that apply to listed securities. Since many of these companies already meet the minimum net worth and earnings requirements for a listing on the Amex, they decide to enjoy the additional advantages of having their shares listed on a major exchange. To see what impact a listing on the Amex might have, *Barron's* charted the price behavior of the 52 issues that moved to the Amex in the last six months of 1966. In the three months leading up to the day of listing, on average, the gain for the 52 issues amounted to about 24 percent, compared with a -2.4 percent for the overall market. Significantly, more than half of these issues declined the day after listing or at least stayed at the same level. In addition, 22 lost at least part of their gain in the following month.

121. "American Board To Begin Renovation This Summer," *Wall Street Journal*, 2 May 1967, p. 14.

The Amex will begin to modernize its trading floor and to expand and improve facilities for its members and public. Eleven large circular trading posts will replace the Exchange's present 28 smaller posts, will reduce floor congestion and provide work space for up to 202 specialists, compared with the current 170. The visitors' gallery will double in size to 4,000 square feet. Trading will not be interrupted during the renovation.

122. "Amex Fireworks," *Financial World* 128 (July 12, 1967): 10, 22.

Volume on the Amex soars to new highs in the first half of 1967. Skyrocketing prices are accompanied by increases in turnover, delayed openings, trading suspensions, and other signs of "feverish speculation." Electronic and data processing issues are popular. Amex officials, who are apprehensive, place 15 "more unruly" stocks under a 100 percent cash margin requirement.

123. "Speculative Spree Alarms Amex," *Business Week* (July 15, 1967): 26-7.

A period of wild speculation on the Amex has resulted in a doubling of prices in the last six months. The Amex's price index is also 50 percent higher than it was in January, while the Dow Jones Industrial Average has only gained around 10 percent. This rise is potentially damaging to the Amex, fighting to shed its image of a speculative market. Wall Street is concerned because it knows too well the outcome of unbridled speculation from the 1961 run-up; small investors bear the brunt of the losses and people blame the brokers. The impact is also likely to spill over to the blue chip issues.

124. "New Leaders of the Financial Community," *Financial World* 128 (October 25, 1967): 26-27, 157.

The financial community witnesses a "game of executive musical chairs" as top men shift at both the NYSE and Amex. At the "Little Board," Ralph Saul has taken on the "big job" as president. He "gives every evidence of thoroughly enjoying the moment-to-moment problems." His attention is going to modernization of the trading floor to handle eight or nine million share days, surveillance procedures, listing standards, and timely disclosure of corporate developments.

125. "Faces Behind the Figures: Ralph S. Saul, Reining in the Amex," *Forbes* 100 (November 15, 1967): 68-69.

Ralph Saul comes to the American Stock Exchange from the Securities and Exchange Commission, where he headed the investigation into wrongdoing at the Amex. During his first year as president of the American Stock Exchange, Ralph Saul has seen a surge in the volume of trading. The surge is the result of thin "floats"--the number of shares available for trading--and low prices. A recent survey by *The Wall Street Journal* found that one of every ten issues on the Amex had tripled in price since 1967. Saul has taken steps to prevent a downward slide, including the suspension of margin buying in hot stocks. The question is whether Saul's improvements will have sufficient impact to prevent a crash.

126. "Big Casino," *Time* 90 (November 17, 1967): 94.

During a seven week autumn period when the stock market is in a "persistent chill," the Dow Jones industrial index climbs to a 1967 high but still loses "more than half of its 1967 gains." A "perplexing puzzle" is a new outbreak of speculation with the Amex serving as the "principal gambling casino." Prediction is that annual volume will pass a billion shares for the first time in the Exchange's 188-year history. Amex officials are concerned by heavy concentration in low-priced issues which "entice speculators because small gains mean hefty profits."

127. Vartan, Vartanig G., "Amex Stiffens Surveillance," *New York Times*, 19 November 1967, sec. III, pp. 1, 10.

With installation of its first computer as a surveillance tool in May, the Amex was able to provide members with weekly and monthly reports of all their transactions in Amex securities, including their percentage of Exchange volume in each security. The reports are a major help to firms in effecting internal controls. The Exchange surveillance staff also scan daily activity reports.

128. Erwin, Ray, "Amex Speeds Stock News Around World," *Editor & Publisher* 100 (December 9, 1967): 14, 58.

The Amex is building a new communications center to speed market information to the news media. Data provided includes volume for current and previous days, hourly reports on the Exchange's Price Level Index, the daily Breadth of Market Index, the number of advances and declines in stock prices, net changes and volume in the trading of active stocks. Information is also relayed on delayed openings and halts in trading, seat sales, special margin requirements, stop-order bans, and large block transactions. Market summaries are transmitted to more than 4,000 radio stations in the U.S. and 300 in other countries. The Center monitors the Dow Jones News Wire and PR Newswire and forwards news items to various market lead writers to assist them in obtaining information on trading activity.

129. Robards, Terry, "American Exchange Planning for Sharp Increase in Volume," *New York Times*, 22 December 1967, p. 47.

Amex's President Saul reports that the Exchange is taking steps to deal with heavy trading volume of 8-9 million shares per day. The 120 new listings in 1967 are a 30-year high. Very heavy trading created problems and underscored the need for modernization of procedures.

1968

130. "Two Stock Exchanges Set Volume Records in 1967," *Wall Street Journal*, 2 January 1968, p. 28.

Trading volume in 1967 totals a record 1,145,157,218 shares, up from 690,518,276 shares in 1966. The pace almost doubled in 1967 from 1966. Friday was the third most active day in trading history.

131. "American Stock Exchange Raises Listing Standards," *Commercial and Financial Chronicle* 207 (March 14, 1968): 1083.

Ralph S. Saul, president of the American Stock Exchange, announces strengthened policies for continued listing. A company now must have net tangible assets of $3 million, earnings of $300,000 ($500,000 pre-tax), 300,000 publicly held shares, 900 stockholders, and 600 round lots. Mr. Saul states: "the Exchange weighs many factors in considering whether a security warrants continued dealing and listing, and each case is considered on its own merits."

132. "Amex Multiples--Caution Signal," *Financial World* 130 (December 11, 1968): 13.

Amex trading records continue to topple. Trading volume, new listings, number of issues, total shares listed, seat prices, and short interest are all hitting new peaks. While the Amex has always had its share of low-priced stocks, the number in the $2-$10 range has "dwindled markedly" because prices have skyrocketed.

1969

133. "Damping Ardour on the Kerb," *Economist* 230 (February 15, 1969): 82-4.

Trading on the New York Stock Exchange has been dominated of late by institutional investors, but individual investors attracted by lower-priced stocks continue to dominate on the Amex. The Amex orders its members to stop trading for their own accounts in 103 issues, indicating concern that the speculation is being fueled in large part by the market-wise members themselves. The feeling on Wall Street is that Amex stocks are now dangerously overpriced, at an average of 25 times earnings compared to the 16 times earnings of the blue chips in the Dow Jones Industrials.

134. "Paperwork Mess Goes into a Think Tank," *Business Week* (February 22, 1969): 126, 128.

In a joint statement, the New York and American Stock Exchanges announce that they have hired the Rand Corporation of Santa Monica, California, to deal with "the intricate web of relationships in Wall Street's paperwork crisis." The exchanges anticipate development of systems which will be able to handle the trading volume expected in the 1970s.

135. "How to Keep an Eye on the Stock Market," *Broadcasting* 76 (June 2, 1969): 69.

Mel Tarr is appointed Amex's manager of media communications. Amex is transmitting market summaries an average of three times a day to more than 5,000 radio stations in the U.S. and 300 outlets in other countries around the world, accounting in all for over 75,000 Amex broadcasts weekly.

136. Rustin, Richard E., "Electronic Stock Certificate Plan Wins Support," *Wall Street Journal*, 21 November 1969, p. 2.

The Amex and NYSE endorse in principle the concept of a machine-readable stock certificate to ease the problems of securities handling bottlenecks and securities thefts. The format of the certificate will resemble a 3 1/2 inch by 7 3/4 inch punch card.

1970

137. Rustin, Richard E., "Membership for Institutional Investors Being Weighed by Two Major Exchanges," *Wall Street Journal*, 2 February 1970, p. 4.

In apparent alarm over defections by member firms, the Amex and NYSE are reconsidering, on a high priority basis, the eligibility of companies like Paul Revere Insurance Co. for exchange membership. Institutions such as mutual funds and insurance companies are currently barred from membership on the Amex and NYSE, because of the exchanges' ban on ownership ties with publicly held companies.

138. "Amex, To Clear from Floor," *Commercial and Financial Chronicle* 211 (May 28, 1970): 1717.

Ralph Saul, president of the American Stock Exchange, announces a plan to develop "a floor-derived clearance system" that is expected to be in place within 20 months. Under the system, an execution report will be teletyped from a floor booth to an Exchange computer. Then, the data will be electronically switched to match with the opposite side of a trade.

139. "Investor Insights: the Amex vs. the NYSE," *Business Management* 38 (June 1970): 26-7.

Although it has been 50 years since the Amex moved indoors, a silent war continues to rage with the NYSE. The Big Board's members still have a "patronizing attitude toward the Amex; Amex members feel the NYSE staff are "hidebound" in their own dignity. The Amex points out that the "lifeblood" of an exchange is its listings. In 1969, the NYSE took 32 companies away from the Amex. Yet, the Amex is growing fast. Over the past ten years, listings have increased from 1960's 931 issues representing 1.5 billion shares valued at $25 billion to 1970's 1,360 issues representing 2.6 billion shares valued at $50 billion. The Amex gained 180 listings in 1969, a record number. Many of these companies qualified for listing on the Big Board. It is noted, however, that the world's largest securities forum is the over-the-counter market.

140. Saul, R. S., "Issues and Interpretations," *Bankers Magazine* 183 (Summer 1970): 9-10.

The president of the American Stock Exchange outlines an expanded timely disclosure policy. The six major disclosure areas are: immediate disclosure of material information; thorough public dissemination of news; corporate response to unusual market activity; unwarranted promotional disclosure; clarification of rumors; and, insider trading. The policy counsels companies to make immediate disclosure of activities or conditions that are likely to have a significant effect on the price of their securities or which will be considered important by a reasonable investor in determining his course of action.

1971

141. "Belling the Fat Cats," *Newsweek* 77 (January 11, 1971): 65.

Wall Street has weathered the crash of brokerage houses and gyrations of stock prices, but now looks forward to results of the Securities and Exchange Commission's study dealing with the impact of institutional investors on markets. Findings of the report include the evolution of separate wholesale and retail markets, the quadrupling of turnover rate in institutional holdings, and reciprocal arrangements between brokers and their banking and insurance clients. The report is delayed when the two Congressional committees who commissioned the study refuse an SEC offer to deliver the report without recommendations.

142. "April 1, 1972, Deadline Set By Amex for Using CUSIP," *New York Times*, 24 February 1971, p. 56.

The Amex Board of Governors sets April 1st as the deadline for member firms to begin mandatory use of the CUSIP numbering system for channeling their trades. The system was designed to make possible immediate identification of stock certificates and related documents.

143. "Wall Street: Time for a Switch," *Time* 97 (March 29, 1971): 78.

Ralph Southey Saul, who recently turned down a Nixon offer to chair the Securities and Exchange Commission, resigns from the Exchange to become vice chair of First Boston Corporation. Saul, in his 4 1/2 years as Amex president, is credited with helping member firms with volume problems and overseeing automation of floor functions.

144. Reilly, Frank K., "Price Changes in NYSE, AMEX, and OTC Stocks Compared," *Financial Analysts Journal* 27(2) (March/April 1971): 54-9.

Reilly compares annual price changes in NYSE, Amex and OTC stocks. Conclusions note that a "significant disparity" exists between NYSE price-indicator series and price changes and those of the Amex and OTC. The Amex and OTC indicator series showed much larger increases than the NYSE series in 1965, 1967, and 1968 and a substantially lower decline in 1966. During the period 1963-1969, the Amex index and OTC average experienced an annual compound rate of increase more than 200 per cent greater than the increase in the S&P Index and NYSE Index, and over 500 percent greater than the rate of increase of the Dow Jones Industrial Average.

145. "Amex To Automate Bond Service in May," *New York Times*, 19 April 1971, p. 58.

Starting in early May, the Amex will implement an automated comparison and clearance service for the more than $3 billion in bonds listed on the Exchange. The program will reduce paperwork and clerical costs at member firms and reduce the physical movement of bond certificates.

146. "Amex To Automate Orders in Odd Lots," *New York Times*, 3 May 1971, p. 60.

The Amex announces that by the end of the year it will install a system for the computerized execution of odd-lot market orders (fewer than 100 shares). The Amex notes this will reduce paperwork for member firms and reduce considerably the traffic on the trading floor.

147. Robards, Terry, "Exchanges Plan a Clearings Pool," *New York Times*, 10 May 1971, pp. 49, 50.

The New York and American Stock Exchanges announce plans to consolidate their clearing departments; this is the first step in a previously announced plan to join service functions now performed independently by each exchange. The reason for this merging of functions is to save member firms money and to eliminate duplicate systems.

148. Robards, Terry, "Big Board Shifts Automation Units," *New York Times*, 12 May 1971, pp. 55, 65.

The New York and American Stock Exchanges and the Association of Stock Exchange Firms announce that they have agreed to mutual sponsorship of a member-firm communications network to be called SECTOR (Securities Telecommunications Organization). The network is expected to offer savings of at least $20 million to member firms in the first five years.

149. Robards, Terry, "Kolton, On Staff of Amex, Is Elected New President," *New York Times*, 21 May 1971, pp. 53, 59.

Paul Kolton, executive vice-president of the Amex for the past nine years, is elected its new president. This is the first time that a professional staff member of the Exchange has been named president. Mr. Kolton had responsibility for administration and operations. Previous presidents have come from outside the Exchange.

150. Robards, Terry, "Half Century Off the Curb: Amex Seeks the Shape of Future," *New York Times*, 6 June 1971, sec. III, pp. 1, 4.

The Amex is celebrating the golden anniversary of its move indoors. The Amex is younger and more speculative than the larger NYSE and, because it has chosen not to get involved in the affairs of its member firms, it has been freer to plan for the future. The story recounts the history of the Exchange, concentrating on electronic enhancements and differences from the NYSE and over-the-counter markets.

151. "Amex Slates Plans For Incorporation," *New York Times*, 23 September 1971, p. 106.

The Amex announces that its membership has approved constitutional amendments to incorporate as a nonprofit organization. The New York Stock Exchange was incorporated earlier in 1971.

152. "Amex Gets Black Member," *New York Times*, 8 October 1971, p. 64.

Travers Jerome Bell, Jr., has become the first black to be approved as an associate member of the Amex. Bell is a principal of the firm of Daniels & Bell, the first black-controlled member firm of the NYSE.

153. Robards, Terry, "Amex Plan Seeks a Single Market," *New York Times*, 18 October 1971, pp. 59, 61.

The Amex announces plans for a new trading system that will link all market-makers in each listed security, will feature a consolidated ticker tape, and will disclose transactions publicly in one place for the first time in securities history. It will bring all regional exchanges into a central market system.

154. "Joint Operations Unit Formed by Big Board, American Exchange," *Wall Street Journal*, 19 November 1971, p. 4.

The Amex and NYSE announce that they will merge their clearing, communications and automation facilities into a jointly owned subsidiary to be called the Securities Industry Automation Corp. (SIAC). It will be operational in mid-1972. SIAC will have a budget of $37.6 million and a staff of 1,100 persons, from both clearing corporations. Ownership shares in SIAC will be two-thirds by the NYSE and one-third by the Amex.

1972

155. Robards, Terry, "Amex Companies Get Louder Voice," *New York Times*, 7 February 1972, p. 45.

> The Amex announces formation of a nine-member Listed Member Advisory Committee to give greater representation to interests outside the brokerage community. President Paul Kolton states that this committee will discuss and evaluate policy matters affecting the interests of companies listed on the Amex, including the development of new listing criteria, conflict-of-interest policies, and disclosure standards.

156. "First Woman Nominee Is Slated for Board of American Exchange," *Wall Street Journal*, 17 February 1972, p. 24.

> Julia Montgomery Walsh, senior vice-president of Ferris & Co., Washington, who was one of the first two women to become members of major stock exchanges, is nominated to the Amex Board of Governors.

157. Rustin, Richard E., "American Exchange Shows Computer Setup That Could Be National Securities Market," *Wall Street Journal*, 29 March 1972, p. 3.

> A new computerized trading, quotation, order-handling and price-reporting system called "Amcode" is being shown to industry leaders by the Amex. Sources say this could be the central national securities market of the future. Using Amcode, specialists on all of the nation's exchanges will be linked electronically and price quotations of each exchange will be visible on a TV screen.

158. "American Stock Exchange Introduces Automated Trading System," *Public Utilities Fortnightly* 89 (May 11, 1972): 54.

> The Amex announces the introduction of Amcode, an automated system for execution of stock orders. The Amcode system is believed by some to have taken the lead in market automation away from the NYSE and "may mean that the American Exchange will be the one eventually to lead the way to a single national market, instead of the NYSE as expected."

159. "SIAC Starts Exchange Operations," *New York Times*, 18 July 1972, p. 43.

> The Securities Industry Automation Corporation (SIAC), a jointly owned subsidiary of the New York Stock Exchange and the Amex, begins operation. It was formed to consolidate operations of key computer and service facilities. An estimated 1,000 people are employed by SIAC.

160. "Amex Sets Up System To Monitor Finances of Listed Companies," *Wall Street Journal*, 22 November 1972, p. 4.

The Amex implements an automated system to track financial data on listed companies. The Exchange also announces that it is compiling a statistical index to serve as an aid in detecting and defining speculative and volatile market trends. The market index is gathering 10-year data on margin trading, volume and types of securities traded. Its purpose is to provide documentation in the event that the Exchange needs to take steps to cool speculation in a volatile market.

161. Robards, Terry, "Boomlet in New Listings on the Amex," *New York Times*, 25 November 1972, sec. III, p. 2.

According to Exchange Chairman Paul Kolton, the great number of new companies migrating to the Amex from the over-the-counter market are disappointed with the volatility of that market. They prefer a market-maker with fixed responsibility. Kolton notes that 164 companies have been added in 1972 with at least 180 expected by the end of the year. The record is 187 new companies in 1969.

Chapter 4

AMERICAN STOCK EXCHANGE: RECENT HISTORY
(1973-1993)

The American Stock Exchange concentrates on expansion through the addition of new trading instruments and automation. Record trading volumes lead up to the "Black Monday" of October 1987. In a quick recovery, old records begin falling in June of 1989.

BOOKS, DOCUMENTS & REPORTS

162. Bruchey, Stuart. *Modernization of the American Stock Exchange 1971-1989.* New York: Garland Publishing, 1991.

Bruchey continues the history of the Exchange begun by Sobel. He describes the reforms of the 1960s, automation of the trading process and floor of the Exchange, the ever-widening markets in trading products and foreign investments, and the "entrepreneurial eighties." He concludes with the "Great Plunge of 1987." A statistical appendix lists presidents and chairmen, trading records, descriptions of Amex listing companies, and trading volumes.

163. Pedersen, Laura with F. Peter Model. *Play Money: My Brief but Brilliant Career on Wall Street.* New York: Crown Publishers, 1991.

Pedersen provides a lesson in options trading interspersed with anecdotes of her childhood, of work in the pit, of pranks on the floor of the Exchange, and of life in Greenwich Village. In the preface, she notes that her reason for writing *Play Money* was to record what she "perceived to be the final gasps of a tradecraft that has been rendered almost superfluous by high technology." She worked at the Exchange for six years, beginning as a $120-a-week clerk and, at the age of twenty, becoming the youngest person in the history of Wall Street to have a seat.

ARTICLES

1973

164. "People and Business: Henri Froy," *New York Times*, 14 March 1973, p. 65.

Henri Froy, senior vice president of Abraham & Co., has been named the first overseas representative for the Amex. Mr. Froy will be based in Lausanne, Switzerland.

165. Jensen, Michael C., "Executives Set Stock Lobbying," *New York Times*, 31 March 1973, p. 45.

More than 100 top executives of companies listed on the Amex meet to organize a lobbying group to influence stock market legislation. The group, called the Committee of Publicly Owned Companies, has hired former Supreme Court Justice Abe Fortas as its general counsel. Members of the group express concern over the trend toward fully negotiated brokerage commission rates and over institutional trading of massive amounts of their companies' stock, which can cause the stock's price to plummet even if its earnings indicate health. It is suggested that a limitation should be placed on the speed of stock disposals by institutional investors.

166. "Wall Street: Valley of Despair," *Time* 101 (June 11, 1973): 78-79.

A week long rally in May raised hopes that the market was pulling out of its five-month slide, but it did not last. At fault were weakness of the dollar, the soaring price of gold, and continued rise of inflation. Trading volume on the Amex is running 40 percent behind 1972. Individual investors are fading from Wall Street leaving more than 70 percent of stock trading to banks and pension funds.

167. Mullaney, Thomas E., "A Fed for the Stock Market," *New York Times*, 5 August 1973, sec. III, p. 11.

Amex chairman Paul Kolton suggests the establishment of a National Board of Exchanges, consisting of representatives of all the present stock exchanges, the broker-dealer community, and the public. Under this arrangement, the SEC would still function as protector of the investing public, while the new group would be responsible for such areas as communicating information on prices, quotations and volume; commission rate structure; performance criteria for stock specialists; access to the system; financial responsibility; and, allocation of costs of the system among the various exchanges represented. It would be patterned after the Federal Reserve Board and look to the proper functioning of the securities industry and to insuring the flow of funds for capital needs in the nation.

168. "Wall Street: a Developing Feud?" *Newsweek* 82 (August 6, 1973): 68-9.

In 1973, not a normal year, the Amex no longer defers to the leadership of the larger and older New York Stock Exchange. The squabble which erupts deals with warrants, a security which gives the owner the right to buy a company's common stock at a specific price within a stipulated range. With Amex volume off 40 percent vs. a 10 percent decline on the Big Board, the Amex opposes the NYSE's proposal to the SEC which would relax listing standards for warrants and make 12 of 84 warrant issues traded on the Amex eligible for the more prestigious Big Board list.

169. "Big Board and Amex Unveil Joint Project for Computer System," *Wall Street Journal*, 10 August 1973, p. 21.

The Amex and NYSE reveal plans for a computer system called Centaur, which will automate communications, trading, reporting and clearing operations. Under the direction of SIAC, it is expected to be fully operational by 1978. Centaur is based on earlier systems, including Amex's Amcode, but is not meant to replace the trading floor.

170. Rustin, Richard E., "Big Board, Amex Circulate Definitive Plan on Switch in Securities-Clearance System," *Wall Street Journal*, 1 October 1973, p. 4.

The Amex and NYSE are about to make a major change in the way their member firms clear securities transactions. The objectives are to align the system with those used by regional exchanges and the over-the-counter market and establish one national clearance and securities depository system. The change would reduce members' securities processing costs by $15 to $25 million annually.

171. "Amex Unit Says End Dual Ban," *Commercial and Financial Chronicle* 218 (November 12, 1973): 1, 5.

The Amex develops and asks for member comments on a proposal to lift the ban on dual trading of Amex issues which have moved to the NYSE. Issues which need to be explored are the flow of orders, automation plans and capabilities, costs and benefits to member firms, and the responsibility of specialists. Other actions taken by the special committee which developed this proposal include placing a high priority on the Exchange's pilot options trading project and reviewing of the Amex role in new market areas. All trading proposals would need the approval of the SEC.

172. DuBois, Peter C., "Trying Harder: the Amex Rates First in Flexibility, Innovation," *Barron's National Business and Finance Weekly* 53 (November 26, 1973): 5, 18-19.

The 1973 third quarter report for the Amex shows a deficit of $443,000 and 31 percent loss of sales volume. However, the Exchange is alive and well and planning for the future. Since its founding on the curb in the 1840s, the Exchange has progressed through a quiet revolution to buying power of more than $500 million. Public representation has been expanded on the board with only two governors being officers of listed companies. In addition to cutting costs, the Exchange is involved in an aggressive marketing effort which includes increased communication with managements of listed companies, a continuing search for new listings including foreign corporations, and proposals for new products.

1974

173. "People and Business," *New York Times*, 20 April 1974, p. 39.

Thomas Johnson, Jr., has been elected the first black floor member of the Amex. He is currently a clerk for Bruns, Nordeman, Rea & Co. on the floor of the NYSE. Mr. Johnson will also begin acting as a commission broker for the firm.

174. "Composite Tape Plan Gets Final SEC Approval," *Wall Street Journal*, 13 May 1974, p. 10.

In a letter to the NYSE, Amex, Midwest, Pacific, and Philadelphia-Baltimore-Washington (PBW) stock exchanges, and the National Association of Securities Dealers, the SEC gives final clearance to a plan to establish a consolidated transaction-reporting tape. The tape is the first step toward a central securities market in which price and volume information will be available for stocks traded on all five of the major exchanges and the over-the-counter market.

175. Watson, Winsor H., Jr., "Global Role for U.S. Stock Exchanges," *Columbia Journal of World Business* 9 (Spring 1974): 42-47.

Because of the recent devaluation of the dollar, foreign corporations are increasingly interested in investing in--and acquiring--U.S. companies. More indications exist of a growing internationalization of securities markets: growth in multinational operations; increasing interdependence of monetary systems; relaxing of controls and opening of freer markets. Banks have of necessity expanded to provide services on an international basis and stock brokerage firms are seeking memberships on exchanges in various countries in order to expand their business. The SEC has established a new Office of International Corporate Finance to supervise securities offerings made by U.S. companies to foreign investors. The Amex, for years the leading securities exchange in the United States for foreign stocks, has also established its own Office of International Securities to deal with all matters relating to foreign securities and the listing and trading of such securities on the Exchange. In December 1973, the Amex announced special listing requirements designed to increase international activity on the Exchange and to attract additional overseas listings. The Amex intends to provide a large base for a viable ADR (American Depositary Receipt) market, permit the listing of non-voting common stock where such listing conforms with overseas corporate practice, extend the period foreign companies have for filing annual and quarterly reports, and permit foreign companies to furnish semi-annual rather than quarterly reports. The intent is to serve the needs of foreigners as well as Americans while helping to facilitate the reemergence of the U.S. as the financial center of the world. The author of this article is the Executive Vice President of the Amex.

176. Leo, D., "NYSE, Amex Extend Hours Despite Pleas from PM's," *Editor & Publisher* 107 (September 21, 1974): 14.

The Amex follows the NYSE in extending trading hours by a half hour to a 4 p.m. closing time. A cry erupts from East Coast newspapers concerned with getting final editions to the commuter crowd. Involved in the outcry are the *Miami News*, the *New York Post*, and the *Philadelphia Bulletin*.

1975

177. Brown, Sidney, "Straight Talk: NYSE-Amex Merger Proposal Is Suspect," *Commercial and Financial Chronicle* 220 (January 6, 1975): 8.

The Securities Industries Association reports that a merger of the New York and American stock exchanges could result in a saving of $2 to $3 milllion in duplicative administrative costs. The Amex chairman has formed a twenty man committee to view options, but no chair has been appointed or date set for the committee to meet. The real savings of a merger could be found in computer and communications systems. Automation amalgamation which has taken place was pioneered by the Amex.

178. Yeaney, Woodrow W. and Robert M. Bear, "The Capital Asset Pricing Model's Applicability to the American Stock Exchange." In: Eastern Finance Association. *Proceedings of the Annual Meeting of the Eastern Finance Association.* Hartford, Conn.: Eastern Finance Association, April 1975, pp. 35-36.

The capital asset pricing model has been widely studied for companies listed on the NYSE. Now, using random samples of securities selected from the Wells Fargo tape, an index has been developed for Amex securities during the period 1964-1969. It is concluded that historical estimates of beta are of limited use in prediction and that stability is not achieved in portfolios of up to 20 securities.

179. Levy, William H., "Paul Kolton Speaks Out: Interview with AMEX Chairman," *Trusts & Estates* 114 (October 1975): 734-7, 762-763.

In an interview, Paul Kolton, the Amex chairman, discusses his concerns and achievements. The major problem of the Exchange is a rapid decline in institutional rates while individual investors continue to pay the same or higher rates. The Prudent Man Rule is applied to options trading. Kolton sees his achievements as automation, increased services to firms and the public, and new products.

180. "Amex Approves Plan to Merge 3 Facilities for Clearing Securities," *Wall Street Journal*, 17 November 1975, p. 18.

The Amex governors approve a plan to merge the clearing facilities of the Amex, NYSE and the National Association of Securities Dealers in order to reduce clearing costs for the industry by several million dollars per year. Currently, clearing is done for the Amex and NYSE by their subsidiary known as the Securities Industry Automation Association (SIAC). The clearing unit of the NASD, called the National Clearing Corp., processes over-the-counter transactions. SIAC will now provide all processing for the new clearing unit.

1976

181. Cole, Robert J., "AMEX Plans $2 Million Expansion Here; Making Long-Range Relocation Study," *New York Times*, 25 March 1976, pp. 53, 54.

The Amex announces that it will spend $2 million over the next two years to expand its facilities, but it also announces that it is examining long-term proposals for a move to New Jersey or Connecticut. Mayor Beame says that he is committed to help the Exchange stay in New York. Chairman Paul Kolton says that the board hopes to remain in New York and will only move for "compelling economic reasons."

182. Aby, Carroll D., Jr., and Fred W. Granger, Jr., "Short Interest on the Amex: Bullish or Bearish?" *Atlanta Economic Review* 26:2 (March-April 1976): 51-54.

Research concerning use of the Monthly Short Interest Ratio (total monthly short sales divided by average daily trading volume) as a predictor of major market turning points, previously confined to the NYSE, is now focused on the Amex. It is reported that the ratio is applicable primarily at market bottoms when ratio levels reach 2.0 or better.

183. "Two More Exchanges Allowed to Fingerprint," *Wall Street Journal*, 12 July 1976, p. 16.

The SEC approves pilot programs by the Amex and the Philadelphia Stock Exchange to fingerprint securities personnel. Fingerprint cards will be sent to the U.S. Attorney General and the exchanges will relay back to member firms any information received about criminal records. Congress authorized the SEC to supervise such fingerprinting in last year's Securities Act amendments, primarily to help brokerage firms combat securities thefts.

184. Rustin, Richard E., "Meeting on Central Market Policy Slated Today by Aides of NASD, Six Exchanges," *Wall Street Journal*, 27 September 1976, p. 5.

Representatives of the New York, American, Pacific, Midwest, Philadelphia and Boston exchanges and the NASD meet to develop a coordinated policy for a national securities market. The meeting is sponsored by the Securities Industry Association and responds to a government mandate to create a competitive system where all stock markets will be linked electronically so that customers can get the best prices for their trades.

1977

185. White, Reba, "Can a Company Find True Happiness in a Dual Listing?" *Institutional Investor* 11 (January 1977): 145.

For many years, the maturity of a growing company could be measured by its progression from over-the-counter trading to an American Stock Exchange listing and, finally, to the Big Board. When the SEC lifted its ban on simultaneous trading, this measure of corporate standing lost significance. The first to dual list was Varo, Inc., a Texas-based electronics company. They were closely followed by Sambo's Restaurants. Owen John, Sambo's chief financial officer, admits that the decision was made because no one could come up with anything against dual listing and the incremental cost is low; an Amex listing is only $7,500 annually.

186. "SEC Clears Plan of Clearinghouse in 3-Way Merger," *Wall Street Journal*, 14 January 1977, p. 2.

The SEC approves merger of the clearing responsibilities of the Amex, NYSE, and the over-the-counter market into the National Securities Clearing Corp. The new organization will be required to establish links with clearing corporations of regional exchanges without charging special fees for the use of its services. It will also be required to: provide at-cost facilities to allow broker-dealers who don't maintain offices in New York to check the accuracy of trade data; share branch facilities with the smaller clearing corporations; and, provide without charge to the regional clearinghouses the computer programs necessary to compare trade data for transactions in the over-the-counter market.

187. "Amex To Get First Female Trading-Floor Member," *Wall Street Journal*, 22 February 1977, p. 34.

Lynne Greenberg, 21, will become the Amex's first woman trading-floor member and its youngest. Miss Greenberg, the daughter of an executive at Bear, Stearns, & Co., purchased the membership on Friday. She intends to become an independent floor broker.

188. Branch, Ben and Walter Freed, "Bid-Asked Spreads on the Amex and the Big Board,"
Journal of Finance 32 (March, 1977): 159-63.

> In this highly technical analysis of price spreads, the authors explore the spread
> between the bid and asked prices of stock--that is, what a buyer is willing to pay vs.
> what a seller is willing to take. This is the first such study to include the Amex. In
> general, a higher volume of trading in a stock means a narrower spread. If a stock is
> inactive, the spread is greater. Low-priced securities tend to have larger spreads than
> higher-priced securities. Volatility also tends to increase price spreads on both the
> NYSE and the Amex. Measurable impact is found on both NYSE and Amex stocks
> which are traded on the third market, i.e. the secondary exchanges. The additional
> volume of trading created by these additional markets tends to reduce the price
> spreads. The authors conclude that while competition plays a larger role in restraining
> NYSE spreads, attempts to limit trading of securities of either exchange from taking
> place off its principal exchange should be discouraged.

189. Eubank, Arthur A., Jr., "Risk/Return Contrasts: NYSE, Amex, and OTC," *Journal of
Portfolio Management* 3:4 (Summer 1977): 25-30.

> A number of information sources including Compustat tapes, *Standard and Poor's
> Corporation Records*, and the *Federal Reserve Bulletin* are used to study corporate
> performance for the period 1960 through 1973. It is determined that there are
> significant differences between the risk-return performances of the NYSE, Amex, and
> OTC markets. However, these differences are not sufficient to provide an opportunity
> for diversification.

190. Salpukes, Agis, "Wall Street Blues," *New York Times Magazine* (December 18, 1977):
42-44, 98-103, 106.

> Article profiles Wilfred (Bill) Tyrrell. Photographs cover a day in his life from 5:30
> a.m. to 5 p.m. Tyrrell is a floor trader; on an average day, he walks 10-15 miles on
> the trading floor, handles 25 to 35 telephone calls, and executes about 450
> transactions. Tyrrell began his career in the securities industry when he joined Merrill
> Lynch, Pierce, Fenner and Beane at the age of 22. He moved to Hayden Stone as a
> floor clerk in 1956, became a vice president and partner at the age of 32, and now
> serves as the head floor trader for the evolved Shearson Hayden Stone, the eighth
> largest and one of the fastest growing securities companies on Wall Street. Tyrrell
> provides honest opinions on mergers which have occurred in the industry and on the
> impact of automation.

1978

191. Reddish, Jeannette M., "People of the Financial World," *Financial World* 147 (February 1, 1978): 32-33.

> Arthur Levitt, Jr., is sworn in as the new chairman of the American Stock Exchange. The 45-year-old son of the New York state comptroller, Levitt leaves his position as president of Shearson Hayden Stone. Levitt believes that his sixteen years at Shearson have given him a "special feel for the individual investor," which will give him a good start at the Amex where 70 percent of trading comes from individuals, making it the "people's market."

192. Cole, Robert J., "Exchanges Ask S.E.C. To Approve 5-Way National Electronic Hookup," *New York Times*, 10 March 1978, sec. IV, p. 7.

> The proposed Intermarket Trading System (I.T.S) will link the NYSE, Amex, Philadelphia, Boston, and Pacific Stock Exchanges and will allow traders at any of the five to determine the best available price when buying or selling stock. The Midwest Stock Exchange has joined a competing system that links it with the Cincinnati and Boston exchanges. According to Richard Walbert, president of the Midwest Stock Exchange, the only time the Midwest exchange will appear on the system is when it has a better price to offer than any of the others. If the price is the same as NYSE, only NYSE will appear.

193. "The Upside-Down Two-Tiered Stock Market," *Financial World* 147:6 (March 15, 1978): 46-47.

> The two-tier market once described the "nifty fifty" (Dow Jones industrial and giant growth stocks) and the rest of the market. Now, two-tier takes a new twist. The Dow, S&P, and premier growth stocks have been declining while the Amex index reaches a new bull market high. The reverse two-tier market has been evolving over the past two years. Some investors are not surprised; they began buying secondary stocks in 1974.

194. "Quiet Bull Market," *Forbes* 121 (May 15, 1978): 50-1.

> The Amex has been in a solid bull market for over three years. The Amex Market Value Index is up 130 percent from its low in December 1974; the Dow Jones Industrial Average is only up 40 percent during that same period. Trading volume has also doubled on the Amex. According to Robert J. Farrell, analyst for Merrill Lynch, larger pools of money are being invested in small companies, with the result that the Amex is now outperforming the Big Board.

195. Loomis, Carol J., "The Irrational One-Tier Stock Market," *Fortune* 98:2 (July 31, 1978): 72-78.

The past five years have seen the collapse of the two-tier market in which a few dozen growth stocks with very high price-earnings multiples formed a top tier much in the image of the few swells living on the hill in a nineteenth century New England mill town. At the end of 1972, the top fifty stocks were selling at an average of 31.5 times earnings while the bottom fifty were at 12.5 times earnings. Now, however, a levelling has occurred with the top fifty showing a p/e average of 10.4 and the bottom just below at 9.8. While it could be that the stock market, as an allocator of capital, is telling us that most companies are pretty much alike, this simply is not true and leaves the market looking irrational.

196. "A Big Step Closer to a National Market," *Business Week* 2547 (Aug. 14, 1978): 28-29.

A composite quotation system, which electronically displays bid and asked prices for the NYSE, Amex, and most regional exchanges, takes an important step toward creating the congressionally mandated national market system. The intermarket trading system formed in April so far includes only about 100 of the 1,000 stocks which are dually listed. The National Association of Securities Dealers remains a holdout. The NYSE and Amex are resisting making their routing system available to other exchanges.

197. Phalon, Richard, "The Small Investor: He's Back--and, for a Change, He's Winning," *Forbes* 122:8 (October 16, 1978): 56-64.

The Street is booming. In the first four months of the year, Merrill Lynch opens 121,907 new accounts. New customers are young, mainly in their 30s and 40s. Emerging growth companies are bullish on the Amex. The Amex indices have risen 172 percent in the past four years compared to 75 percent for the NYSE. Arthur Levitt, Jr., chairman of the Amex, who sees his chief function as "bringing Main Street back to Wall Street," concedes that the investment quality of issues appearing on the Amex is not quite up to the previous year's and that signs of increasing speculation are obvious. Some the Amex's biggest gainers reflect a faddish interest in gambling and resort stocks.

198. "What Kept the Amex at Home," *Business Week* (November 20, 1978): 38.

The Amex has called off a three year study to move across the Hudson River to Jersey City. The stay-in-New York plan includes having state agencies build a $40 million facility. The Exchange would lease the building for $2.6 million annually for 25 years. Merger talks with the NYSE may resume; the Big Board says that only a move into the new Amex facility is being considered. In competition between the exchanges, the NYSE has begun merger discussions with the Commodity Exchange, Inc., the nation's third largest futures market, while the Amex Commodity Exchange is talking to the New York Cocoa Exchange, which ranks second in the world behind the London cocoa market.

1979

199. Eckenrode, Robert T., "Forecasting--How To Keep Your Head When All About You Are Losing Theirs," *Planning Review* 7:2 (March 1979): 23-26.

Robert Eckenrode, executive vice president and chief financial officer for Amex, discusses the state of planning when he joined the Exchange staff. A 1968 forecast of trading volume was evaluated using the "reductio ad absurdum" technique. A variety of forecasting techniques are discussed: judgment methods, extrapolation of trends and cycles, methods based on causality, analogy and innovation, and interaction methods. Eckenrode concentrates on facts, getting as broad an input as possible. Factors which must be considered in the securities industry are possible merger of the NYSE and Amex in 3-10 years, relocation of Amex outside of New York City within five years, evolution of the market system linking the largest seven or eight of the 11 U.S. exchanges, increasing automation, and the proliferation of trading products.

200. "Amex Advisors Urge Changes," *New York Times*, 15 June 1979, sec. IV, p. 5.

An outside advisory board suggests changes in the governing structure of the Amex. The 21-member Board of Governors should add two more members and more representation should be given to members working on the floor in order to cover more adequately the diversity of floor trading. The Board also suggests that governors' terms be increased to three years instead of the current two. The suggestions are part of a 39-page report made by a group headed by William J. Casey, former chairman of the SEC.

201. "St. George of the Small," *Time* 114 (August 13, 1979): 42.

"Small business" now includes firms with revenues of $5 - $350 million. Arthur Levitt, Jr., chairman of the American Stock Exchange, where 95 percent of the 964 listed companies have revenues under $350 million, wants to be the champion of small business and proposes establishing a lobby that would be patterned after the Business Roundtable, whose members include the chiefs of 190 of the nation's largest corporations. Levitt lists special needs of the companies as dealing with government regulation and compliance with environmental, safety and other rules.

202. Goldman, Ari L., "American Exchange Wins State Backing To Build New Home," *New York Times*, 3 November 1979, pp. 1, 24.

The New York state legislature approves a plan to build a $53 million home for the Amex at Battery Park City in lower Manhattan, just west of the World Trade Center. The $53 million will be financed principally by the Urban Development Corp. and bonds floated by Triborough Bridge and Tunnel Authority. The Exchange will have two parts, a 12-story office building and a 50,000-square-foot trading floor. The Exchange hopes to break ground in April and finish the project in late 1981 or early 1982.

203. Bleiberg, Robert M., "People's Exchange: a Critical Note on the Amex Expansion Plans," *Barron's National Business and Financial Weekly* 59 (November 5, 1979): 7.

An editorial decries the mix of government and business. Arthur Levitt, Jr., chairman of the board of the Amex also serves as chairman of the federal Small Business Conference Commission. In another joint venture, the "People's Exchange" is looking forward to new quarters to be financed by the Triborough Bridge and Tunnel Authority, a state grant, and a U. S. Treasury approved contribution through an Urban Development Action Grant. The Amex has agreed to a 25-year lease for the new facility at an annual rental of $2,575,000.

204. Smothers, Ronald, "City Receives Federal Funds To Assist Commercial Construction Projects," *New York Times*, 29 December 1979, p. 25.

New York City receives five Federal grants to aid commercial construction; one grant is an expected $10.35 million award to supplement state and private funds needed to build new headquarters for the Amex in Battery Park City. The announcement is the last step of a three-year effort by state and city officials to keep the Exchange and its 2,100 jobs in the city; it will also create an additional 2,600 jobs. Construction of the $69.3 million building to replace the 86 Trinity Place headquarters is scheduled to start in Spring 1980 and be completed within two years.

1980

205. Chakravarty, Subrata and Jane Carmichael, "Death of What?" *Forbes* 125:4 (February 18, 1980): 40-42.

Trading volume on the NYSE has increased by 86 percent during the first month of 1979, but the Amex has surged up 191 percent over the last year. The Amex Market Value Index is setting new highs almost on a daily basis. Options trading has also risen from an average of 66,000 contracts daily in 1979 to an average of 121,000 so far this year. The authors contend that investors have finally recovered from the market crashes of 1970 and 1974 and are once again seeking out the stock of small companies. Amex Chairman Arthur Levitt, Jr., calls it a "resurgence of entrepreneurial spirit." Speculative run-ups are becoming common once more. Many analysts see this as dangerous in a market like the Amex which has a "thin float"--not enough shares to satisfy the demand. Other analysts are seeing this as a beginning of a new bull market, as investor confidence spreads to the NYSE.

206. Greenebaum, Mary, "How the Amex Rose to Superstardom," *Fortune* 101 (February 25, 1980): 153, 156.

In 1979, the Amex Market Value Index rose 64 percent compared to 12.3 percent for the S&P 500 and 15.5 percent for the New York Stock Exchange composite. The reason for the jump on the Amex is the popularity of oil companies, most of which trade on the Amex. Since 488 of the 500 companies on the S&P index are listed on the NYSE, these two indexes move in tandem. Both indexes were hurt last year by a fall of 14 percent in the prices of IBM and AT&T. The bull market in small companies began in 1976 and both the Amex and NASDAQ have been beneficiaries. Institutional investors especially have been selling off the old glamour stocks and turning their attention to fast growing high tech stocks and to oil companies.

207. Hawawini, Gabriel A. and Ashok Vora, "Evidence of Intertemporal Systematic Risks in the Daily Price Movements of NYSE and AMEX Common Stocks," *Journal of Financial and Quantitative Analysis* 15:2 (June 1980): 331-339.

Earlier research with New York Stock Exchange securities concluded that monthly returns of securities did not precede or follow monthly returns on the market index. This study extends the research to daily returns for securities listed on the Amex. Strong and all pervasive lead/lag effects were found for daily returns. However, the relationship for stocks listed on the Amex is weaker than for those on the NYSE.

208. Hershman, Arlene, "Here Come the Customers' Yachts," *Dun's Review* 116:4 (October 1980): 48-51, 55-56.

The individual investor is the winner in the 1980 bull market that has seen the Dow Jones industrial average zoom. Individuals are the biggest buyers of the small, secondary issues that dominate the list of leaders on the American Stock Exchange, where the average has climbed 31 percent for the year. However, a correction is expected. Discussion includes the relationship between the market and politics and the number of eighteen year olds entering the job market each year.

1981

209. Fabozzi, Frank J., "Does Listing on the AMEX Increase the Value of Equity?" *Financial Management* 10:1 (Spring 1981): 43-50.

Fabozzi describes the procedure for listing on the Amex and the analysis a company should conduct prior to making a listing decision. Benefits to be anticipated include improved marketability of shares, fairer and more specific prices, and lower cost of capital to the firm.

210. Levitt, Arthur, Jr., "Self-Regulation at the Amex: Protecting the Endangered Entrepreneur," *Directors & Boards* 6:1 (Summer 1981): 31-32.

The Chairman of the American Stock Exchange notes that "corporate governance" is not a single subject, as though complaints against corporations are all the same as are the remedies for those complaints. Neither large nor small companies have a "monopoly on virtue or iniquity;" they must all be held to the same standards. When the SEC asked that exchanges require listed companies to appoint independent audit committees, the Amex took a different approach. The Amex board adopted a policy of encouraging audit committees composed of outside directors and established a director pool for companies seeking directors with specific talents or experience. Under the plan, regulated managers still feel that they have control of their companies. In a related action, the Amex establishes its own audit committee.

211. "Amex Board Expected To Weigh Expanding Trading Room Space," *Wall Street Journal*, 26 August 1981, p. 16.

The Amex board is expected to consider an expansion plan that is much less grandiose than the previous plan, which called for the building of a new facility in Battery Park City. The State of New York had planned to contribute $53 million to the project, but the Amex was unable to raise the $17 million needed for its share. Plans for the new building were shelved last year, and the Amex began to explore other avenues for expansion. The Amex recently bought an adjacent building at 22 Thames St., which will be used for offices.

212. Kichen, Steve, "The Amex Nobody Knows," *Forbes* 128:6 (September 14, 1981): 230-232.

The NYSE is known as the home of the blue chips and NASDAQ is the place to find small company bargains. The Amex now has an image problem. Few of the Exchange's stocks are household names. Of the 950 stocks traded on the Amex, 68 are oil and gas related. But these account for more than 45 percent of the Amex's total market value. The author contends that there are as many bargains to be found on the Amex as on the OTC and many Amex stocks are underpriced because they do not get much attention from the analysts.

213. Feder, Barnaby J., "Amex To Expand Floor by 35%," *New York Times*, 15 September 1981, sec. IV, p. 21.

The Amex governors approve a $6.98 million construction project to expand the Exchange's trading floor capacity. The new trading space will contain room for four large trading posts and 140 new booths for member firms in the area which is now the visitors' gallery. The plan is the result of a study commissioned a year ago after exchange and state officials decided not to build in the Battery Park City development.

214. "Success Story," *Working Woman* 6 (October 1981):100.

Sarah P. Boehmler serves as a Vice President of the Amex in charge of liaison with member firms. Her big project for 1981 is to encourage foreign investment in Amex firms. Boehmler graduated from Sweet Briar College in 1965 with a liberal arts degree and spent three years as a social worker on the way to a job with Reynolds Securities of Charlotte, N.C., in 1968. A new position with Smilen and Safian, Inc., a Wall Street brokerage firm, in 1972 provided a bridge to employment with the Amex marketing department in 1973. There are now 27 female brokers who are members of the Exchange.

1982

215. Slemrod, Joel, "Stock Transactions Volume and the 1978 Capital Gains Tax Reduction," *Public Finance Quarterly* 10:1 (January 1982): 3-16.

This research tests the hypothesis that the capital gains tax cuts in the Revenue Act of 1978 caused an increased volume of stock transactions. Transaction volume on all exchanges has risen substantially. Average daily volume for the first five months of 1981 was more than three times higher than it was from 1972 through 1977. While the association between the tax cut and increased transaction volume is strong for the NYSE, it is not supported for the Amex.

216. Lease, Ronald C. and Wilbur G. Lewellen, "Market Efficiency Across Securities Exchanges," *Journal of Economics and Business* 34:2 (1982): 101-109.

This paper adds to past empirical evidence concerning efficiency of the American capital market. Securities traded on the American Stock Exchange show return rates that imply more frequent price departures from equilibrium than do those of the NYSE. The study sample includes trades by 2,500 customers of a large national retail brokerage house between January 1964 and December 1970.

217. Grant, James, "Current Yield: Looking Back at a Forecast," *Barron's National Business and Financial Weekly* 62 (December 13, 1982): 62-63.

> Buried in an article on bond prices is an interview question: What about the Treasury bond market on the Amex? A broker is puzzled. Many don't know or care; quotations aren't included in newspapers. But they're on the tape--between Wang Labs B and The Pep Boys are common and long bonds. The Amex trading share is small--$1.4 billion on a daily volume of $35 billion. Since it started in 1975, Amex trading volume has grown steadily--to $321 million in 1979 and to four times as much in 1982.

1983

218. Wonderling, David, "Data Communications Edges Its Way onto the Stock Exchange Floor," *Telephony* 204 (April 4, 1983): 30, 34, 79.

> The American Stock Exchange has developed a data communications system to serve the 18 trading posts on the exchange floor. Contel Information Systems is helping to make the system even more efficient. Stock purchase orders are routed from a member firm's own computer system to a message switching host at the Securities Industry Automation Corporation (SIAC). When SIAC and the Amex began, in late 1980, looking for new designs and technologies to support trading, a LAN proved the most effective solution. ContelNet, a system which is fast and cost-effective, will easily handle installation of new protocols.

219. "Business Bulletin: Stock Exchange," *Wall Street Journal*, 12 May 1983, p. 1.

> The Amex introduces a new board game called *Stock Market Specialist*, which simulates action on the trading floor. It is being marketed by John N. Hansen Co. of Anaheim, CA, and will cost about $20.

220. Klein, Joe, "Sweet Sweetback's Wall Street Song," *New York* 16 (September 5, 1983): 42-43.

> In the 1960s, when Melvin Van Peebles was in an angry period making movies like "Sweet Sweetback's Baadasssss Song," many were aware of his business acumen. He is newly reincarnated as the only black trader on the floor of the Amex. Now 51 years old and "well turned out . . . at once funky and distinguished: straw Panama hat, pink-striped button-down shirt, pink-and-brown bow tie, tan slacks, and salmon socks," Van Peebles explains that he is "doing just what I've always done--making deals." Van Peebles notes that he ended up on Wall Street after losing a bet with Dr. Henry Jarecki, chairman of Mocatta Metals and "one of the most respected men on Wall St." Jarecki also has "an interest in" Timber Hill, Inc., Van Peebles' employer; the three other Timber Hill traders are all women.

221. Deemer, Walter, "You Ain't Seen Nothin' Yet - More Speculation for Wall Street?"
Barron's National Business and Financial Weekly 63:40 (October 3, 1983): 66-67.

Judging from past experience, a bull market is near. On one day in the spring, Amex
daily volume was 20 percent of the Big Board's. This is not excessive based on past
history when the ratio ranged from 40 to 60 percent. In 1961 and 1968, weekly
volumes reached 88 and 73 percent, respectively. Mr. Deemer advises that investors
can lose valuable positions if they give in to speculation jitters and risk selling too
soon.

222. Ambler, John., "American Stock Exchange Trades Old Network for Streamlined Setup,"
Data Communication 12:11 (November 1983): 255-258, 261-262.

Over a period of years, the Amex network grew in response to increases in trading
levels on the floor. Hardware and wiring needs began to intensify the space shortage
on the floor. In 1980, Amex and its subsidiary Securities Industry Automation
Corporation (SIAC) began looking for a more efficient network design. A local area
network was chosen as the most effective way of coping with the problem of
connecting devices and computers while efficiently using space on the trading floor.
The network is called AMNET (American Stock Exchange Network) and is designed
to be implemented in stages. The first stage is a network called ACARS (Amex Card
Reader System), which only supports card readers. Printers continue to be handled by
each host. Both ACARS and AMNET use microcomputers called bus interface units
(BIUs) for connections to devices and hosts. These BIUs provide the hardware and
software interface between the card readers and the cable bus. The local area network
results in a significant reduction in the number of dedicated lines and modems and will
also help to reduce future wiring and installation costs. Thus, it provides a relatively
inexpensive incremental growth path.

223. Eubank, Arthur A., Jr., and John D. Markese, "Listing Changes from the AMEX to the
NYSE and Stock Return Behavior," *Akron Business & Economic Review* 14:4 (Winter 1983):
18-22.

In the past twenty years, as companies moved their listings from the Amex to the
NYSE, they were assumed to be seeking benefits from enhanced prestige and a more
liquid market for their equity issues. This study examines daily stock returns for a
seven year period, June 1962 to July 1969. It concludes that the market initially reacts
positively to a listing change from well in advance of the announcement week through
the listing week. However, once listing occurs, cumulative average residuals have a
tendency to decline.

1984

224. Rosenberg, Hilary, "NYSE vs AMEX vs OTC - a Bitter Triangle," *Financial World* 153:2 (January 11-24, 1984): 16-19.

> As the over-the-counter market grows, both the NYSE and Amex are actively recruiting new listings. Amex's game plan has started to pay off with 56 newly listed companies in 1983, a record volume of shares, and an all-time high net income. The exchanges are also vying for new products. Amex has diversified more than the other exchanges since the mid-1970s and now is in the forefront with index options products, trading market indexes and narrow-based industry indexes.

225. Kalogerakis, George, "How To Be Better Than the Pack," *Communicator's Journal* 2:3 (May/June 1984): 18-22.

> In an interview, Arthur Levitt, Jr., chairman of the board of the American Stock Exchange, comments on the flow of information in the financial community. To improve communications, the Amex has founded 22 American Stock Exchange Brokers Clubs around the world; has established a pool of potential corporate directors which includes Cabinet officers and university presidents; encourages brokerage firms to write reports on Amex firms; and holds regional forums to help Amex companies develop management techniques and understand communication with shareholders and investors. A unique program provides CEOs, Amex board members, and heads of brokerage firms the opportunity to participate in an Outward Bound wilderness education course for personal growth, self-reliance and outdoor skills. The Amex considers the investing public as their most important constituency while other exchanges place their member companies in this position.

226. Mamis, Robert A., "Taking Stock," *Inc.* 6:6 (June 1984): 57-64.

> In the days "when ticker tape was made of real paper," the daily message in the Amex test run just before the opening bell read "Good morning. Reject old ways." The tradition took its own advice when the Exchange converted to high speed tape. Now the Exchange may be haunted by companies remembering the advice. Listings have decreased a third from 1,249 to 913. Dropouts have not been replaced by the new, emerging public companies the Exchange seeks. Some 1,600 of the 4,025 companies in NASDAQ meet the financial requirements to list on the Amex, the traditional home of promising young companies, yet remain with the over-the-counter system. A war of words is erupting in the search for listings. NASDAQ is prepared to publish a booklet, "Why NASDAQ," which "freely takes potshots at the listed exchanges." Amex prepares to respond with a publication of its own, "Amex vs. OTC."

227. "Innovation at Amex Aids Traders with a Touch," *Wall Street Computer Review* 1:10 (July 1984): 25-26.

The Amex continues to establish "firsts" in automation. AUTOPER, a touch sensitive screen display, developed by Fluke Manufacturing Co. of Seattle, allows brokers in branch offices anywhere in the world to buy and sell stocks on the Amex and receive return reports within seconds. Both the number of screens in use and the scope of transactions handled have increased since the first AUTOPERs were installed on the exchange floor in June 1983. In addition to increasing order execution speed, the system has improved transaction accuracy.

228. Kichen, Steve, "Where the Aisles Aren't Crowded," *Forbes* 34:2 (July 16, 1984): 166-167.

Even during the first half of 1984 when most indexes were down, the Amex performed relatively well. Investors seeking small company bargains are shopping on the OTC, but many companies selling under book value are to be found on the Amex. Many of these companies have had superior earnings growth or have benefited from special situations--mergers, buyout offers--which have increased the price of their stock. The author argues that there are bargains to be found on the Amex.

229. Bleakley, Fred R., "Big Board May Open 24 Hours," *New York Times*, 19 July 1984, sec. IV, pp. 1, 8.

The NYSE and Amex say that they are thinking of instituting 24-hour trading to accommodate increasing international trading. Many foreign investors are accumulating more shares in U.S. stocks and vice versa. The change to 24-hour trading would cause major changes at brokerage firms and professional money management organizations.

230. "How the Amex Is Luring Newcomers to Its Trading Floor," *Business Week* (July 30, 1984): 96-97.

Robert Blau, a "cheerful, slightly rumpled former college professor," is one of 31 survivors from 95 newcomers who paid $15,000 apiece for a new class of options trading membership. Over the years, he has used rights offerings to bring onto the floor his brother-in-law, two fraternity brothers, and a hometown friend. Now, the Amex's 661 members have approved plans to add up to 108 new options memberships beginning July 23d. Under the plan, current exchange members will be issued rights. With several accumulated rights, one can obtain a two-year trading permit. In informal trading, rights have been worth $5,500 making the value of a permit approximately $38,500. This compares with the $50,000 needed to lease a regular options membership for a year and the $180,000 needed to buy one. The system can be considered an installment plan for purchase of a membership.

231. "One Record the Market Will Keep Breaking," *Business Week* (August 20, 1984): 135.

Record trading volumes are expected to continue. Volume on the Amex has tripled in the past decade. Computers run smoothly on heavy volume days.

232. Antilla, Susan, "Wall Street: Battle of the Stock Exchanges," *Working Woman* (September 1984): 82-83.

The New York and American Stock Exchanges are experiencing increased competition in listing companies from the over-the-counter market (OTC), also known as the National Association of Securities Dealers. The NASD was once the home of companies too small to list on the NYSE or the Amex. Now, it claims that 700 of its companies meet the financial criteria to list on the NYSE and 1,700 qualify for the Amex, but they prefer to stay where they are. The progression was once OTC to Amex to NYSE, the advantage being that the last two had a central place where price quotes could be obtained. In 1971, the National Association of Securities Dealers Automated Quotation system (NASDAQ) was established and prices of the "unlisted" stocks were available to all on computer screens. In 1982, the National Market System (NMS) was set up as a further improvement; the price and volume of selected OTC stocks were reported 90 seconds after a transaction occurred. Amex Executive Vice President of Marketing Walter H. Liebman says that the reason for the NASD's growth is the increased number of companies going public. Over a ten year period ending in 1983, the Amex's listings were down 34 percent at 822 companies and the NYSE was down one percent with 1,550 listings. NASD gained by 60 percent to 3,901 companies during that same period. In 1983, the Amex published a brochure titled *Why your company should list on the American Stock Exchange*. It told of lower transaction costs for investors and more attention from brokerage research analysts. Since 1975, the Amex has added options, corporate and government bonds, options on indexes, and a gold coin exchange to its offerings in an effort to increase revenues. William G. McGowan, chairman of MCI, suggests that if a system like the NYSE were to be designed today, it would probably look more like NASD.

233. McConnell, Donald K., Jr., "Are the Big 8 Increasing Their Share of the NYSE, AMEX, and OTC Audit Markets?" *Journal of Accounting, Auditing and Finance* 7:2 (Winter 1984): 178-181.

During 1974 and 1975, Big 8 firms audited 92 percent of companies listed on the NYSE and 76 percent from the Amex. This study finds statistically significant Big 8 audit client gains in the NYSE and Amex markets, but not in the OTC. Amex companies exhibited 43 percent of changes between auditor tiers, the highest percentage of the three groups. Big 8 auditors had a net gain of 35 clients; 74 percent of Amex changes resulted in retention of a Big 8 firm while 26 percent ended in re-engagement of a non-Big 8 firm.

1985

234. Antilla, Susan, "Wall St. Woos the Nation's Most Powerful Women," *Working Woman* 10 (January 1985): 38-40.

On the floor of the Amex are the "glad-handing" chairman of the Exchange, smiling floor traders, quality label booze, flower arrangements. The target audience is the Committee of 200 of the Women's Forum, Inc. The Chicago-based committee promotes entrepreneurship and researches women's management styles. Eighty percent of its members have built, own, or run their own businesses. President of the forum, Donna Shalala, an Amex governor, noted that "I told the women who were working at the Amex a few years ago that women would take over the floor of the Exchange." The evening includes lectures on the success of mid-sized growth companies and training in the trading of stocks, as well as the drinking and dining. The Exchange's interest is in the companies which are or may become large enough to list on the Amex.

235. Branch, Ben and Kyungchun Chang, "Tax-Loss Trading, Is the Game Over or Have the Rules Changed?" *Financial Review* 20:1 (February 1985): 55-69.

Research on tax-loss trading, seasonal influences, or the January effect flourished in the 1980s. This study examines four questions: Does the December/January return pattern persist? Can tax-loss candidates be identified by other means? Does the observed return pattern differ with the size of the firm? Does the December/January pattern occur in other months? The researchers conclude that Amex and OTC December-decliners tend to perform significantly better in January than is the case for NYSE issues.

236. Gilpin, Kenneth N. and Todd S. Purdum, "Amex Picks No. 3 Man; He'll Focus on Strategy," *New York Times*, 15 February 1985, sec. IV, p. 2.

The Amex announces a restructuring of top management and promotes Kenneth R. Leibler to the new position of senior executive vice president of marketing, administration and finance. The new job makes him the No. 3 man after chairman Arthur Levitt, Jr., and president Robert J. Birnbaum. In his new position, Leibler will oversee marketing and strategic planning, including seeking new issues for the Amex. He will also be chairman of the Amex Commodities Corp., which was created to oversee trading of options on gold bullion. Mr. Leibler says his main goal will be to make the Amex more competitive in the increasingly diverse financial services industry.

237. "Amex Stocks Found To Outperform Issues of OTC, Big Board," *Wall Street Journal*, 6 March 1985, p. 60.

A study done by the consulting firm Wilshire Associates for the Amex finds that stocks listed on the Exchange posted a 617 percent return for the past ten years, compared with a 353 percent return for the over-the-counter market, and 339 percent for Big Board issues. The study tracked the performance of all stocks and American Depositary Receipts, which represent stocks of foreign companies. Both the NYSE and the NASD challenged the findings, stating that results of this type of analysis would vary greatly depending on the time period selected.

238. Kessler, G. A., "The Battle for the Exchange Floor," *Institutional Investor* 19:5 (May 1985): 81-84.

A battle for control of the Exchange floor may be imminent. At war with the specialists are full-service brokerage houses who want to become specialists making markets in listed stocks. The Big Board and Amex feel that the change is feasible provided that there is "an impregnable 'Chinese Wall' between the downstairs specialist unit and the upstairs brokerage concern." SEC approval is needed.

239. McMurray, Scott, "At a Crossroads: Continued Survival of Amex Is Threatened as Its Listings Decline," *Wall Street Journal*, 2 July 1985, p. 1.

In the bull markets of the late 1960s and the late 1970s, the Amex was a prime place to speculate, especially with energy stocks. More recently, activity on the Amex has cooled and the Amex's roster of listed companies has declined by more than a third because of mergers and acquisitions, graduations to the NYSE, and delisting for failure to meet financial criteria. Only the thriving options business has slowed the Exchange's slide. Some say the Amex's problems are compounded by the fact that Chairman Arthur Levitt, Jr., has spent much of his tenure away from the Exchange. Mr. Levitt, however, says that his efforts have been directed toward narrowing the prestige gap with the NYSE. He has created a network of 24 domestic and foreign Amex Clubs, where listed companies make pitches to local brokers. In the past year, newly listed Amex companies won the right to choose the specialist for their stock from a list of seven provided to them by the Exchange. The Amex has also formed a trading link with the Toronto Stock Exchange and plans to open an office in London to attract foreign listings and investors.

240. Miller, William H., "Levitt," *Industry Week* 227:1 (October 14, 1985): 57-58.

Arthur Levitt, Jr., chairman and CEO of the American Stock Exchange, admits to a fear of lightning as he prepares to lead a group of businessmen on a six day Outward Bound expedition into the Colorado mountains. He has exhibited no such fears in the Amex's relations with governments. He devotes approximately 20 percent of his work schedule to the American Business Conference, an association of midsize, high-growth companies he established in Washington, D. C. In his first year at the Amex, he visited 100 mayors, governors, and political leaders because "so much of what we do in the securities industry depends on Congress, the Administration, and the Securities and Exchange Commission . . . [who] care very little about brokers, exchanges, specialists, and traders. They care passionately, though, about growth, jobs, and capital formation."

241. "Instinet and Amex To Offer Overseas Trading Hookup," *Wall Street Journal*, 10 December 1985, p. 6.

The Amex and Instinet have agreed to offer foreign investors access to the Amex trading floor through Instinet's electronic order-execution system. The link will be available to investors in stocks and options who have access to the financial information network of Reuters Holdings PLC and will cost institutional customers an average of up to $1,000 per month. The new system will allow immediate two-way communication between the foreign investor and the Amex floor specialist. At present, it takes between a few minutes and several hours for trades to be confirmed. As part of the agreement, Instinet will become a member of the Exchange. It was previously announced that Reuters has agreed to acquire a 27 to 28 percent interest in Instinet.

1986

242. Schmitt, Eric, "Acquisitions Helped Some Amex Leaders," *New York Times*, 2 January 1986, sec. IV, pp. 9, 12.

The Amex posts record trading figures for 1985 and a marked increase over 1984. Over 2.1 billion shares were traded, compared with 1984's 1.56 billion. Some of the top performers made key acquisitions to expand existing operations or to shift their primary business to more lucrative fields. The Exchange also listed 74 new companies in 1985, bringing total listings to 941.

243. Phalon, Richard, "And Then There Were Three," *Forbes* 137:8 (April 21, 1986): 31-32.

A surging OTC market is taking volume from both the NYSE and the Amex. Listings on the NYSE and the Amex have been slipping, losing companies to mergers and buyouts, while the OTC has climbed to 4,136 issues. A new flood of initial public offerings is adding to the OTC numbers, since few new issues meet the listing requirements of either the Amex or the NYSE. Both of the major exchanges are marketing their services more aggressively, diversifying into futures and options contracts.

244. Benway, Susan Duffy, "Dogged Curb: the Amex Is Alive and Well," *Barron's National Business and Financial Weekly* 66:22 (June 2, 1986): 42, 74.

The Amex is rebutting stories that it is losing ground to the over-the-counter market. (Especially hurtful was a recent *Forbes* article which included the photo of a graveyard.) Current records cite the year's first quarter stock volume as 43 percent above the previous year's, records in options trading, new listings expanding by 63 percent, and profits of $2.9 million, up from $1.7 million in 1985's first quarter. Perhaps most important is the price of seats; a recent sale was at $220,000. While down from the 1983 high of $325,000, this is $85,000 more than the last sale in 1985.

245. Schmerken, Ivy, "Amex Eyes Tandem, Stratus for New Market Data System," *Wall Street Computer Review* 3:11 (August 1986): 6, 8.

Although the Digital Equipment Corporation (DEC) is one of the most actively traded issues on the Amex, it will lose this important customer when the Amex converts to Tandem and Stratus computers during the first quarter of 1987. DEC does not offer fault-tolerant architecture which includes redundant components within the computer to serve as a back-up should any computer element fail. Such design is considered critical to future development of the Market Data System which captures quotes and last-sale figures for 900 listed stocks, 130 stock options, and stock index options. Current computer systems of the Amex provide a "Who's Who" of computer manufacturing: Fluke Manufacturing of Everett, Washington, provides Quick Quote, a computerized touch sensitive screen system; a prototype of a new electronic specialist's limit order book runs on an IBM AT; Kiel Corp. of Amherst, New Hampshire, makes hand held keypads for updating quotes and last sales; and Votrax of Troy, Michigan, makes a voice synthesizer which alerts SWAT, the Stock Watch Automated Techniques market surveillance systems which run on an IBM 4341, a small mainframe.

246. "The Specialist System Gives Amex the Edge," *Euromoney* (September 1986): Amex Supplement, 19-20.

Brokers explain why the Amex is dominant in dually listed options. Fred van der Scheer of Bear Stearns in Amsterdam says "the specialist system is advantageous as compared to the market maker system [used on other exchanges]." Gerald Kuschuk, a senior vice president of Prudential Bache, adds that "in most situations the American Stock Exchange specialists and traders have made a strong commitment to make or maintain a fair and orderly market with reasonable spreads and depth." The Amex imposes strict responsibilities on its specialists. Used to maintain orderly markets are tight pricing, uniform pricing, efficient block trading, quick solutions to "don't know" problems, and accountability.

247. "In Technology, Other Exchanges Are Playing 'Catch Up'," *Euromoney* (September 1986): Amex Supplement, 21-22.

> Mark Smith, vice president in charge of Amex's Planning Division, notes two main thrusts for the Exchange's technology: "to make trading as efficient as possible" and "to electronically extend the marketplace." Amex is ahead of other exchanges in automation, annually spending one third of its income on development of new systems. In 1978, the Amex developed AMOS (Amex Options Switching System). AMOS has recently been extended by AUTO-EX, which provides automatic and instant execution of market orders, and certain marketable limit orders, in the Exchange's Major Market Index. Quick-Quote, introduced in 1984, allows specialists to update a number of options quotes simultaneously.

248. Sonenclar, Robert, "Hanging on at the Amex," *Financial World* 155:19 (September 16, 1986): 82-83.

> The Exchange has a mandate to innovate or die. Long term viability is being questioned; company listings are a third lower than they were ten years earlier. This is in spite of past pioneering efforts: cultivating major foreign firms, dealing in American Depositary Receipts, listing stock options, admitting female members, leading in use of computer technology. Successes include options trading, the Major Market Index, and the value of an Amex seat.

249. Ruffel, Charles, "Evolving To Survive with the Fittest," *Euromoney* (November 1986): 80F-80H, 81.

> After years of struggling in the shadow of the NYSE, the Amex becomes a "hybrid" exchange offering an options program, electronic trading systems, and international linkages. However, the Amex dilemma may be hiding in the "dust of this year's thundering bull market." Records have been set in daily, weekly, and monthly trading; new listings are running ahead of previous years; and seat prices are as high as they have been in the past three years. On the Exchange floor, there is concern that initial public offerings and professional trading are obscuring the fundamental problem that mergers, bankruptcies, and takeovers are eroding Amex listings.

250. Blum, Gerald A., William A. Kracaw, and Wilbur G. Lewellen, "Determinants of the Execution Costs of Common Stock Trades by Individual Investors," *Journal of Financial Research* 9:4 (Winter 1986): 291-301.

> The researchers' opening premise is that "among the underpinnings of much of modern portfolio theory, and of the resultant pricing models for common stocks, is the assumption that the costs associated with securities are negligible." They study nine years of data, 139,548 transactions by 8,000 individual investors trading on the NYSE and the Amex. They conclude that odd lot trades are more costly than round lots, but

that only in relatively low-priced stocks is the extra cost really noticeable. Consistently, trades on the Amex were more costly to execute than those on the NYSE.

251. Atchison, Michael D., "Non-Representative Trading Frequencies and the Detection of Abnormal Performance," *Journal of Financial Research* 9:4 (Winter 1986): 343-348.

In the past, numerous studies used betas computed with the ordinary least squares technique and daily returns. However, these betas are considered biased and inconsistent due to nonsynchronous trading periods or differences in trading frequency. This study examines 250 samples from each of 20 firms trading on the NYSE and the Amex using the Scholes and Williams beta estimator and tests developed by Brown and Warner. It finds that the bias in the OLS beta estimate is largest for less frequently traded firms and concludes that future researchers employing the event study technique may use OLS estimates rather than the more involved Scholes and Williams technique.

1987

252. Mahar, Maggie, "Big Winners and Bad Losers: 1986's Best and Worst Performing Stocks/Summing Up: the Financial Highlights of 1986 in Tabular Form," *Barron's National Business and Financial Weekly* 67:1 (January 5, 1987): 16-17, 47-48.

Marty Zweig, publisher of *The Zweig Forecast* describes 1986's two-tier market as "brutal." Blue chips boomed while smaller stocks slumped. On the Amex, Lee Pharmaceuticals is reporting record sales--primarily based on false fingernails which come in "nine fetching colors." Home owners bought heavily from the company heading the Amex's list, Crown Crafts, a manufacturer of bed coverings. In a year when scandals were big news on and off Wall Street, the Amex's list included two companies with bad news. In May, Conner Corporation, a mobile home manufacturer, pleaded guilty to a criminal charge of defrauding the Veterans Administration. Professional Care was indicted in a Medicaid fraud case.

253. "The Puzzle in Post-Listing Common Stock Returns," *Journal of Finance* 42:1 (March 1987): 119-140.

Negative stock returns immediately following listing on the NYSE are pervasive. Negative returns are not affected by trading locale; they impact equally on OTC, Curb/Amex and regional exchange stocks being listed on the NYSE and on OTC stocks listing on the Amex. Explanations explored include data peculiarities, biases in first trading price, loss of market maker support, issues of new stock shortly after listing, and insider dumping of the stock.

254. Wayne, Leslie, "Innovative Amex Fights Back," *New York Times*, 16 June 1987, sec. IV, pp. 1, 5.

The Amex is still a distant third in volume of trading among the major U.S. exchanges; however, recent strategic steps have moved it ahead of the competition with a variety of new products. Earnings are up 90 percent over 1986. The most recent seat sold went for $400,000, up from $285,000 at the end of 1986. In addition, the Amex has attracted listings away from the NYSE, because it is the only exchange to allow companies to trade two classes of stock with different voting rights. Many see this as an anti-takeover measure. In its options business, the Amex has continually increased its market share at the expense of the Chicago Board Options Exchange.

255. Pierog, Karen, "The 'Kid' in the Amex Pit," *Futures* 16 (July 1987): 37.

A brief profile of Laura Pedersen lists accomplishments: at 11, she was trading stocks and at 20 became the youngest specialist on the Amex floor. Disappointed with college, she headed for the Amex, got a job as a data clerk, became a clerk for the Market Value Index, and became a specialist for Major Market Index options. Along the way, Pedersen obtained her bachelor's degree in finance from New York University and now teaches an arbitrage and strategy course at the New York Institute of Finance.

256. "Vote Proposal Is Opposed," *New York Times*, 23 July 1987, sec. IV, p. 5.

The SEC's proposal to impose a uniform one-share, one vote standard on stock exchanges is greeted with opposition by the Amex. Chairman Arthur Levitt says the proposal will create a legal and administrative nightmare and would probably be unworkable.

257. Reiter, Glenn M., John D. Lobrano, Richard M. Kosnik, and James M. Bergin, "New U.S. Listing Procedures for Non-U.S. Issuers," *International Financial Law Review* 6:9 (September 1987): 11-14.

The United States Securities and Exchange Commission has approved rule changes by the NYSE and the Amex which will allow waiver or modification of certain financial reporting and corporate governance listing standards for non-U.S. issuers. Four categories which may be waived when they conflict with the laws, customs or practices of a non-U.S. issuer's home country include quarterly reporting of interim earnings; composition and election of the board of directors; shareholder approval requirement and voting rights; and quorum requirements for shareholder meetings.

258. Parker, Marcia, "2 Exchanges in Works for Foreign Securities," *Pension and Investment Age* 15 (September 7, 1987): 3, 74.

The Amex is developing a proposal which will help institutional investors target good opportunities in international equities. Operating guidelines for handling foreign securities not registered in the U.S. have been drafted. Apfel & Co., a New York financial research firm, is designing clearing and settlement procedures. The SEC must provide approval. Richard Scribner, Amex executive vice president, notes "we have had a great deal of interest from institutional investors and foreign issuers."

259. Fischel, Daniel R., "Organized Exchanges and the Regulation of Dual Class Common Stock," *University of Chicago Law Review* 54:1 (Winter 1987): 119-152.

Firms raising funds from capital markets must decide whether to sell common or preferred stock and under what circumstances investors other than common stockholders will have the right to vote. The Amex allows trading of dual classes of stock provided that the inferior voting stock has some voting rights. Legislation has been introduced in both houses of Congress that would require the Amex and NASD to adopt the NYSE prohibition against trading of dual class common stock. Critics of competition among exchanges believe the result is a "race to the bottom," in which investors and corporate managers will choose the exchange which provides the greatest opportunity to exploit investors. The author concludes that it is not necessary for all exchanges to have the same governance rules. It is unclear if a prohibition on listing of dual class common stock is harmful or beneficial to investors.

260. Leibler, Ken, "At the Helm on 'Black Monday;' Why Dad Was in Such a Bad Mood," *New York Times*, 6 December 1987, sec. III, p. 3.

An article by Amex president Ken Leibler describes his reaction to the stock market crash and Amex's role in dealing with it. He stayed in Manhattan every evening, and wore a beeper with an 80-mile radius to stay in constant touch with what was happening. People knew they were going to lose money; the important thing was to maintain confidence in the system. It was important to keep the market open to prevent the chance of a panic. He further adds that there is no coordinated mechanism in place to deal with a market crash.

261. Cowan, Alison Leigh, "Amex Seeks New Network," *New York Times*, 28 December 1987, sec. IV, pp. 1, 3.

The SEC is reviewing an Amex proposal to allow sophisticated investors in the U.S. to trade securities issued by foreign corporations that do not register with the Commission. The plan would create a closed network of several hundred eligible investors who could freely trade among themselves. Traders would not be protected by the usual disclosure requirements.

1988

262. Palmer, Jay and Diana Henriques, "Winners and Losers -- Which Stocks Performed Best and Which Performed Worst," *Barron's National Business and Financial Weekly* 68:1 (January 4, 1988): 18-22.

While "economic historians of the 26th century, looking back on the antics of their ancient ancestors in the 20th century," may rate 1987 as a good year for investors, *Barron's* dubs it "downright horrible." The American Stock Exchange Index rose 7.5 percent compared to a 2.26 percent gain in the Dow Jones Industrial Average. In the final quarter, Amex stocks were either takeover targets or losers. Losers were headed by the Dino De Laurentiis family of entertainment companies.

263. Rogers, Ronald C., "The Relationship Between Earnings Yield and Market Value: Evidence from the American Stock Exchange," *Financial Review* 23:1 (February 1988): 65-80.

A series of papers have examined empirical anomalies referred to as the size effect and earnings/price (E/P) effect in the pricing of common stock. In the E/P effect, portfolios of stocks with high E/P ratios earn higher risk-adjusted returns than those of a randomly selected portfolio. In the size effect, small firms earn higher risk-adjusted returns than do large firms over a long period. An empirical method used by Basu is replicated and applied to firms that traded on the Amex from 1963 to 1982. Evidence from the Amex study suggests that both the E/P and size effects exist but that the size effect is predominant.

264. Linn, Scott C. and Larry J. Lockwood, "Short-Term Stock Price Patterns: NYSE, AMEX, OTC," *Journal of Portfolio Management* 14:2 (Winter 1988): 30-34.

The study aims to document three patterns which prevail in markets of the NYSE, Amex, and OTC: a monthly pattern in which returns during the first half of the month are consistently higher than those during the last half; a weekly pattern in which returns for the first two days of the week are consistently below those of the last three days; and, the persistence of a negative return for the Friday to Monday close period. Four portfolios are drawn representing 1,510 stocks from the NYSE, 990 from the Amex, 2,400 from OTC, and 2,500 from NYSE/Amex. They conclude that the patterns do hold true and test two trading rules: time purchases so that they occur toward the end of the month and sales so that they occur around the middle of the month, and time purchases so that they occur toward the close on Monday or Tuesday and sales so that they occur toward the close on Friday. Neither strategy led to excess gains over a passive buy-and-hold rule.

1989

265. Goldenberg, Susan, "Strategies: Foreign Exchange," *Canadian Business* 62:3 (March 1989): 103-105.

Deterred by steep fees and stringent listing requirements, Canadian corporations have avoided foreign market listings. Only 14 of *Canadian Business*'s top 50 companies and only 200 Canadian firms of any size are listed on the 125 foreign stock exchanges. However, Canadian representation is increasing, forming almost one-third of foreign listings on the major American exchanges. While the Amex charges Canadian companies half of what it charges U.S. firms, fees still range from $5,000 to $30,000, depending on the number of shares outstanding. Other Amex requirements include a $750,000 pretax income and $4 million in shareholder equity.

266. Wong, Betty, "Amex 'Window' Is Opened a Bit by State Judge," *Wall Street Journal*, 3 April 1989, sec. C, p. 15.

A New York State judge rules that a loophole in the Amex constitution allows an investor to bring a dispute with a broker to the independent American Arbitration Association, rather than the Amex. This may occur even under an existing agreement that disputes will be brought before a self-regulating organization of the securities industry. The ruling will allow Amex investors to file for arbitration in a form more impartial than the industry body. The American Arbitration Association is the only arbitration board not linked to an exchange. Disputes stemming from Black Monday have increased the volume of pending arbitration proceedings.

267. "Other Indexes Set Records Before the Industrials Did," *Wall Street Journal*, 25 August 1989, sec. C, p. 16.

The Dow Jones Industrial Average finally closes above its 1987 pre-crash record. It was the last indicator to climb to a new high; the Amex was the first to surpass its pre-crash record on June 8th, the S&P 500 Index and the NYSE Composite followed on July 26th, and the NASDAQ Index on August 3d.

268. Ritter, Bradley Scott and William R. Dauber, "The Present and Future Role of the Electronic Trading Linkage in the Developing International Securities Markets," *George Washington Journal of International Law and Economics* 22:3 (1989): 639-670.

Advances in computer and communication technology have reduced the barriers of distance between nations, creating worldwide profit-making opportunities. Few industries have been affected as extensively as the securities industry. International exchange linkages are examined using the Amex-Toronto Stock Exchange (TSE) plan as an example. Seven problems to be addressed by international linkage schemes are discussed: investment communities of the world must desire participation in the global market; lack of uniform regulation between nations; need for an effective surveillance and enforcement mechanism; implementation of an efficient international clearance and settlement system; existence of varying time zones; development of a consolidated reporting system so that investors can obtain information regarding the trading of a particular security in every country in which it is traded; and, finally, the potential reluctance of foreign exchanges to deal with the United States. The authors conclude that internationalization of the securities markets will continue because of the many benefits gained by trading in a much larger, more diversified marketplace. This well documented article provides a wealth of further references.

269. Savitz, Eric J., "Winners and Losers: a Rundown of the Biggest Gainers and Sorriest Losers," *Barron's National Business and Financial Weekly* 69:40 (October 1, 1989): 22, 24.

Overall, 1989 on Wall Street is described as "the year that gave mortgages a bad name." Real estate, savings and loan, and financial institutions were hard hit. Amex's biggest loser is Sorg, a financial printer which filed for Chapter 11 in August. Mission Resource Partners, an oil and gas limited partnership, starred among takeover targets. The best acting stock was Graham Corp., a vacuum and heat-transfer equipment company, which saw the price of its shares advance more than fourfold.

270. "Tap Dance Kid," *Forbes* 144 (November 20, 1989): 164.

Amex board member and former Oklahoma congressman, James R. Jones, is named new chairman of the American Stock Exchange. One of Jones's jobs will be to lobby for laws that will bring back the small investors and defend the specialist trading system. Another task will be to bring the Amex back into favor with middle-sized companies, which are now listing with NASDAQ.

271. Barclay, Michael J. and Clifford G. Holderness, "Private Benefits from Control of Public Corporations," *Journal of Financial Economics* 25:2 (December 1989): 371-395.

Trades of blocks involving at least five percent of the common stock of NYSE and Amex listed companies are typically priced at substantial premiums to the post-announcement exchange price. The average premium is 20 percent, which represents approximately four percent of the total value of the firm's equity. Previous assumption was that shareholders are homogeneous and corporate benefits are distributed to shareholders in proportion to their ownership. However, block premiums suggest that large-block shareholders use their voting power to secure private corporate benefits that do not accrue to other shareholders.

1990

272. Cowan, Alison Leigh, "Market Value Index Set Record During the Year," *New York Times*, 2 January 1990, sec. D, p. 11.

> The Amex was a big winner in 1989. Companies listed have improved earnings. The Market Value Index hit an all-time high on October 10th and closed the year up 23.5 percent, exceeding the 19.3 percent rise of the NASDAQ Composite Index. The Dow Jones Industrial Average was up 27 percent and the NYSE Composite, 24.8 percent.

273. Canna, Elizabeth, "SRO at First AMEX Conference on Shipping Stocks," *American Shipping* 32 (February 1990): 75.

> In one of its regular industry specific conferences for investors, the Amex sponsors a presentation by Costas Grammenos, a director of one of the world's few post-graduate programs in shipping, trade, and finance at London's City University. Grammenos told an audience of more than 100 analysts and portfolio managers that investors are encouraged to participate in shipping but should not repeat the mistakes of the late 1960s and 1970s. In that period, cheap bank credit combined with a view of shipping as a glamour industry led to excess supply and related necessary corrections. Now, a rapidly aging fleet brings opportunities for long-term investment in long-term growth companies. Amex has several shipping stock listings; eight of them are new listings from the past two years.

274. "AMEX May Ease Standards in Bid To Lure OTC Firms," *Wall Street Journal*, 1 March 1990, sec. C, p. 6.

> Amex Chairman James Jones says that the Amex is making a special effort to identify companies that would not normally meet listing standards, because they reinvest earnings in research and development. This would include some of the over-the-counter market's most promising stocks.

275. Friedman, Jon, "Jim Jones Will Need More Than Volcker," *Business Week* (April 16, 1990): 72.

> Five months into his term as Amex chairman, Jim Jones scores a coup by getting Paul A. Volcker, former chairman of the Federal Reserve Board, to serve on the Amex Board of Directors. *Business Week* reports that Jones will need all the help he can get. Small investors are reluctant to buy stocks. Although trading volume is up because of trading in the new Nikkei put warrants, all other trading is down 17 percent from 1987. Seats are going for only $215,000, down from $420,000 in 1987. About 15 companies are leaving the Exchange each year to go to the NYSE where volume is 12 times higher. A Georgetown Law School graduate, Jones is seen as a man of

Washington. He served as chief of staff during the Johnson presidency and was a Democratic representative from Oklahoma for 14 years.

276. Sanger, Gary C. and James D. Peterson, "An Empirical Analysis of Common Stock Delistings," *Journal of Financial & Quantitative Analysis* 25:2 (June 1990): 261-272.

Paper presents an investigation of stock returns, bid-ask spreads, and trading volume for common stocks delisted from the NYSE or the Amex. For firms with prior announcements, equity values decline by approximately 8.5 percent on announcement day. When there are no prior announcements, the same adjustment occurs between the last day of trading in the initial market and the close of the first day of trading in the new market. Four hypotheses are examined: the liquidity, the management signalling, the exchange certification, and the downward sloping demand curve hypothesis.

277. Hershey, Robert D., Jr., "4 Exchanges to Test Trading O-T-C Issues," *New York Times*, 1 June 1990, sec. D, pp. 1, 4.

The SEC approves a test program to allow 100 stocks now traded over-the-counter to be traded on the American, Midwest, Philadelphia and Boston stock exchanges. The new program is a benefit to investors, because the competition will generate better prices for OTC stocks, and OTC companies will have an opportunity to sell to a larger group of investors. Companies will not have to pay additional fees to list and trade stocks on the exchanges. The NYSE will not participate, because it relies heavily on listing fees. The Amex is the largest exchange in the pilot program.

278. Norris, Floyd, "3 Exchanges Set Plan for All-Night Trading," *New York Times*, 19 June 1990, sec. D, p. 2.

The Amex, Cincinnati Stock Exchange and Chicago Board Options Exchange announce plans with Reuters for all-night trading of stocks and options to stake out a leading position in global trading, starting in 1992. The NYSE announces a similar system. Electronic trading will be done 6 p.m. to 6 a.m., eastern time. Amex says that the new system will have higher transaction costs than daytime trading, because they will need to pay fees to Reuters and to the exchange whose products are traded. The initial focus will be on stock index options and the largest stocks and then to options on products traded in Chicago and on the Amex.

279. Steedley, Filbert and Warren Midgett, "Treasure Hunt," *Forbes* 145 (June 25, 1990): 242.

The authors discover undervalued stocks on the Amex. They argue that investors mistakenly view the Amex as a dumping ground for stocks that can't quite make it on the NYSE. Their criteria are: more then 10 percent return on equity, a strong balance sheet (debt-to-equity not to exceed 80 percent), and a share price above five. The list is to be seen as a starting point for an Amex "treasure hunt."

280. Kulkosky, Victor, "On-Line Transaction Processing: Real Time Is Money," *Wall Street Computer Review* 7:10 (July 1990): 12-24.

During a general downturn in the midrange computer market, sales of online transaction processing (OLTP) computers are better than ever. Recent developments at the Amex and Boston Stock Exchange indicate that systems strategy is away from fault tolerance toward a predominantly DEC architecture. There are three levels to both the old and new architectures: a data repository into which trades enter the exchange and out of which they are reported for execution; a second layer where trades are executed; and a third layer on the floor, where traders and market makers use PC workstations linked through local and wide area networks. At the Amex, the first tier, where every transaction must be logged in and out, will be redundant and probably remain fault tolerant. John Diesem, Amex's senior vice president for systems technology, notes that "There, the consequences of going down are pretty significant, so we say, fine, make those machines fault tolerant, but let's have redundancy as well." Elsewhere, the need for fault tolerance is less obvious and the Exchange is moving to an approach where backup machines can be booted up in less than a minute in the event of hardware failure.

281. Savitz, Eric J., "The Quick and the (Near-) Dead: High Tech Shone, Debt-Heavy Firms Didn't, in Half," *Barron's National Business and Financial Weekly* 70:27 (July 2, 1990): 20-21, 42.

For the first half of 1990, the biggest loser list is headed by companies which have filed for Chapter 11. Heading the list on the Amex is EECO, a computer keyboard manufacturer. Sharing in an overall slide of financial institutions is Trust America Service, a Florida mortgage banking company. On the bright side is OEA, with stock up nearly 120 percent. Profits come from manufacture of automobile airbag initiators, the "gizmos used to make the bags inflate," and escape systems (ejection seats) for military aircraft.

282. Torres, Craig and William Power, "Turf War: Markets Fight for Private Placements," *Wall Street Journal*, 11 July 1990, sec. C, pp. 1, 9.

The Amex, in a joint venture with Reuters Holdings PLC and the NYSE, launches a system for trading privately placed stocks and bonds in an effort to unseat NASD's new electronic PORTAL system. The Amex seeks to share in the expected boom in the $170 billion private placement market under SEC Rule 144a passed in April. With companies exempted from normal disclosure requirements, there is a promise of more income and a toehold in the market for exchanges whose electronic systems dominate.

SEC's Rule 144a is designed to encourage capital raising and trading in the private placement market. Only several hundred institutional investors and several dozen investment banks qualify. The Amex's SITUS system (System for Institutional Trading of Unregistered Securities) will be more flexible than PORTAL, because it builds on Reuters' technology and a huge share of financial market data. Reuters' worldwide securities database, software capabilities, and links to big investors via Instinet's electronic trading system could challenge PORTAL.

283. Baker, H. Kent and Martha Johnson, "A Survey of Management Views on Exchange Listing," *Quarterly Journal of Business & Economics* 29:4 (Autumn 1990): 3-20.

The study surveys the chief financial officers of 608 companies to obtain opinions about exchange listing. Included are companies newly listed on the NYSE from 1985 to mid-1987, those that listed on the Amex between 1982 and mid-1987, and NMS companies eligible for listing on the NYSE or Amex as of August 31, 1987. Respondents agreed that listing increases a company's visibility, enhances its prestige, and improves the marketability of its stock. There was a high correlation between the responses of NYSE and Amex managers. NYSE and Amex respondents said that the most important party in the listing decision is the CEO/ president. Amex companies' next ranked response, the investment banker, may reflect that the Exchange's firms are frequently seeking initial public offerings or secondary offerings.

284. Weiss, Lawrence A., "Bankruptcy Resolution: Direct Costs and Violation of Priority of Claims," *Journal of Financial Economics* 27:2 (October 1990): 285-314.

Weiss examines the resolution of bankruptcy for 37 NYSE and Amex companies that filed petitions under the 1979 Bankruptcy Code. Direct costs average 3.1 percent of the book value of debt plus the market value of equity at the end of the fiscal year preceding bankruptcy. Priority of claims is violated for 19 of the 37 firms studied; this happens more frequently for cases filed in New York.

285. Savitz, Eric J., "The Slaughter Quarter: Except for Oils, July-September Was Murder on Stocks," *Barron's National Business and Financial Weekly* 70:40 (October 1, 1990): 20-24.

Nikkei put warrants take eight of the top 10 spots on the quarter's list of winners reflecting the "devastation to Japanese shares." Gains in most cases were over 100 percent, and in some instances over 200 percent. Some former "wunderkinds" showed up on the list of Amex losers: Catalina Lighting, a maker and distributor of lighting fixtures, and ECI Environmental, a California asbestos-abatement firm. Top performer was Maxxam, parent of both Kaiser Aluminum and Pacific Lumber, which was boosted by soaring aluminum prices.

286. Ambrosio, Johanna, "Fault-Tolerance Out, DEC In at the AMEX, *Computerworld* 24:41 (October 8, 1990): Section 1, 31.

   The Amex is trading its high-cost Stratus and Tandem computer systems for Digital Equipment Corp. machines. Instead of having hosts with huge applications, smaller machines will pinch hit for each other in case of failure. Software will be broken down into small, easier to maintain modules. The goal is to add flexibility and have the Exchange's architecture able to respond quickly to changing needs.

287. D'Ambola, Thomas and Antonia Alafouza, "AmEx Seeks a World Beyond Wall Street," *Management Review* 79:11 (November 1990): 10-11.

   Interview with CEO and Chairman of the Board James R. Jones focuses on Amex's plans for global expansion. Jones is also chairman of the U.S.-Japan Trade Task Force and a member of the House International Trade Subcommittee. He sees the democratization of Eastern Europe as an opportunity to divert military-related spending to education and job training and to capital investment such as infrastructure building. He suggests tax incentives to encourage people to save, through IRAs or other vehicles. Jones sees the Amex as emissary of its listed companies and as a market searching to broaden liquidity and create new financial opportunities for investors. He would like to see reciprocity with the European community and with Japan to enable U.S. companies to trade their stocks in foreign markets.

288. Torres, Craig, "AMEX Sees Way To Make Inroads in Foreign Issues," *Wall Street Journal*, 18 November 1990, sec. C, p. 20.

   The Amex hopes to challenge the OTC market's dominance in trading in unregistered foreign stocks in 1991, an action that would be expected also to increase the number of options and warrant issues on the same securities. Currently, many major foreign companies trade in American Depositary Receipts (ADRs) in an OTC market separate from the NASDAQ system. Prices are now listed daily in the pink sheets by the National Quotations Bureau, Inc. The SEC has restricted trading and price dissemination because the companies that issue ADRs do not follow accounting and disclosure requirements mandated in the U.S. The Amex believes that the SEC ruling establishing an OTC Bulletin Board creates a loophole that will allow more active trading in unregistered stocks. The Amex says that it plans to trade unregistered foreign securities with its specialist system or on its SITUS system, which is still in development. NASD President Joseph Hardiman says that if the Amex is cleared to trade electronically, it's an endorsement of what NASD is doing.

289. Foltz, Kim, "Advertising: Aggressive Campaign for the Amex," *New York Times*, 28 December 1990, sec. D, p. 4.

Because of a slowdown in business and increased competition from rival markets, the Amex will launch a $1 million print campaign and join the advertising battle raging between the NYSE and NASDAQ for listings. The basic differences between the Amex and NASDAQ are that the Amex has a physical location in lower Manhattan and each stock is handled by a specialist whose job is to create a continuous market for the stock. NASDAQ has no specialists, just a group of dealers; no one has responsibility for the quality of the market. Business on the Amex dropped considerably as a result of the crash and then during the Middle East crisis.

290. Dutt, Jill, "Wall Street Stock Exchanges Woo the International Firms," *Multinational Business* 4 (Winter 1990-1991): 12-20.

The exchanges are scrambling to convince international companies to list shares for trading in U.S. markets. Only 840 foreign companies have American Depositary Receipts, but the number is growing fast. The most formidable barrier to listing is not cost but compliance with U.S. securities laws. Donald Panoz, chairman of Dublin-based Elan Corporation, explains their attraction to trading on the Amex: "The American market offered the kind of distribution and recognition of the true capital value of a company we were looking for . . . the mix of institutional and individual shareholders are a good balancing act." Choice of the Amex is driven by the company's ability to choose the specialist for its stock.

1991

291. "Wall Street Wakes Up to Image Management," *Wall Street Computer Review* 8:4 (January 1991): 39-44.

The Amex, one of the pioneers of computing in the securities industry, looks at image management technology. A pilot system called COINS (Computer Output Information System) from Imtech will record a year's worth of daily trading reports on an optical disk. While paper is heavy and microforms deteriorate, the optical disk technology offers advantages in accuracy, quality, productivity, and reduced need for expensive storage space.

292. Nickel, Karen, "The Best & Worst Stocks of 1990," *Fortune* 123:2 (January 28, 1991): 58-63.

In a year described as "The Ecstasy and the Agony," the Dow Jones Industrial Average "galloped to giddy new highs," and, finally on "one dismal day" in October was 14 percent behind for the year. On the Amex, best stocks were OEA, which with zooming sales of air-bag triggers, provided a 165 percent return to investors.

Following were Thermo Cardiosystems (medical equipment) and Tech Ops Sevcon (controls for electric vehicles). Topping the worst list is Price Communications, with a -97 percent return to investors and difficulties servicing debt.

293. Dubofsky, David A., "Volatility Increases Subsequent to NYSE and AMEX Stock Splits," *Journal of Finance* 46:1 (March 1991): 421-431.

Paper extends to the Amex previous research which provides evidence that NYSE stock return variances increase subsequent to stock distribution days for splits of 100 percent or greater. Items believed to contribute to the phenomenon include: attributes of the stock and/or company (Amex stocks are smaller and lower priced), specialist behavior, and ownership factors (institutions dominate ownership and trading of NYSE stocks but not of Amex). The variance of daily returns behavior is found to be true for the Amex also, however post-split volatility is found to be less.

294. "Politician Does Well," *Forbes* 147 (March 18, 1991): 140.

After just a year on the job, James R. Jones has turned the Amex into a serious competitor of the NASDAQ. Amex's stock volume for 1990 was up more than six percent, while the NYSE fell five percent and NASDAQ fell slightly. To become more competitive, Jones has Amex staff working with member brokerage firms to create new instruments to trade on the Exchange, for example, warrants that allow investors to trade puts and calls on broad foreign market indexes. Another project is an incubator market for small companies that spend heavily on research and development; these companies would eventually graduate and be fully listed on the Amex enabling the Exchange to compete directly with NASDAQ.

295. Torres, Craig, "AMEX Aims To Lure 'Emerging' Companies by Setting a Lower Standard of Listing," *Wall Street Journal*, 13 September 1991, sec. C, p. 1.

The Amex Board approves the Exchange's "emerging company marketplace" initiative and the plan goes to the SEC for clearance. The Amex posted a loss for the first half of 1991 and is desperate for new listings. The Amex is looking for the hot new companies of the future and will target some of the 1,000 companies currently traded on NASDAQ as well as emerging private companies. Its proposed new standards will be the lowest of any major exchange.

296. Eckerson, Wayne, "Network Security Lacking at Major Stock Exchanges," *Network World* 8:37 (September 16, 1991): 23-24.

The Government Accounting Office (GAO) finds a total of 68 computer and network security and control problems at five of the nation's six major exchanges and concludes that the nation's largest stock exchanges are vulnerable to power outages and data tampering. The most security problems, 24, were noted at the Midwest Stock

Exchange. There were no problems at the National Association of Securities Dealers, three at the New York Stock Exchange, and five at the Amex. The report says that four of the stock markets do not have contingency plans outlining the procedures and responsibilities for managing automated systems and trading floor operations during various emergencies; the Amex is cited for lack of onsite backup generators. As a result, the Exchange has contracted with an outside firm to haul in generators to supply power in the case of an extended outage.

297. Lux, Hal, "Change or Die: Can the Shake-'em Up Style of Jim Jones Rejuvenate the American Stock Exchange?" *Investment Dealers Digest* 57:46 (November 18, 1991): 12-17.

In his two year tenure as Amex chairman, James Jones has floated or promoted projects such as a satellite trading floor in Hawaii, a joint venture to promote foreign trade for Amex companies, a 24-hour trading project with Reuters and the Chicago Board Options Exchange, an Amex sponsored research subsidiary, and a long line of new products. Now, he announces a top-to-bottom reorganization of the Exchange refocusing everything from members to customers. While listing fees are the big money maker for the NYSE, at the Amex they account for only 12 percent of revenue, while 40 percent is contributed by communication fees, money paid by information services like Quotron to get real time Amex data. As the Exchange continues to add new business lines, it has announced plans for an Emerging Company Marketplace, an incubator for smaller companies. One tradition which is surviving, although it does "not exactly promote the hauteur and exclusivity of the American Stock Exchange," is the lunch hour ceremony in which a male trader who gets engaged is shackled to the loading dock while fellow brokers and clerks lob eggs, tomatoes, mustard, and mayonnaise from Greenwich Street windows.

298. Baker, H. Kent and Richard B. Edelman, "Valuation Implications of AMEX Listings: a Joint Test of the Liquidity-Signaling Hypothesis," *Quarterly Journal of Business & Economics* 30:1 (Winter 1991): 87-109.

Baker and Edelman examine stock price behavior for 62 common stocks that moved from NASDAQ to the Amex during a five year period from 1982 to 1987. The study tests the joint liquidity signaling hypothesis which states that a stock's prelisting liquidity and performance affect the market's response to news of an Amex listing. The results reveal significant differences between companies with low liquidity and low performance and those with high liquidity and performance. Firms with low liquidity and past performance before listing appear to benefit from listing on the Amex. Abnormal gains are realized but additional costs are incurred by listing.

1992

299. Weiss, Gary, Gail DeGeorge, and David Greising, "The Amex: a Questionable Seal of
Approval," *Business Week* (April 13, 1992): 78-79.

The Amex fights losses to NASDAQ in the secondary stock market by inaugurating an
Emerging Company Marketplace (ECM) of 23 small companies. The ECM companies
are top heavy in areas of high tech innovation ranging from cancer therapy to air-
cooled krypton lasers. Although the companies were "handpicked by a 'blue-ribbon'
committee" of Amex members and managers, *Business Week* found "dubious" listings:
Printron, Inc. and Cancer Treatment Holdings, Inc.

300. Hoffman, Thomas, "CASE Project Melds Stock Exchange's Data," *Computerworld*
26:20 (May 18, 1992): 95, 97.

The Amex is integrating its computer systems through use of Oracle Corp.'s computer
aided software engineering (CASE) tools. This is an upgrade of the Oracle relational
database management system installed in 1985. The Exchange is handling 160,000
options contracts and 35,000 equity transactions daily. The next two stages will
address move of networked applications into a Windows environment and provision of
more marketing information.

301. Barsky, Neil, "Big Board, Amex Discuss Sharing a New Home," *Wall Street Journal*,
12 June 1992, sec. C, pp. 1, 11.

For almost a year, executives from the NYSE, Amex, J. P. Morgan, and New York
City have been discussing Morgan Bank's proposal for a joint home for the exchanges
at the corner of Broad and Wall Streets, directly across the street from the present
home of the NYSE. This would mean construction of a new office tower in the space
occupied by Morgan's former headquarters and three other office buildings. The cost
could be as high as $1 billion and is seen as a way to reverse business exodus and
secure lower Manhattan's standing as the world's center of finance while expanding
and upgrading exchange trading floors. No agreements have yet been signed.

302. Lueck, Thomas J., "7 Giants of Finance May Share Quarters," *New York Times*, 13 June
1992, sec. I, p. 27.

The NYSE, Amex, and New York's five commodities exchanges are talking about
building a new trading complex. Endorsed by New York's City Hall, the joint
complex could insure that New York's most important financial institutions remain in
the city and give an economic boost to lower Manhattan. The site would cover the
entire block bounded by Wall Street, Broad Street, Exchange Place, and William
Street. It is located four blocks east of the Amex and just east of the NYSE building.
The two exchanges would occupy the block, with the commodities exchanges in a

separate building connected by a bridge across Exchange Place. Olympia & York, which has spent over $1 million on planning documents, has asked to be designated as developer of the project. Another proponent is J. P. Morgan and Co., which owns more than half of the existing office space on the site proposed for the complex. All buildings on the 1 1/2 block site would be bought and demolished to make way for the complex. On the other hand, the NYSE has already spent $600 million in the last 10 years to install new computers and upgrade the trading floor in its existing building. The five commodities exchanges (the New York Mercantile Exchange, the Commodity Exchange, the Coffee, Sugar & Cocoa Exchange, the New York Cotton Exchange, and the New York Futures Exchange) have all grown rapidly in the last decade and have been exploring sites in the TriBeCa section of New York City and in New Jersey.

303. O'Brien, Timothy L., "Dicey Dealings: Amex's New Market for 'Emerging Firms' Faces Embarrassments," *Wall Street Journal*, 1 July 1992, sec. A, pp. 1, 4.

The Emerging Company Marketplace (ECM), launched earlier in 1992, has less stringent listing requirements in order to lure new business to the Amex. Most ECM companies are unprofitable and two have been cited for questionable management. Such problems raise questions about the Exchange's screening process. In the past decade, the Amex has lost business steadily to the NYSE and NASDAQ; share of total volume plunged from 6.4 percent in 1981 to 3.7 percent. Alfred Avasso, controlling shareholder of PNF Industries, Inc., was barred permanently six years ago from any association with the Amex. PNF is one of 25 companies in the EMC; it has lost money for the last four years and expects no profit this year. The company now has a market value of $15 million because of its EMC listing, although its sales last year were only $870,000. Mr. Avasso's original $2 million investment has increased in value to over $9 million.

304. Jones, James R., "Easing the Way for Young Companies," *New York Times*, 12 July 1992, sec. 3, p. 13.

Amex Chairman and CEO James R. Jones says venture capital money has dried up and growing companies, a major source of job growth, have been hit the hardest. Among the Amex's plans to help these companies is a new stock market called the Emerging Companies Marketplace, which opened last spring. It has 25 listed companies, taken out of the OTC market and brought to the auction market. The cost of trading the companies' stock has been reduced because it is traded directly to investors instead of via middlemen. This benefit has been limited until now to large and mid-sized companies.

305. Norris, Floyd, "Problems Emerge in New Amex List," *New York Times*, 13 July 1992, sec. D, p. 6.

A majority of the stocks' prices have plunged since the opening of the Emerging Companies Marketplace. Of the 22 companies that began trading on March 18th, 19 now trade for less than their closing price on the first day. The Amex argues that investors get a better deal because the difference between the bid and ask prices is narrower than when they traded on the OTC, enabling them to buy for less and sell for more. The one star is Media Logic, which makes machines that test the quality of floppy disks for makers of the disks. It began trading on the Amex at $6.375 and closed last week at $12.75. In the year ending March 31st, Media Logic turned its first profit and now has a promising product which tests the quality of computer tapes. Most of the attention has focused on the questionable listing of firms like PNF, a maker of fire-retardant chemicals, which has a major shareholder who is a convicted arsonist. The Amex has changed its procedures for reviewing companies since listing this firm so that it now looks at the history of large shareholders as well as officers and directors.

306. Harrell, Wilson L., "The Third Market: the Entrepreneurial Movement Will Save America," *Success* 39:6 (July/August 1992): 9.

The American Stock Exchange has created a second tier exchange specifically for Third Market firms. The Third Market has been spawned by entrepreneurs in an economic revolution over the past two decades. Third Market participants include about one million companies that are growing 15 percent a year or more and that are responsible for over 44 percent of all business-to-business sales in the U.S.

307. O'Brien, Timothy L., "Amex Acts To Delist PNF Permanently, Offers It a Hearing," *Wall Street Journal*, 21 August 1992, sec. C, p. 13.

The Amex halts trading in PNF Industries, Inc., and moves to delist the stock permanently. In a suit filed by PNF's board, the company alleges that recently ousted Chairman Otis H. Hastings tampered with the company's flame retardant, causing substandard coatings to be shipped to three customers. It also alleges that Mrs. Hastings, the former treasurer, improperly issued checks in the company's name. The SEC is also investigating the company. PNF is one of the companies on the Amex's new Emerging Company Marketplace.

308. Cronin, Xavier A., "Limits of Market Surveillance," *Wall Street and Technology* 10:1 (September 1992); 15-20.

The SEC and major exchanges concede that they cannot catch all "schemers:" some countries have "blocking statutes," dummy corporate accounts shield identities, and accounts are set up in "other" names. Yet, regulators feel the market is not a "den of thieves." Over the past 10 years, the exchanges have set up high-tech computer surveillance systems. At the Amex, detection happens automatically. The robotic voice of SWAT (Stock Watch Alert Terminal) makes a "terse, reverberating announcement," which is followed by a computer print of the suspect trading. SWAT reacts an average of 80 times a day; 75 percent of the cases are dismissed as insignificant. If further investigation indicates violation of federal securities law, the case is referred to the SEC.

309. "Amex Lifts Price of Stocks To Trade in Sixteenths," *Wall Street Journal*, 1 September 1992, sec. C, p. 9.

The Amex announces it will allow stock prices up to $5 per share to trade in increments of one-sixteenth of a dollar. Currently, Amex shares trade at eighths of a dollar if they are $1 or more per share. Only shares under a dollar trade in sixteenths. The Amex says the new rule will apply to 370 issues and will promote greater liquidity in cheaper stocks.

310. O'Brien, Timothy L., "Amex Investigates 2 Exchange Specialists as Part of Inquiry into Listing of PNF," *Wall Street Journal*, 11 September 1962, sec. C, p. 9.

The Amex says it is investigating specialists Robert Van Caneghan and Louis Miceli in the trading of PNF stock. The Amex investigation revolves around their role in obtaining a listing for PNF in the Emerging Companies Marketplace and the nature of their financial involvement with the company.

311. O'Brien, Timothy L. and William Power, "Amex Chief's Actions Anger Some Members," *Wall Street Journal*, 14 September 1992, sec. C, pp. 1, 11.

Amex Chairman James Jones is a former Oklahoma congressman and Washington lobbyist. He was lured by the Amex in hopes that he would bring quick regulatory approval for new Amex ventures and trading instruments. Jones won approval from the SEC for the new Emerging Company Marketplace. He is still seen as a Washington insider with a limited grasp of Wall Street. There is speculation that if Clinton is elected, Jones will leave the Amex to become budget director or head of the SEC. Jones, who wants to see the Amex customer-driven, is more popular with companies listed on the Amex and with Wall Street brokerage firms than he is with floor members. Jones says his goal is to make the Amex the primary market for options and all kinds of derivatives. The Amex is already the second largest options exchange behind the Chicago Board Options Exchange.

312. Eichenwald, Kurt, "An Outsider's Amex Stewardship: Some Mixed Results in 3 Years at Helm," *New York Times*, 29 September 1992, sec. D, pp. 1, 22.

In an attempt to gain ground as a stock exchange and to win favor in Washington, the Amex recruited James Jones, former Democratic congressman, as chairman. He is being criticized by Amex floor traders for failing to grasp the Exchange's workings. Instead of compensating by hiring Wall Street executives for top posts, Jones has hired former congressional aides. Rumors are circulating that Jones is a candidate for a job in the Clinton administration. Business at the Amex, NYSE, and NASDAQ has been flat for years. Jones has won praise for advocating more electronic systems on the floor of the Exchange and for promoting projects for hand-held terminals and touch screen technology.

313. Eichenwald, Kurt, "Amex Planning To Enter Nontrading Business," *New York Times*, 30 September 1992, sec. D, p. 5.

The Amex plans to branch out into pensions and insurance as part of its long-term strategy. Chairman James Jones says this direction is an extension of the Amex's customer-driven strategy adopted in 1990, in which the Amex focuses on the needs of listed companies and retail investors rather than member firms.

314. Barsky, Neil, "Big Board, Amex New Home Plan Advances a Step," *Wall Street Journal*, 1 October 1992, sec. B, p. 7A.

J. P. Morgan & Co. retains a team of developers to advise it on a major building project. The plan has been a subject of discussion between the NYSE and the Amex, Morgan, and New York City officials during the past year. Morgan senior vice president David W. Singleton says this will be more than an office building; it will draw business and revitalize lower Manhattan. Neither of the exchanges has yet to sign a contract.

315. O'Brien, Timothy L., "Amex Finds No Evidence of Wrongdoing in Listing of PNF on Small Firm Market," *Wall Street Journal*, 15 October 1992, sec. C, p. 13.

Amex Chair James Jones says human error was responsible for the PNF listing on the Emerging Company marketplace, as two specialists are exonerated. No sanctions against the two men are deemed necessary. Mr. Jones also says that the Amex is planning to implement a new policy requiring Exchange staff to disclose any financial interest in companies introduced for listing.

1993

316. Power, William, "Despite Setbacks, Amex Mulls Yet Another Market," *Wall Street Journal*, 24 February 1993, sec. C, pp. 1, 2.

In spite of a rocky first year for the Emerging Company Marketplace, which has second tier listings with lower standards, Amex officials are talking about creating another tier for tinier, riskier companies. The market won't be available for a year, but it will aim at true startup companies without sales or earnings. Chairman James Jones says that, aside from PNF Industries, the ECM has been a success; the Amex is now gearing up for the next phase.

317. "Securities Industry's Self-Regulation Toughens," *Wall Street Journal*, 23 March 1993, sec. A, p. 4.

A study by the American Bar Association says that the five self-regulatory organizations which police the securities industry--the National Association of Securities Dealers, NYSE, Chicago Board Options Exchange, Amex, and Midwest Stock Exchange--are getting tougher on rules violations. Nearly 1,400 disciplinary cases were brought against brokerage firms in 1992 and 1,409 in 1991. But the fines levied rose 17 percent from $37 million in 1990 to $47 million in 1991. Among them was a record $15 million fine by the NYSE against Drexel Burnham Lambert, Inc.

318. Strauss, Cheryl Beth, "Exchanges Shuffle Staffers in Bid for International Listings," *Investment Dealers Digest* 59:15 (April 12, 1993): 7-8.

In the race for international listings, the major exchanges have shuffled their staffs. At the Amex, George Avril, founder of the London office, returns to New York. Europe is slow and the London office is expensive. Avril will take a new position as the Amex's first industry group specialist and will concentrate on a few industry groups.

319. Lux, Hal, "NASDAQ and AMEX Draw Up Sides in a $3 Billion Spat," *Investment Dealers Digest* 59:17 (April 26, 1993): 4, 6.

Amex researchers, in an attempt to quantify excess trading costs for public customers in NASDAQ, estimated $3 billion. National Association of Securities Dealers chairman Joseph Hardiman dismisses the claim as "marketing puffers." He notes that the OTC market making industry did not generate $5 billion over the past year, let alone excess costs. The competition comes at a time when Congress and the SEC are conducting reviews of the equities markets.

320. Affleck-Graves, John, Shantaram P. Hegde, Robert E. Miller, and Frank K. Reilly, "The Effect of the Trading System on the Underpricing of Initial Public Offerings," *Financial Management* 22:1 (Spring 1993): 99-108.

The authors study whether the underpricing of initial public offerings previously documented on NASDAQ also applies to the NYSE and the Amex. Additionally, they consider the effect of the quantitative and qualitative listing standards of the exchanges. Underpricing does extend to all exchanges, although the levels for the NYSE (4.82 percent) and the Amex (2.16 percent) are less than those found on the NASDAQ/NMS (5.56 percent) and NASDAQ/non-NMS (10.41 percent). They advance the proposition that listing standards certify the quality of IPOs, reduce uncertainty, and lower expected underpricing.

321. Golden, Tim, "Clinton Names Head of Stock Exchange as Envoy to Mexico," *New York Times*, 13 May 1993, sec. A, p. 6.

Amex Chairman James R. Jones is named by the Clinton Administration to the post of U.S. Ambassador to Mexico. Jones is a former Democratic congressman from Oklahoma and was a senior aide to President Johnson. A senior Mexican official says it is a good appointment, because Jones is close to Clinton, to the Administration, and to Congress. Jones joined the Johnson administration straight out of Georgetown University Law School. He was promoted to special assistant and appointments secretary to the President, a position now called Chief of Staff. He ran unsuccessfully for the Senate in 1984. After practicing law in Washington for almost three years, he became Amex chairman in 1989.

322. Hoffman, Thomas, "Amex Seeks Wireless Trades," *Computerworld* 27:20 (May 17, 1993): 6.

The Amex tests off-the-shelf hand-held computers on the trading floor. In the conversion to paperless trading, the biggest benefit is expected to be access to real-time market position analysis. In the first phase of testing, options traders are using equipment from Granite Communications, Inc., of Amherst, New Hampshire. A second pilot project in equities trading will test Fujitsu-ICL Systems pen-based devices and Grid Systems Palm Pals.

323. Rublin, Lauren R., "The Trader," *Barron's* 73:23 (June 7, 1993): 66-68.

With bond and commodities markets leading the market, the Amex's Market Value Index scores new highs, adding 2.73 points to 440.95. At midday on May 20th, the Exchange bans purchases of Andrea Electronics shares on margin in an attempt to cure the stock's volatility. This marks the first time in seven years that the Amex has enacted such a prohibition.

324. Lux, Hal, "American Stock Exchange Begins Hunt for New Chief," *Investment Dealers Digest* 59:23 (June 7, 1993): 6-8.

> The Exchange begins the hunt for a replacement for James Jones who is named U. S. Ambassador to Mexico. The last two chairmen were selected from outside the Exchange and the pattern could repeat. Jones' departure raises questions for one of his pet projects, the Emerging Company Marketplace (ECM). While the ECM has generated trading volume for the Exchange, it has also generated negative publicity concerning the quality of some of the listings.

325. "American Hero," *New York Times*, 1 July 1993, sec. D, p. 6.

> The Amex outperforms the Dow Jones Industrial Average and other major market indexes in the first half of 1993. It peaked at 440.95 on June 5th, after breaking its all-time high 20 times. New listings double to 52. The average daily volume was 3 million above 1992, at 17.3 million shares.

326. Raghavan, Anita, "Amex Specialists Test Hand-Held Computers," *Wall Street Journal*, 9 July 1993, sec. C, p. 1.

> Hand-held computers made by Granite Corp. of Nashua, New Hampshire, are part of an experiment aimed at saving time and giving specialists price information and allowing them to execute trades. The major drawback seems to be that many specialists are reluctant to enter the world of electronic trading.

327. "Amex Names Acting Chief," *New York Times*, 27 August 1993, sec. D, p. 4.

> The Amex names Jules L. Winters acting chief executive while the Exchange seeks a replacement for James R. Jones, who becomes the Clinton Administration's Ambassador to Mexico. Mr. Winters has been the Amex's chief operating officer since 1992. He started at the Exchange in 1965 as a floor page. The Amex has appointed a search committee to find a new chairman.

328. "Two Stock Exchanges Drop Plan for Office Building," *Wall Street Journal*, 27 September 1993, sec. B, p. 10A.

> The Amex and NYSE announce that they are dropping plans to build a new headquarters building for both exchanges on a square block in the heart of Manhattan's financial district. The plan, which included a large office tower, fell through because of the continued weakness of the lower Manhattan office market.

329. Lux, Hal, "American Stock Exchange Names Its First Chief Economist," *Investment Dealers Digest* 59:45 (November 8, 1993): 9.

The Amex names Steven Bloom, a Harvard PhD in economics and one of its senior product development specialists, as the Exchange's first chief economist. Exchange chief economists are known as "the ideological torch bearers for their trading systems. That often means coming up with research papers that bash the competition." Bloom has served as second-in-command to Nate Most, the Exchange's new products head, and has participated in development of successful products, including the Japan Index and Standard & Poor's Depositary Receipts (SPDRs).

330. Kimball, James G., "NASDAQ Ads Lead Way in Exchange War," *Business Marketing* 78:12 (December 1993): 9.

The battle for market supremacy is heating up. The Amex changes ad agencies from DeVito/Verdi to McCann-Erickson. Joan Allen, vice president for corporate communications at the Amex, says the Exchange intends to use all the marketing tools and be more aggressive in reaching both the individual investor and the listing environment. Amex strengths include high-quality trading, superior technology, and personal services.

331. Lucas, Henry C., Jr., "Market Expert Surveillance System," *Communications of the ACM* 36:12 (December 1993): 27-34.

At the Amex, the responsibility for monitoring trading so that SEC rules are not violated is shared by two departments, Stock Watch and Equities Surveillance. Lucas, research professor of information systems at the Leonard N. Stern School of Business at New York University, describes his experience of sharing in, with the manager of the Equities Surveillance Department, the development of an expert system for the Amex. Meetings were held weekly for six to eight months. MESS (Market Expert Surveillance System) was developed to assist in initial screening of insider trading referrals. Once the system is activated, trading data (the stock's current price and volume, data from two days following the alert, and 50 days preceding it) is retrieved from Amex records and downloaded into a Lotus spreadsheet program. An analyst uses the spreadsheet to calculate a number of statistics and graph price and volume data. Finally, EXSYS, a rule-based expert system shell for a personal computer, evaluates data using approximately 160 rules. Result is one of two weighted responses: "open an investigation" or "do not open an investigation." A major advantage of the system is that the same set of rules is applied for each case.

Courtesy of The American Stock Exchange

Courtesy of The American Stock Exchange

332. Lux, Hal, "Riley Leaves Amex To Head Hong Kong Futures Exchange," *Investment Dealers Digest* 59:49 (December 6, 1993): 6.

Ivers Riley is named chief executive of the Hong Kong Futures Exchange. He replaces Gary Knight, another American options official. With the scheduled takeover of Hong Kong by China, Riley may be the last American to fill the position. Ivers has been active in the U.S. options market since its advent in the 1970s, serving as an executive for options floors at the Chicago Board Options Exchange and New York Stock Exchange. During his term as head of derivative products for the Amex, the Exchange has developed its first successful stock basket product, SPDRs, and entered the international derivative product market with the Japan Index, the Hong Kong Index, and Nikkei stock index warrants.

333. "Amex Board Adopts Rule for 'One-Share, One-Vote'," *Wall Street Journal*, 17 December 1993, sec. C, p. 2.

A new Amex rule, strongly opposed by former chairman Arthur Levitt, now has his support. Levitt, now Chairman of the SEC, says that his new job helped him see that one-share, one-vote is the best way to protect shareholders' voting rights. It prohibits listed companies from issuing new batches of common stock that would dilute the voting power of existing stockholders. The rule was proposed during the 1980s takeover frenzy when companies tried to ward off unfriendly acquisition by issuing new stock with lesser voting rights.

334. Harlan, Christi, "Market 2000 Sets Its Sights on the Present," *Wall Street Journal*, 31 December 1993, p. 15.

The SEC is expected to release its Market 2000 report early in 1994. The report is not meant to address global issues but to talk about the market as it is, focusing on issues of technology and competition. The study is the SEC's first look at the equity market in 20 years, when turmoil in the securities business led to a study by an independent commission of industry leaders and experts. Their report was responsible for the elimination of broker-dealers' fixed commissions. One of the issues to be addressed is the move toward electronic trading systems, which are not regulated like exchanges. The Amex issued a comment letter in response to the study proposal in which the new trading systems were called a threat to the livelihood of established exchanges and investors. Instinet, a proprietary trading system owned by Reuters Holdings PLC, said in its comment letter that this system is technologically superior to the exchanges and that the exchanges may be obsolete.

Chapter 5

TRADING INSTRUMENTS AND INDICES

The Amex sees the road to expansion and profitability in new trading instruments: indices, options, commodities, and foreign issues. This chapter is devoted to these trading instruments.

ARTICLES

1966

335. Kirk, J., "American Exchange's Market Indicator Explained," *Banking* 59 (Spring 1966): 4.

The Amex has unveiled a new stock market indicator--the Price Level Index (PLI). The PLI reflects daily the average price of the Exchange's more than 950 common stocks and warrants. On April 29th, the base price was set at $16.88. On May 23rd, it stood at $13.15. Amex officials have also developed a daily breadth of market report which will show the extent to which the day's price changes were spread across the market. The Exchange also publishes a price-earnings index which indicates the current price level of all common stocks traded on the Amex relative to their current corporate earnings. In June, the median price-earnings ratio for all common stocks was 13.5.

1974

336. Rustin, Richard E., "Pivotal Project: Amex Options Venture May Help It to Avoid a Big Board Merger," *Wall Street Journal*, 15 November 1974, pp. 1, 31.

After incurring losses amounting to $931,000 over the last 18 months, the Amex is about to begin a new venture which is expected to bring a rebound. Amex will allow investors to trade in call options, which give the trader the right to buy 100 shares of a stock within a specified period at a set price. The investor pays a premium of five percent to 20 percent of the cost of the stock. He makes a profit if the price of the stock rises more than the cost of the premium. If the venture does not succeed, the Amex will be forced to consider merging with--or being absorbed by--the Big Board.

1975

337. Brown, Sidney, "Amex Looks for New Profitability," *Commercial and Financial Chronicle* 220 (January 13, 1975): 1, 6.

The Amex looks forward to improved profitability with the inauguration of options trading. In the future is options trading in government securities, gold, mortgage futures, and foreign currency.

338. Wax, A. J., "Options Trading Begins on Amex," *Commercial and Financial Chronicle* 220 (January 13, 1975): 1, 7.

A new era begins at the Amex with the trading of six call options; a total of 20 series of options will be traded before the end of the month. The stocks of all the listed companies are traded on the New York Stock Exchange. The Amex has been conducting a simulation of options trading involving the trading floor, its nationwide communications system, and order entering execution and clearing procedures. Tests show that the Exchange can handle 5,000 orders per day for contracts involving a total of 1.5 million shares of underlying stock.

339. "Options on the Amex," *Time* 105 (January 27, 1975): 77.

Faced with slumping sales volume, the Amex introduces trading in stock futures hoping to lure small investors. The Amex is handling options trading for 13 companies including DuPont, Union Carbide and U.S. Steel, and plans to expand to 20 stocks.

340. "People and Business," *New York Times*, 19 May 1975, p. 51.

More than fifty executives attend the Amex's first seminar on options.

341. Cole, Robert J., "Amex Sells Options-Only Memberships," *New York Times*, 14 November 1975, p. 50.

Encouraged by its successful entry into options trading, the Amex will soon sell 200 special memberships solely for the use of options traders. Chairman Paul Kolton says the memberships will cost $15,000 each and would support options specialists by enabling them to spread the risk on large transactions. These specialists closely resemble the market makers on the Chicago Board Options Exchange who specialize in the buying and selling of specific stocks. These special memberships are part of the Amex's attempt to provide more investment opportunities for the small investor. The Amex started with seven options and now trades in 40; subject to approval by the SEC, it plans to add 20 more.

1976

342. Liebman, Walter, "New Curb Service: Odd-Lotters May Trade in Treasuries Safely and Cheaply," *Barron's National Business and Financial Weekly* 56 (March 22, 1976): 11, 19.

A year following the advent of negotiated commissions, both large institutions and small traders appear to be gainers. Being developed at the Amex is change in the way individuals trade U.S. government securities. Amex's Depository Trust Co. (DTC), which actually consists of a large computer, a vault, and 800 employees, debits in and credits out securities electronically. However, it has never handled bearer certificates. By exercising its inactive membership in the Federal Reserve System, the DTC completes a circuit linking the Amex and its members to the Fed and gains the ability to deal in huge quantities of Treasury issues electronically. The advantage to the investor is in not having to handle bearer certificates. The man behind the system is Al Patti, an assistant vice president who was put in charge of new products in 1974.

343. "Amex's New Products," *Business Week* (October 25, 1976): 122.

The Amex brings out a "bunch" of services that provide new interest for investors and new business for all of the Exchange's members. Included are a program for trading options on commodities and a continuous spot market in gold bullion and silver. On the horizon is options trading in government bonds. Buyers and sellers are expected to be both speculators and end users--jewelers or metal refiners in the case of gold and silver options, and pension funds or bond dealers in the case of government bond options.

344. "AMEX Board Clears Put, Call Option Mart for Debt Securities," *Wall Street Journal*, 12 November 1976, p. 29.

Subject to SEC approval, the Amex Board authorizes the development of a market for trading options on debt instruments. Initially, the trading will be on U.S. government notes and bonds, but it may be expanded. Chairman Paul Kolton states that options on debt securities will "redistribute risks and provide investment opportunities."

1977

345. "An Options Race Goes to the Amex," *Business Week* (February 7, 1977): 76, 78.

The Amex wins a head-to-head battle with the Chicago Board Options Exchange when it lists MGIC Investment Corp. On December 14, 1976, the first day of the listing, Amex trading reached 6,226 contracts compared to the CBOE's 2,440. The lead has widened each week since with most volume coming from brokers rather than individuals. The battle was over when Merrill Lynch, Pierce, Fenner & Smith and E. F. Hutton switched orders to the Amex.

346. "State of War in Options Trading," *Business Week* (March 7, 1977): 60.

The Amex and Chicago Board Options Exchange are at war. Amex fired the first shot when it announced plans to trade options on National Semiconductor, CBOE's third most active account. The CBOE fired back by announcing it would begin trading in six options listed on the Amex. Amex specialists for the six options are expected to rely on the greater liquidity of their established markets.

347. "Trading Options: Is Amex Spoiling Chicago's Rattle?" *Economist* 163 (April 9, 1977): 103.

The Chicago Board Options Exchange has a superior form of market mechanism in that it can have multiple designated market makers trading for their own accounts. This results in higher volume of trading and thinner price spreads. Deals made for outside customers are more often executed on the Amex. The next tests for both exchanges will come on June 3rd, when trading will begin in put options in addition to the current call options. Clients will then be able to buy or sell a stock at a prespecified price. Brokers will continue to get commissions on the share purchase and on the options trade.

348. "AMEX To Widen Access to Its Options Mart to Head Off Competition by the Big Board," *Wall Street Journal*, 13 May 1977, p. 11.

Sources say that Amex officials are concerned that the NYSE's plan to move into the lucrative options market could cool its desire for a merger with the Amex. If the NYSE directors approve a merger, the process could take up to two years. In January, the NYSE announced plans to begin trading options on the Big Board; such a plan might diminish desire to merge with the Amex in order to get into options. Therefore, the Amex has announced plans to provide low cost and efficient access to the Amex options market to other exchanges and their members.

349. Hamilton, Kevin J., "Options: the Dual Trading War," *Institutional Investor* 11 (June 1977): 30-32.

A Chicago Board Options Exchange official leaks to the press that when the Amex begins trading National Semiconductor, the CBOE will begin trading six Amex options: Merrill Lynch, Digital Equipment, Burroughs, Disney, du Pont, and Tandy. The options war is renewed. Some in the business question the timing when the advent of trading puts and calls is due within a month. It is felt that the continuing clash may squeeze smaller regional exchanges which have unique portions of the business. Of even greater importance are plans of the NYSE to launch its own options program later in the year. Reasons may include size (CBOE, the larger rival, has 1,300 floor members, including 600 market makers against the Amex's 450 specialists, brokers, and traders), territory (New York looking for a victory over Chicago), or system (the Amex's specialist system vs. the CBOE's market makers).

350. "Amex Prepares To Trade Commodities," *Business Week* (October 3, 1977): 89.

The Amex announces a new commodities exchange. Amex Commodities Exchange, Inc. (ACE) will appoint officers and directors at an October 6th meeting and then seek approval of the SEC. Plans call for ACE to begin trading in gold and silver bullion and in financial instruments contracts.

1978

351. Gross, LeRoy and Alan C. Snyder, "Options Outlook: the Raging War," *Financial World* 147 (January 1, 1978): 36.

A dual-listing war breaks out between the Amex and the Chicago Board Options Exchange as the Amex begins to market an exclusive CBOE issue. CBOE responds by listing six Amex options. The number of dually traded options rapidly escalates to ten. CBOE publishes a booklet reporting its advantages while the Amex president indicates that the Exchange's share in the ten options has grown from 47.3 to 51.3 percent. The competition is expected to benefit investors as long as the exchanges "compete with services and not fictitious trades or market maker/specialist churning."

352. "Markets and Investments: the CBOE Loses Its Edge in Options," *Business Week* (June 12, 1978): 114, 116.

The winner in a mid-May market surge in options is the Amex. With trading level quadrupled, the Amex, which assigns a single specialist to each option, handled order flow smoothly while the CBOE, which allows traders to make a market through competition on the Exchange floor, did not fare as well. Merrill Lynch, Pierce, Fenner & Smith, Inc., and Bache Halsey Stuart Shields, Inc., thought the Amex did a sufficiently better job that they moved all their business on four dually traded options from the CBOE.

353. "Chicago's Finesse," *Economist* 267 (June 24, 1978): 121-122.

The Amex renews war with the Chicago Board Options Exchange over share of the options trading market. CBOE plans to take over options facilities of the Midwest Stock Exchange. Since summer, the SEC, which is investigating irregularities, has had a ban on expansion of the traded options market. The Amex has protested to the SEC about the violation of rules. CBOE argues that merger is not expansion, merely consolidation.

354. Mahon, Gigi, "Amex vs. CBOE: Competition Has Stiffened in the Options Trade," *Barron's National Business and Financial Weekly* 58:26 (June 26, 1978): 4, 5, 10.

The Amex and CBOE trade in common options on ten stocks with the CBOE the principal market for American Express, Bally, DEC, and National Semiconductor. On May 22d, Merrill Lynch switched trading to the Amex; Bache had already done so and Dean Witter followed suit. Stated reason was operational difficulties at the CBOE, however some observers feel that Merrill Lynch made the switch to save face and shift blame for its own slip-ups in handling orders during the market rally. The new Amex chair, Arthur Levitt, Jr., declares that he won't settle for second best, so a trend toward more dual listings can be expected when, and if, the SEC lifts its moratorium on new listings. To be ready, the Amex is unveiling a big-bucks, multi-media educational tool to help brokers teach their customers about options.

355. "Markets and Investments: Bidding for the Action in Options," *Business Week* (July 3, 1978): 84.

When the SEC placed a freeze on new stock option listings, it expected the market to cool until it could complete a massive study of options. Instead, it touched off a three-way battle for listings between the Amex, the NYSE, and the CBOE. On June 16th, the CBOE and Midwest Stock Exchange announced a proposal to consolidate their trading on the CBOE's floor. Minutes after hearing of the plan, Amex Chairman Arthur Levitt, Jr., fired off a telegram to the SEC objecting to the proposal.

1979

356. "Building the Financial Marketplace of the Future: the Race To Be First," *Business Week* (February 19, 1979): 68-72.

In the "hurly burly" securities industry of the Seventies, the Amex has the momentum while the Big Board is only beginning to give pursuit. The Amex has entered the "rich, alluring" markets for stock options and commodities. The Amex began trading stock options in 1975 and now trades options in 69 stocks, nearly all of them listed on the NYSE. In 1978, the Amex took another step with opening of the Amex Commodities Exchange, which trades contracts on Government National Mortgage Association (GNMA) futures and has filed with the Commodity Futures Trading Commission to add trading in Treasury bills, bonds, notes, and domestic bank certificates of deposit. Many believe that the Amex is creating the financial market of the future: a single exchange which trades stocks, bonds, options and futures.

357. Patti, Alfred J., "A Future on ACE: GNMA Options," *Mortgage Banker* (September 1979): 61-64.

Early in 1976, the Amex saw the need for an independent financial futures exchange to complement traditional commodities trading on Wall St. ACE (the Amex Commodities Exchange) was conceived to offer products countercyclical to the equities and options already being traded on the Amex. Trading began in GNMA futures in September 1978. In June 1979, 90-day T-bills were added. Still pending approval of the Commodity Futures Trading Corporation are contracts for T-bonds and notes.

1980

358. Arenson, Karen W., "2 Futures Exchanges To Merge," *New York Times*, 22 March 1980, pp. 27, 28.

The Amex Commodities Exchange and New York Futures Exchange announce that their boards have agreed to merge the two exchanges under the name of the NYSE entity. The agreement will allow Amex Commodities Exchange members to acquire seats on the Futures Exchange and will give them partial or full credit for what they paid for their ACE seats. The Amex Commodities Exchange was established in 1978 to trade futures contracts in Treasury securities and other financial instruments. The Exchange found that it could not compete with the Chicago commodity exchanges, which had been trading futures contracts for several years. Amex chooses to merge with the NYFE rather than the New York Commodity Exchange, because they perceive that the NYFE is the more successful.

1983

359. Pacey, Margaret D., "New Index Options Bow at the Amex," *Barron's National Business and Financial Weekly* 63 (July 11, 1983): 70-71.

The Amex, which already trades cash-settlement index options on its Major Market Index (MMI), introduces puts and calls on the Amex Market Value Index (AMVI). The underlying contracts are entirely different. The MMI consists of 20 stocks listed on the Big Board, while the AMVI is made up of all of the more than 800 issues which trade on the Amex. It is a highly volatile index with stocks in natural resources and high technology accounting for more than half its value. The largest components are Wang Laboratories, Imperial Oil, Texaco Canada, Gulf Canada, Dome Petroleum, Mitchell Energy, Washington Post, Amdahl, the New York Times, and TIE/Communications.

360. Pacey, Margaret D., "The Striking Price: Industry Index Options To Bow," *Barron's National Business and Financial Weekly* 63 (August 16, 1983): 76-77.

The Amex pioneers the first options on an industry index--a computer technology index of 30 stocks. IBM accounts for 53.9 percent of the weighting, followed by Hewlett Packard with 7.9 percent, and Digital Equipment with 4.1 percent. Also included are Commodore International, Computer Sciences, Control Data, Honeywell, and Texas Instruments. In September, a second "narrow-based" option will appear with puts and calls on an oil and gas index also consisting of 30 stocks.

361. Pacey, Margaret D., "The Striking Price: Options on Amex Oil & Gas Index Bow," *Barron's National Business and Financial Weekly* 63 (September 12, 1983): 92, 94.

The Amex begins trading options on its Oil and Gas Index of 30 stocks. Included are Exxon with 17 percent of the weighting, Standard of Indiana with 7.9 percent, and Shell and Standard of Ohio with 7.3 percent each. The Amex has filed for another nine such index options.

1985

362. "How AMEX XMI Options Provide Portfolio 'Insurance'," *Futures* 14 (1985): Index Guide, 28-31.

For many years, stock indexes were used for technical analysis and performance measure. Now, they are becoming the underlying basis for new financial instruments, such as stock index options. Amex's Major Market Index, trading as XMI, is a broad-based market index based on 20 leading blue chip stocks that measure the performance of U. S. industrial corporations. Of all the broad-based indexes, XMI bears the greatest correlation with the Dow Jones Industrial Average. Also trading on the Amex is the Market Value Index (XAM), which measures the collective performance of the more than 800 issues traded on the Exchange. Narrow-based options on the Exchange include the Computer Technology Index (XCI), Oil Index (XOI), and Transportation Index (XTI). Scenarios for investment strategies are provided.

1986

363. Ring, Trudy, "'European' Settlement Draws Funds' Interest," *Pensions and Investment Age* 14:10 (May 12, 1986): 41-42.

Options with European-style settlement are attracting interest on the part of pension fund executives and money managers. In European-style settlements, options can be exercised only on the expiration date, while in American-style, settlement can be exercised any time during the life of the contract. On April 10, 1986, Amex introduced a European-style option on 13-week Treasury bills. The option traded slowly in its first three weeks, but Exchange officials remain hopeful.

364. "The Amex Has the Momentum," *Euromoney* (September 1986): Amex Supplement, 1-6.

Amex has the momentum as trading in options on the Major Market Index (XMI) rises more rapidly than trading for the Chicago Board Options Exchange's Standard & Poor's 100 (OEX). While OEX volume was up 30 percent in 1985, XMI increased by an even more impressive 110 percent. The Amex also excelled in dually traded issues. For Digital Equipment and Merrill Lynch, Amex's share exceeded 99 percent. Overall use of options has increased rapidly because of revived investor interest in paper instruments, a broad move toward "derivative" securities, increased respectability of options as investment tools, development of new options instruments, and effect of the preceding factors on bringing in large numbers of new market participants.

365. "The 'Red Hot' XMI," *Euromoney* (September 1986): Amex Supplement, 8-10.

Interest in Amex's Major Market Index is growing rapidly. On top of a gain in volume of more than 100 percent in 1985, XMI has gained an additional 50 percent in the first half of 1986. Logical reasons include the make-up of XMI itself and the increased use of XMI by European options investors. XMI was specifically designed to correlate with the blue chip market and consists of far fewer stocks than any of its rivals. Advantages generated are close relationship to "the market," fewer stocks to recreate the index, buying XMI puts for portfolio protection, using an XMI combination to profit from anticipated market volatility, and using XMI call options to reduce or eliminate possible currency loss.

366. "How We Employ Options: Top Users Discuss Strategies," *Euromoney* (September 1986): Amex Supplement, 11-15.

Three fund managers and brokers explain use of options. Sumner Abramson, senior vice president of the Putnam Management Company, notes that options and futures are used extensively by mutual funds to produce high returns with minimum volatility. Steve Hardy, a principal with Balch, Hardy and Scheinman, explains two techniques available to the options overwriting manager: options rolling (the options manager buys back options previously sold and simultaneously sells new options) and the continuous varying of the number of options bought and sold. Michael Trup of Dean Witter Reynolds in London describes three basic options strategies which can be employed when stocks on which options are traded begin to rise due to takeover speculation: hold stock and sell calls against it; sell the stock and buy calls; or keep the stock and buy puts.

367. "More Opportunities for Foreign Investors . . . ; an Interview with Kenneth R. Leibler, President of the American Stock Exchange," *Euromoney* (September 1986): Amex Supplement, 16-17.

> Leibler successfully guided the Amex's entry into competitively traded over-the-counter options, a market in which the Amex has captured nearly all customer volume. Leibler sees order flow in the Exchange's premier contract, options on the Major Market Index, as a benefit of Amex's upcoming link with the European Options Exchange. For the first time, European investors will be able to trade a major index option based on U. S. stocks during European trading hours.

368. "A New York Expert Answers Questions Put Frequently by European Investors," *Euromoney* (September 1986): Amex Supplement, 24.

> Louis Margolis, a managing director of Salomon Brothers, explains that "options allow you to do things that you cannot do in the futures markets." This includes removing "the bulk of the downside" while participating in up moves in the market. During the past 15 years, markets have gone higher and lower than could have been expected. Investors have done well buying volatility. If they buy calls and the market goes up substantially, they'll participate in the gain. But if they're wrong and the market goes down, risk is limited to the premiums.

369. "Hunting for User-Driven Contracts," *Euromoney* (October 1986): Futures and Options Supplement, 20-21.

> The American Stock Exchange has the second largest trading volume of any exchange in the United States. It is noted for oil, gas, and foreign shares traded. Stock option listings began in 1970. In 1983, options trading on the Major Market Index opened. Recently, agreement has been reached for the MMI to trade on the Amsterdam European Options Exchange. Options contracts are also developed from three industry-based stock indexes: the Computer Technology Index (XCI), the Oil Index (XOI), and the Airline Index (XAI). Looking toward the future, executive vice president Paul Stevens "predicts a radical leap forward in trading technology. A key development will be what futurologists call 'locked-in trading' or, more prosaically, the advent of the instant and automatic trade execution, which many feel will radically alter the entire market."

370. "Amex Options Dealers Seek Greater Control," *Wall Street Journal*, 1 October 1986, p. 57.

> Options dealers petition the Exchange's Board of Governors for a seat on the Exchange's nominating committee and for the elimination of the guaranteed two seats for specialists on the 25-person board. The rift between the two groups is a result of

the growth in importance of the options business. During the 1980s, it has accounted for about a third of the securities trading dollars.

371. Szala, Ginger, "AMEX Hits Hot Button with New Index," *Futures* 15 (November 1986): 14,16.

Based on its first day of trading, October 3d, the Amex's new Institutional Index options contract (XII) is a hit. The index is based on the 75 stocks most held by institutions and has European-style exercise which means an option cannot be exercised until expiration day. First day trading totalled almost 30,000 contracts-- 15,554 calls and 14,037 puts.

1987

372. "Creative Options," *Banker* 137 (January 1987): 96-97.

The Amex, New York's second stock exchange, is quickly becoming the "agile prince" of stock options. Average daily total volume has grown over 42 percent in 1986 with 56 percent growth on the stock indices. One of the early successes was the Major Market Index, which is based on the stock performance of 20 leading blue chip companies. In October 1986, Amex pioneered the Institutional Index, which is based on 75 stocks most widely held by institutions in the U. S. Companies represented vary from Coca-Cola to Salomon Brothers.

373. Morgello, Clem, editor, "Paul Kolton, Former Chairman, American Stock Exchange," *Institutional Investor* 21:6 (June 1987): 431-432.

Kolton discusses the planning and implementation of options trading. The SEC raises numerous issues: how do you bring an unregulated put-and-call market under control? would there be a separate clearing operation or would Amex buy a piece of the Chicago Board Options Exchange clearing house? Also, lengthy negotiations occurred before New York state and city officials determined that the stock transfer tax did not also apply to options.

374. Marton, Andrew, "Transatlantic Equity Options: Dutch Treat," *Institutional Investor* 21 (October 1987): 23-24.

John Shad, the new U.S. Ambassador to The Netherlands and former chair of the SEC, smiles for dignitaries on the floor of Amsterdam's European Options Exchange (EOE) and purchases a September call on the Amex Major Market Index. Concerned about the inability to police trading on the EOE, the largest options market outside of the U.S., had delayed inauguration of trading. Following an agreement between the Amex and EOE to share market surveillance information and collaborate on investigations, trading gets underway.

1988

375. Siler, Julia Flynn, "Options Customers Will Get $1 Million in an Amex Refund," *New York Times*, 11 February 1988, Sec. I, p. 1, Sec. IV, p. 13.

Investors lost hundreds of millions of dollars in trading stock index options during the crash. The refunds represent the first time that the Amex and the Chicago Board Options Exchange have made refunds to a large group of investors who complained about losses, citing problems with pricing and order execution during the turmoil. Much of the blame for investors' index option losses is placed on market makers, whose effectiveness in maintaining an orderly market during the heavy trading has been questioned.

376. Pierog, Karen, "Refunds for Index Options," *Futures* 17 (April 1988): 18, 20.

In an unprecedented move, CBOE S&P 100 Index options (OEX) market makers and Amex Major Market Index options (XMI) specialists and market makers will refund more than $2 million to customers. The payments result from an SEC report on the market crash which noted that "the options markets did not provide an effective, continuous market for the most actively traded index options classes at certain times on October 19th and for virtually all of October 20th." The "adjustment" covers all series and classes of index options which had "too high premiums." The money will be collected on a voluntary basis from specialists whose trades fell outside the parameters of normal pricing.

377. Stein, Jon, "CBOE, AMEX Spinning with Automation," *Futures* 17 (May 1988): 53.

Autoex, the Automated Execution System of the Amex, aims at automatic processing of quick fills for retail customers while allowing market makers to concentrate on large orders. Autoex is currently in place for emergency situations on all but three issues. The Amex has filed with the Commodity Futures Trading Commission to go floorwide with the system and implementation will occur first in the more active option posts.

1989

378. "Equity-Index Participation Begins Exchange Trading," *Wall Street Journal*, 15 May 1989, Sec. C, p. 15.

The SEC lifts a temporary stay on baskets and trading begins on the Amex and Philadelphia Stock Exchange. The securities are based on the S&P 500 stock index and other indexes, giving the investor the equivalent portion of the stocks in those indexes. Each stock is represented in the basket in the same proportion as it is represented in the index. Baskets have elements of mutual funds, futures and stocks. The Chicago Mercantile Exchange and the CBOE have argued that the SEC does not have jurisdiction over their trading, because they are actually futures. The Amex says that trading on the first day was done primarily by institutions; Paine Webber, Inc. bought a 10,000 unit block, almost 25 percent of the total volume.

379. Nathans, Leah J. and Joseph Weber, "Will the Amex and Philly Team Up Against Chicago?" *Business Week* (July 31, 1989): 78.

The Amex is negotiating with the Philadelphia Stock Exchange to combine all options trading under one roof in New York. In May, an SEC ruling that options may be traded on more than one exchange was good news for the Chicago Board Options Exchange, which has 44 percent of the stock option trading volume, as well as to the Amex, with 28 percent of the market. Both are after some of the heavily traded options listed only in Philadelphia and on the Pacific Stock Exchange. Members of the Philadelphia Exchange want an even trade of seats, a problem when PHLX seats are worth about $50,000, while Amex seats are going for $180,000. Any deal must be approved by members of both exchanges and by the SEC.

380. Power, William, "Exchanges' Basket Investment-Vehicle Battle Continues," *Wall Street Journal*, 31 August 1989, Sec. C, p. 13.

In mid-August, a Federal Appeals Court in Chicago invalidated the three-month old basket products of the Philadelphia Stock Exchange and the Amex as a result of a suit brought by the Chicago futures exchange. The argument was that the product was more like a futures contract than a security. The court ruled that the SEC should not have approved them. The Philadelphia exchange has a revised proposal for its Cash Index Participation (CIP) shares which will allow investors to cash out their positions anytime without penalty. Amex officials say they are also working on new alternatives but will not be more specific. The Philadelphia Stock Exchange has filed a new proposal with the SEC that, it says, will "make clear" that its new basket product is a security, not a future instrument.

381. Eichenwald, Kurt, "Amex and Philadelphia Markets End Talks," *New York Times*, 10 October 1989, sec. IV, p. 8.

Merger talks have broken off between the Amex and the Philadelphia Stock Exchange. No merger agreement is expected for the next three to five years. Discussions were spurred in large part by a recent rule adopted by the SEC allowing multiple exchanges to trade a single option; currently, each option is allotted to only one exchange.

1990

382. Weiss, Gary, "The Nikkei Nosedives? Break Out the Bubbly!" *Business Week* (March 12, 1990): 103.

Nikkei put warrants begin trading on the Amex providing investors an opportunity to cash in on the sharpest decline in Japanese stocks since Bloody Monday. Four new warrants are pegged to the Nikkei Stock Average of 25 major Japanese stocks. In the first weeks of trading, volume sometimes exceeds one million per day in trading by small investors. Institutions have the funds to buy and sell Japanese index futures directly. If the Tokyo exchange's problems continue, the warrants are expected to soar.

383. "AMEX Is Hoping To List U.S. Stock-Index Warrants," *Wall Street Journal*, 2 May 1990, Sec. C, p. 21.

The Amex announces that it wants to list warrants on its 20-stock Major Market Index to let investors gamble on the market's direction over the next three years. Long term warrants are popular new products. The only stock index warrants currently traded in the U.S. are based on Japanese or British indices. The Nikkei warrants are popular because it is difficult for most U.S. investors to find any other way of betting on the decline of the Japanese market.

384. "Amex-Europe Trading Accord," *New York Times*, 19 October 1990, Sec. D, p. 11.

The Amex works on expanding its trading globally. An agreement with the European Options Exchange and Paris Bourse will expand the number of international products trading on the Amex. It will allow the Amex to trade warrants on the Bourse's CAC-40, an index of 40 leading blue chip French stocks. In exchange, the Bourse will trade Amex's Major Market Index. In a second agreement, the Amex receives exclusive rights to trade the European Options Exchange's EuroTop-100 Index, which contains 100 stocks from nine European countries. The Amex is already trading warrants on the Nikkei 225, which is the blue chip index of the Tokyo stock market; warrants on the Financial Times-Stock Exchange 200 Index, which is the main index of the London market; and, options on its own Japan Index, which is similar to Tokyo's Nikkei 225.

385. "AMEX Seeks Talks on the Acquisition of Options Business," *Wall Street Journal*, 26 October 1990, Sec. C, p. 11.

The Amex is trying to strengthen its market share of the options business because of the new SEC rule that breaks monopolies on certain stock options. They move to reopen talks on the acquisition of the Philadelphia Stock Exchange's stock-options business.

386. Torres, Craig, "Foreign Market Offerings Revive Amex's Fortunes," *Wall Street Journal*, 9 November 1990, Sec. C, pp. 1, 13.

The Amex loses 19 issues to the NYSE, but trading volume is up 10 percent based on a new product--warrants which allow investors to bet against the Japanese stock market. The Amex now has eleven stock-index warrant listings, far more than any other U.S. exchange. The Amex is the biggest trader of these warrants and other derivative securities. When stock and bond trading slumped in the years after the crash, international products became a high priority. Soon after the Amex listed the first Nikkei warrants, the Tokyo stock market began to fall and trading volume swelled in the warrant. Although the Amex now has a dominant position, the NYSE is reluctant to concede that it is an insurmountable lead.

1991

387. Torres, Craig, "Amex Cuts MMI's Value in Half Hoping To Attract Small Investors," *Wall Street Journal*, 1 August 1991, sec. C, p. 1.

In an effort to beef up volume in one of the Amex's main products, the 20-stock Major Market Index, the Exchange plans to cut the value of the index in half. Making MMI options less costly is expected to make them more accessible to small investors, thereby increasing trading volume. Developed by the Amex in 1983, the MMI is designed to look like the Dow Jones Industrial Average; it is traded in the form of options on the index at the Amex, and MMI index futures at the Chicago Board of Trade.

388. "AMEX Wins License To Trade in Options on MidCap Index," *Wall Street Journal*, 8 October 1991, sec. C, p. 11.

The Amex signs a contract with Standard & Poor's Corp., a unit of McGraw-Hill, to begin trading stock-index options of S&P's new 400-stock MidCap Index. The Amex, which is building a reputation for trading derivative securities such as options and warrants, wins the right to the trading over the four other U.S. exchanges. Sources say that the Amex won the bid because of its commitment to technological and market making support. The MidCap 400, which includes stocks such as Sun Microsystems and U.S. Surgical Corp., was introduced in June and quickly became popular as an investment representing the sector of the market between the big stocks of the S&P 500 and small stocks. Its total return for the first nine months of the year is 33.57 percent, compared with 20.37 percent for the S&P 500.

389. Goldman, Kevin, "Amex Will Limit New Stock Options It Lists on Exchange," *Wall Street Journal*, 9 October 1991, sec. A, p. 10.

In response to member firm concerns about the proliferation of options, the Amex says it will refrain from listing any new stock options that aren't traded on at least one other exchange. The announcement precedes the relaxing of options listing criteria which takes effect October 21st. The Amex currently trades 227 stock options, including 55 options on OTC stocks; options on four broad market indexes--the Major Market Index, the LT-30 Index, the Institutional Index, and the Japan Index; as well as options on two narrow-based indexes--the Oil Index and the Computer Technology Index.

390. Torres, Craig, "Rival Exchanges Gird for October Options War," *Wall Street Journal*, 14 October 1991, sec. C, p. 1.

An August 1991 SEC decision to lower listing standards on common stock options is expected to cause a full scale options war beginning October 21, 1991. Five U.S. exchanges will be battling to control the market in as many as 32 new stock options. The competition expected among the Chicago Board Options Exchange, the NYSE, the Amex, the Philadelphia Stock Exchange, and the Pacific Stock Exchange marks the end of the old monopoly system for trading options. The Amex is first to announce its intent to trade 16 new options, all of which are wanted by other exchanges. The SEC recommends that the exchanges link up electronically so that prices remain the same across all markets. The exchanges have filed a plan for an Option Intermarket Communication Linkage system to comply. The exchange that dominates the market in the first few weeks is thought to be the likely leader in the trading in a given option. Opponents of deregulation fear this proliferation of options might be confusing to investors.

391. Lux, Hal, "Derivative Products: Bringing Back the Crowds," *Investment Dealers Digest* 57:42 (October 21, 1991): 24-28.

During the summer, with industry officials predicting an end to the four year slump in the options pits, trading volume took a dive. Options exchanges, including the Amex, make staff cuts. To woo back investors, the Amex is trying to convince them they can make money in new options products. In addition to new foreign indices, the Amex plans to launch options on a new index of pharmaceutical companies. The Exchange also implements a two-for-one split of its Major Market Index to bring the price down for small investors.

392. "Amex Begins Trading Capped Options Tied to Two of Its Indexes," *Wall Street Journal*, 15 November 1991, sec. C, p. 8.

The Amex begins trading in put and call capped index options tied to its Major Market Index and on its Institutional Index. Because the options offer more limited potential for profit, they will cost less.

1992

393. "Amex and Chicago Merc to Sell Products Tied to S&P 'Midcap 400'," *Wall Street Journal*, 29 January 1992, sec. C, p. 19.

The Amex and Chicago Mercantile Exchange announce that they plan to trade financial products based on the MidCap 400 Index of medium-sized companies, starting February 13th. The Index comprises 400 companies with median capitalization of $750 million and a total market value of $425 billion. The Exchanges say more than $2 billion in investments is linked to the index. The Amex will trade options and the Chicago Merc will trade options and futures. The Amex plan has been approved by the SEC; the Merc's plan is expected to be approved soon by the Commodity Futures Trading Commission.

394. "Amex Begins Trading Warrants on Dollar in Relation to Pound," *Wall Street Journal*, 24 February 1992, sec. C, p. 11.

The Amex begins trading the first U.S. currency warrant based on the performance of the dollar relative to the British pound. Warrants rise in price when the dollar strengthens and fall when it weakens. The Exchange already trades 15 other foreign currency warrants, ten based on the Japanese yen and five on the German mark.

395. Lux, Hal, "American Stock Exchange Eyes Trading of Pure Volatility," *Investment Dealers Digest* 58:14 (April 6, 1992): 6, 8.

The Amex is developing a new contract which would trade against an underlying index of stock index volatility. Menachem Brenner and Dan Galai, finance professors at New York University and the Hebrew University of Jerusalem, proposed the idea to the Exchange. They are completing development work on a volatility index which could become the basis for the product.

396. "Amex Says SEC Clears Plan to Trade Options on Drug Stocks Index," *Wall Street Journal*, 23 June 1992, sec. C, pp. 20, 6.

The Amex announces clearance from the SEC to trade options on its Pharmaceutical Index. The Index was created last year, is based on U.S. and European pharmaceutical companies, and is intended to represent a cross-section of widely held, high capitalization companies of the drug industry. The Amex currently trades options on its Oil Index and Computer Technology Index.

397. Neal, Robert, "A Comparison of Transaction Costs Between Competitive Market Maker and Specialist Market Structures," *Journal of Business* 65:3 (July 1992): 317-334.

Bid-ask spread and some properties of transaction prices for equity call options are compared in two market structures: the specialist environment of the Amex and the competitive market maker structure of the Chicago Board Options Exchange. Results reveal several differences. When trading volume is low, the specialist structure has lower bid-ask spreads than the market maker. As volume rises, the difference appears to diminish. Transaction prices in the specialist market structure are closer to the midpoint of the bid and ask prices. The findings have important implications for the regulatory debate about the options allocation plan. The SEC has proposed to eliminate the allocation plan and permit direct competition among the options exchanges. The exchanges are opposed. However, an important difference in transaction costs between the two structures provides a strong economic reason to eliminate the regulatory barrier.

398. "Amex Seeks Approval from SEC to Trade Option-Like Security," *Wall Street Journal*, 17 July 1992, sec. A, p. 6.

To replace hybrid options contracts called PRIMEs and SCOREs, the Amex is seeking approval for long-term option-like securities called BOUNDs (buy-write option unitary derivative). BOUNDs give investors the equivalent of selling a call option on their common stock. They will allow investors to participate in stock price gains, up to a preset amount, while receiving the equivalent of dividends on the underlying stock. The LEAP, another Amex security, gives the investor the right to benefit from the appreciation of a stock or index, above and beyond the preset price. LEAPs and BOUNDs are expected to trade in a close relationship to their underlying stock.

399. "Amex to List Warrants Tied to Tokyo Stock Market," *Wall Street Journal*, 28 August 1992, sec. C, p. 11.

The Amex will soon defy the Tokyo Stock Exchange by listing and trading its first warrants on the Japanese stock market in more than two years. In April 1990, the Amex stopped listing warrants tied to the Tokyo Stock Exchange at Tokyo's request. Investors profited when the Nikkei 225 stock index fell. U.S. brokers suggest the new attitude reflects the weakened position of the Japanese--the economy has slowed and the stock market has plunged 60 percent in the last several years.

400. "Amex Asks the SEC for Blanket Approval of Industry Indexes," *Wall Street Journal*, 24 September 1992, sec. C, p. 21.

The Amex is asking the SEC for blanket approval of criteria to develop industry indexes for options trading so that any index which meets the criteria can be traded without further approval from the Commission. The SEC says this is the first time such a request has been received from an exchange.

401. "Amex, CBOE to Start Trading in Options on Biotech Indexes," *Wall Street Journal*, 28 September 1992, sec. B, p. 8.

The Amex and the Chicago Board Options Exchange plan to begin trading in competing indexes of biotech stocks. The Amex index is comprised of 15 of the most active biotech manufacturers traded on the OTC, particularly those with strong growth potential. Each has equal dollar weighting, meaning equal amounts invested in each to avoid dominance by any one company. The CBOE's index is composed of 20 stocks, weighted according to price, and each stock carries an equivalent number of shares. The CBOE will also list LEAPs (long-term equity anticipation securities), long term options for the biotech index with expirations of more than two years. The Amex offers options on three industry indexes: oil, computer technologies, and pharmaceuticals.

402. Lux, Hal, "The Big Stretch for U.S. Exchanges," *Investment Dealers Digest* 58:40 (October 5, 1992): 18-22.

As the Chicago Board Options Exchange announces new Flex (Flexible Exchange Options) derivatives which will allow investors to pick and choose expiration, strike and exercise style for S&P 100 and 500 options, the Amex restarts development of a new index that will allow traders to buy and sell volatility.

403. Smith, Craig and Michael Williams, "Amex Seeks to Expand Japanese Indexes; Tokyo Argues Derivatives Are Detrimental to Stocks," *Wall Street Journal*, 19 October 1992, sec. B, p. 6A.

In spite of objections from the Tokyo Stock Exchange (TSE), the Amex is planning to list stock index warrants, similar to options, that will allow American investors to bet on the rise and fall of the Tokyo market. TSE officials claim the derivatives, especially futures, options and warrants based on the indexes of Japanese stocks, are swinging their stock market around wildly and that it has become too volatile for small investors. Tokyo succeeded in getting the Amex to stop listing Japanese index warrants in 1990 but this time the Amex enjoys the support of U.S. regulators and is not likely to back down. According to the Japanese, the main problem is index arbitrage, in which large investors take advantage of price discrepancies between derivatives representing an index of stocks and the stocks themselves by buying one and selling the other simultaneously. Such speculative trading can drive down stock prices if trading volume is light. Americans say this is a convenient explanation of the Tokyo market's extended malaise.

404. Lux, Hal, "Another New Product Caught in Options-Futures Tangle," *Investment Dealers Digest* 58:50 (December 14, 1992): 8.

BOUNDS, a new "buy-write" product announced by the Amex in July, remains caught in a regulatory tangle between stocks, options, and futures. The conflict is between the Amex and Options Clearing Corporation over whether the options exchange is trying to offer something which is, in fact, a futures contract. The fight has similarities with a 1980s disagreement over Index Participations, a product killed off by a regulatory authority split between the SEC and Commodity Futures Trading Commission.

1993

405. Raghavan, Anita, "Amex To Set 'Spiders' on Small Investors," *Wall Street Journal*, 22 January 1993, sec. C, pp. 1, 19.

The Amex is expected to unveil a new security which allows investors to track the performance of the S&P 500 Index. The "Spider" (Standard & Poor's 500 Stock Index Depositary Receipt) is traded like common stock, but looks like an index fund. It gives the investor an interest in a trust holding shares of stocks in the S&P 500. It promises to match investment returns of the S&P 500 without the high management fees and trading costs of trading the underlying stock. Amex's latest effort to attract the small investor is expected to be approved by the SEC and begin trading within a week. An Amex spokesman says the Spiders represent the first in a large new category of securities. According to AMG Data Sources, investments in stock index funds rose to $13.1 billion at the end of 1992, up from $8.1 billion at the start of the year. The big difference between an index mutual fund and Spiders is that the investor in Spiders can buy or sell their interests in the trust when the Amex is open. Mutual fund investors must cash out or buy into a fund at each day's closing price. Unlike options and futures, Spiders do not expire in weeks or months or years, but in 25 years, when the underlying unit investment trust expires.

406. Cochran, Thomas N., "The Striking Price: Flying Spiders," *Barron's National Business and Financial Weekly* (February 1, 1993): 57.

Spiders begin trading on the Amex with ticker symbol SPY. They are valued at 1/10 the value of the components of the S&P 500.

407. Lux, Hal, "Second-Generation Spiders at Amex Already in Works," *Investment Dealers Digest* 58:7 (February 15, 1993): 12.

The Amex's new basket product, Spiders, is off to a good start and the Exchange is eying a whole line of similar products. The Spiders are descended from an earlier product, Index Participations, which were killed off in a regulatory fight soon after their debut in 1989. The underlying product of Spiders is the Standard & Poor's 500 index; holders can trade the market the way they might trade a stock. In the first nine days of trading, Spiders have been among the most active Amex stocks, averaging 380,000 shares daily.

408. Roth, Harrison, "The Striking Price: the End-of-Quarter Index," *Barron's National Business and Financial Weekly* 73:10 (March 8, 1993): 59-60.

The American Stock Exchange and Chicago Board Options Exchange introduce stock options trading on end-of-quarter indexes (EOQs). Listed on the Amex are the Major Market Index (XMI), the Institutional Index (XII), and the S&P MidCap Index (MID). While standard contracts expire on the third Friday of the month, the new options will expire on the first business day after the end of each calendar quarter in March, June, September, and December. The major purpose of the new options is to allow institutional users to hedge positions with an instrument that corresponds to the ends of their fiscal year and quarters.

409. "Risk Management Buyer's Guide," *Global Finance*, 7:4 (April 1993): 91-96.

Global Finance's second annual directory of key risk management providers includes the Amex among the 25 organizations listed. Included in the Exchange's products are long-term options, LEAPS, currency, and stock index contracts; warrants for yen, British pound, and Deutschmark currencies; and equity products based on a number of indexes--the Major Market, EuroTop 100, Institutional, Japan, S&P 500, S&P MidCap, Oil, Computer Technology, Biotechnology, and Pharmaceutical. It also trades Spiders and LOR SuperUnits.

410. Taylor, Jeffrey, "Options Exchanges Renew Listings Fight," *Wall Street Journal*, 9 September 1993, sec. C, pp. 1, 26.

Together, the Chicago Board Options Exchange and the Amex control 75 percent of all U.S. options trading. Multiple listing of options, proposed by the SEC, threatens the former exclusive options business of the Philadelphia and Pacific exchanges. Because the competition will allow for varying prices on the same option, it has been called an arbitrager's dream and a market maker's nightmare. An option can be bought on one exchange and immediately resold on another, at the expense of the second market maker. The Committee on Options Proposals (COOP) has called for safeguards to protect investors.

Chapter 6

REGULATORY ASPECTS

The United States Securities and Exchange Commission provides primary surveillance of the American exchanges. However, the American Stock Exchange has also been the subject of examination by government agencies at all levels, including Congressional committees, the Government Accounting Office, and the courts. This chapter summarizes this attention. Here, also, are some people--the cheats, the scoundrels, the crooks.

REPORTS

411. United States. Securities and Exchange Commission. Division of Trading and Exchanges. *Staff Report on Organization, Management, and Regulation of Conduct of Members of the American Stock Exchange.* Washington: U. S. Government Printing Office, [1962].

> After an SEC order revoked the broker-dealer registration of Re, Re & Sagarese and expelled Gerard A. Re and Gerard F. Re from the American Stock Exchange, the Commission directed its staff to investigate the facts of the case and of the adequacy of the rules, policies, practices and procedures of the Amex concerning the regulation and conduct of specialists and other members. The Res were repeated violators of the securities acts and the constitution and rules of the Exchange. Most of the violations were apparently known to Exchange officials, but few penalties were imposed. This was a clear manifestation that the financial community was failing to exercise its share of responsibility for self-regulation in the public interest. As a result of the investigation, the rules and policies of the Exchange underwent important changes. Further, it was recommended that the Commission's supervisory powers be strengthened for the future to insure proper performance of the Exchange as a major American financial institution.

ARTICLES AND CASES

1932

412. "Curb Exchange Tightens Rule on Trading by Bank Employees," *New York Times*, 20 December 1932, p. 27.

> The Curb Exchange requires written consent of employers before employees of banks, trusts, insurance companies, and firms dealing in stocks may deal in trading activities. Also barred is the giving of gratuities to employees of these companies and of newspapers.

1933

413. "Curb Tightens Rule on Company Reports," *New York Times*, 12 January 1933, p. 31.

The Curb's Committee on Listing adopts a rule requiring corporations applying for listing to agree to issue annual reports audited by independent accountants. Eighty five percent of listed companies do so.

414. "Curb Will Reform Unlisted Trading," *New York Times*, 6 July 1933, pp. 27, 36.

To correct ills discovered in an inquiry by the Attorney General, trading in unlisted securities is no longer permitted if it is opposed by the issuing company because it works harm against the company. The new rules also control the number of shares which must be available for trading so that no one will be able to corner a stock.

415. "Curb Adopts New Rules Like Stock Exchange's," *New York Times*, 10 August 1933, p. 27.

The Curb Exchange amends its rules to require member firms and partners to submit, by August 18th, reports on all pools, syndicates, joint accounts, and options held. The Committee on Business Conduct is empowered to set minimum margin requirements.

1934

416. "Exchanges Prepare To Go under New Federal Law," *New York Times*, 23 August 1934, p. 25.

The Curb Exchange votes to treat violations of the new Securities Exchange Act and the rules and regulations of the SEC in the same manner as infringements on its own rules.

1937

417. "S.E.C. Moves To Stop Inside 'Free Rides'," *New York Times*, 25 February 1937, pp. 31, 35.

SEC President James M. Landis suggests that full margin rules for brokers will place them on the same basis as their clients and will curb speculation. Broker dealers will have to put cash on stock transactions both on and off the trading floor and make daily records of margin calls to eliminate taking advantage of the three-day period for posting. The SEC is looking for voluntary adoption of the new rules by the exchanges.

1940

418. "Securities Law Attacked by Rea," *New York Times*, 22 March 1940, pp. 31,35.

At a luncheon of alumni from the Harvard Business School, Curb Exchange President G. P. Rea asks for a congressional revision of the Securities Acts of 1933 and 1934. He argues that the acts retard business and finance and are the cause of the national unemployment problem. He further states that adequate employment will come only through the development of new enterprises and the construction and rehabilitation of plants; this will only occur with new capital. An average of $3.3 billion of securities was issued each year from 1923-1932. Since 1932, and the new laws, a yearly average of only $700 million has been issued. Idle funds are now lying on deposit. Fraud and manipulation must remain prohibited but their definitions in the securities laws must be clarified.

1941

419. "Rules of Curb under Fire by S.E.C.," *New York Times*, 24 January 1941, p. 30.

The SEC orders a general investigation into the rules of the Curb Exchange. They claim that the Curb's Committee on Business Conduct failed to act on fee-splitting charges against J. C. Cuppia.

420. "Disciplinary Steps To Be Aired by Curb," *New York Times*, 5 February 1941, p. 27.

The Curb's Board of Governors begins to give fullest publicity to disciplinary actions against members. The change results from earlier failure to discipline members who were involved in fee-splitting with J. C. Cuppia. The Curb did not act because actions concerned members only and did not directly involve the public interest. The case was examined by the SEC which determined that the Curb must apprise the public of the commission of any material offense, whether or not it involves financial loss by the public.

421. "Hutton & Co. Fined for Rule Violation," *New York Times*, 8 February 1941, pp. 21, 23.

W. E. Hutton & Company is fined $250 for not conforming to SEC procedures when making stabilizing purchases in the stock of Raymond Concrete Pile Co. and for carelessness in preparation of SEC forms. The announcement results from the Curb's new policy of full publicity for all disciplinary actions. No willful violation of SEC rules is disclosed.

422. "SEC Hears Curb Head on Splitting of Fees," *New York Times*, 21 February 1941, p. 31.

> In SEC hearings into an allegation that J. C. Cuppia had secret rebate and fee-splitting arrangements with other brokers on the Curb, President George P. Rea testifies that the Curb concluded its investigation by permitting Cuppia to transfer his seat and by reprimanding the other members involved. He notes that the Curb felt they never had sufficient evidence on the fee-splitting.

423. "Curb Expels 2 Members," *New York Times*, 6 April 1941, p. 35.

> J. S. Reardon and W. J. Hennessey are expelled for violations of the Curb constitution in the Cuppia fee-splitting case. Reardon is expelled for fee-splitting, Hennessey for giving false testimony before the SEC subcommittee.

1942

424. "Cuppia and Whitney Cases Cited by S.E.C. in Demand for More Power," *New York Times*, 28 January 1942, p. 29.

> The Curb's laxity in disciplining J. C. Cuppia convinces the SEC that it should have the power to take direct action. Instead of suspension or expulsion, the Curb allowed Cuppia to sell his seat and reprimanded other members involved in the case. The SEC claims that this case, like the case of Richard Whitney, former president of the NYSE, points to the need for a residual governmental power which will assure that the rules of the exchanges affecting the public receive thorough and unequivocal enforcement. Existing legislation gives the commission no express power to compel compliance.

1943

425. "Broker Is Disciplined," *New York Times*, 23 April 1943, p. 27.

> John A. Borg, a Curb specialist in the stock of George A. Fuller Co., is fined $200. On April 7th, 100 shares sold at 13 3/4; Mr. Borg made a $12 market bid, $14 asked; a floor broker received a market order to sell 200 shares, which Borg bought at 12. The Curb finds that the specialist failed to make an adequate effort to get a better price for the stock.

1945

426. "Four Curb Members Fined Total of $850," *New York Times*, 27 July 1945, p. 25.

Investigations by the Committee on Stock Transactions result in fines of $25 each for specialists Max Winchel and William B. Steinhardt because their June 22nd purchase of 5,000 shares of Red Bank Oil Co. was not "reasonably necessary" to maintain a fair and orderly market. Murray Furman is fined $250 for assuming the duties of alternate specialist in the stock of Technicolor, Inc., without being registered or receiving approval of the Committee. Charles Foshko, a commission broker, is fined $100 for not using proper diligence in the execution of an order; the name of the security is not disclosed.

1947

427. "Curb Suspends Member," *New York Times*, 27 September 1947, p. 23.

In a hearing before the New York Curb Exchange Board of Governors, M. D. Fox is found guilty of violations of the antibetting provision of the constitution of the Exchange. He is suspended for 60 days on one charge and for one year on a second. Three specialists are fined $100 each for not using due diligence in establishing an opening price; they are instructed to adjust the opening price of Aluminum Co. of America from 58 1/2 to 58.

1948

428. "Suspension Voted for Curb Broker," *New York Times*, 5 May 1948, p. 41.

Broker Jack J. Dreyfus, Jr., partner in the firm of Dreyfus & Co., is found guilty on four charges of not using due diligence in supervision of employees and suspended for three months. Dreyfus claims no knowledge of the alleged misconduct. The disciplinary action results from Curb investigations of sales in the common stock of Kaiser-Frazer Corp.

429. "L. W. Herman Fined by Curb Exchange," *New York Times*, 4 November 1948, p. 47.

A total of $750 in fines is imposed on the specialist in Gray Manufacturing Co. and Atlantic Coast Fisheries Co. common stock. The action is a result of a Committee on Business Conduct investigation conducted between 1943 and 1946. The Committee finds that Herman violated the Exchange's constitution by failing to make a record of certain orders and by making a speculative transaction without either his employer's knowledge or the prior consent of the appropriate committee.

1952

430. "SEC 'Clarifies' Insiders' Status," *New York Times*, 25 September 1952, p. 47.

The SEC votes amendments intended to "clarify and enlarge" reporting requirements and exemptions under the Securities Exchange Act's provisions governing activities of insiders. The new amendments require officers, directors, or ten percent owners to report all holdings and transactions in the securities of their companies.

431. "Rules Are Revised for Prospectuses," *New York Times*, 11 October 1952, p. 53.

New rules dealing with registration and prospectus requirements of the Securities Act of 1933 permit advertising by newspaper, postal card, or other medium. The advertising statement is to attract, through disclosure of pertinent financial information, the attention of persons interested enough in a security to request a prospectus.

432. "S.E.C. Announces Some Proposed Changes in Requirements on Quarterly Reports," *New York Times*, 15 October 1952, p. 51.

New rules require, after the close of each quarter, the filing of a report containing a profit/loss statement and related statement of earned surplus for the quarter and current fiscal year. Previous rules required the filing of quarterly reports on gross sales and operating revenues.

1956

433. J. Erwin Hyney, Appellant, v. Marie Nielsen et al., as Executors of Gerald B. Nielsen, Deceased, et al., Respondents, 1 N.Y. 2d 823 (1956).

J. Erwin Hyney, the plaintiff, in March 1953, loaned $17,000 to Gerald Nielsen for purchase of a seat on the American Stock Exchange, under an agreement that the seat should remain the property of Nielsen as a guarantee for payment of the loan and that the seat could not be transferred or assigned pending repayment of the loan. Before payment of the loan, Nielsen died on June 13, 1953 leaving an insolvent estate. The American Stock Exchange was allowed to pay into the court $12,243.45, the net proceeds from sale of Seat Number 490 and was discharged as a party defendant. (135 N.E.2d 606, 153 N.Y.S.2d 77)

1959

434. "ASE Restricts Floor Traders Much as the Big Board Does," *Business Week* (June 13, 1959): 148.

At the suggestion of the Securities and Exchange Commission, the American Stock Exchange has tightened its regulations governing floor traders. The Amex's new rule limits the volume and timing of purchases that floor traders are allowed to make in order to keep them from causing sharp run-ups in stock prices. Brokers and SEC officials say that floor trader activity both on the Amex and the NYSE has quieted down considerably.

1960

435. "The Markets: Curb Specialists in Doghouse," *Business Week*, (May 21, 1960): 161-162.

"A bizarre trio" is listed by the Securities and Exchange Commission as playing an important role in an alleged scandal by serving as front men for Re, Re & Sagarese in a complicated series of financial maneuvers lasting over six years. The three include Charles A. Grande, a retired horse trainer; Jose Mirada, a former official of the deposed Batista regime in Cuba; and Benjamin C. Wheeler, the head of I. Rokeach, a Kosher meat-packing company. Re, Re & Sagarese engaged in fraudulent distribution and trading of stock worth more than $6 million.

1961

436. Bedingfield, Robert E., "Suspended Brokers Here Accused of Stock Rigging," *New York Times*, 28 April 1962, pp. 1, 34.

The SEC begins prosecution of Gerard A. Re and his son, Gerard F. Re, for the biggest stock manipulation since the 1920s.

437. "Stocks: Two Touts," *Newsweek* 57 (May 8, 1961): 74.

A six-year, $10 million rigging operation on the American Stock Exchange is operated by "men as close to the 'inside' of the market as an insider can get"--Gerard A. (Jerry) Re, 64, and his son, Gerard F., 38. Victims of the Res' bad touts include restaurateur Toots Shor, baseball manager Charlie Dressen, and Amex president Edward McCormick, who "should have known better."

438. "At American Stock Exchange: SEC Broadens Its Stock Manipulation Probe," *Business Week* (May 20, 1961): 31-32.

As Wall Street is concerned about a rise in speculative activity, the SEC orders a full-scale investigation of the American Stock Exchange. Brokers were expecting that the SEC's announcement would bring a sharp reaction in the market. The price of most stocks showed little change although trading volume dropped off sharply.

439. "Wall Street: Curbing the Curb," *Time* 77 (May 26, 1961): 89-90.

As the Dow Jones industrial average bursts through the 700 mark, the Securities and Exchange Commission announces a full-scale probe of the American Stock Exchange, the first publicly announced proceedings against any U.S. exchange since 1938. The investigation grew out of charges against Gerard A. Re and his son, Gerard F., who, from their privileged position as specialists on the American exchange, made an estimated profit of $3,000,000 in five years of market rigging and price fixing. Policing on the Amex is less strict than on the Big Board. Amex growth from 112 million shares traded in 1951 to 186 million traded in 1960 helped to weaken controls.

440. "Business and Finance: Sleuths on Wall St," *Newsweek* 57 (May 19, 1961): 75.

In the wake of the Re scandal, the Securities and Exchange Commission enters into an investigation of the rules, policies, practices, and procedures of the Amex. A House subcommittee is inquiring into stock exchange procedures to see if securities laws need tightening. After the SEC announcement, Amex volume drops off sharply (from 4.5 million to 3.4 million shares) even as trading increases on the Big Board.

441. "New Troubles for the ASE," *Business Week* (June 17, 1961): 141.

In the wake of the Re and Re scandal, the Amex gets another jolt as the SEC stops a proposed offering of 1.3 million shares of Hazel Bishop, Inc., the cosmetics concern. The SEC questions the role of Gilligan, Will, the Exchange's specialist in the company stock, stating that a "conflict may exist" between Gilligan, Will's role as a specialist (with a duty to maintain a fair and orderly market) and as a selling stockholder.

442. "American Exchange Discloses Re Vote," *New York Times*, 14 July 1961, pp. 29, 33.

The Amex reveals a vote by the Governors on December 16, 1959 in connection with the trial of Gerard A. Re and his son, Gerard F. The Governors voted 18 to five that the Res had not willfully violated securities laws. Five governors were not present, and three who served on the committee preparing the case did not vote.

443. "Wall Street: Amex at Bat," *Newsweek* (July 24, 1961): 56, 58.

At a House subcommittee's hearings, it seemed a "foregone conclusion" that American Stock Exchange president Edward T. McCormick and chairman Joseph F. Reilly would be two "embarrassed witnesses." When they took witness chairs in Washington, however, they presented a "picture of hearty self-confidence and a study in skillful public relations." The subcommittee votes to ask Congress for $750,000 to finance an investigation.

444. "Senate Approves S.E.C. Study of Stock Exchange Rules and Regulations," *Wall Street Journal*, 28 August 1962, p. 2.

The Senate authorizes an SEC study which marks the first formal proceedings against any of the nation's stock exchanges since 1940. The Senate proposal now goes to the President for approval. The SEC plans to hire a 65-man staff of experts to conduct the study, which will look into market and trading practices as well as rules and regulations of the exchanges. The SEC announces it will make extensive investigations into operations of the Amex; the Exchange says it welcomes this thorough check of its operations.

445. Bedingfield, Robert E., "American Board 'Closing Ranks'," *New York Times*, 14 October 1961, p. 27.

The Amex plans a full-scale review of its rules, practices, and procedures. Gustave Levy, a partner in Goldman, Sachs, will chair the new committee.

446. "ASE Names Committee of Brokers To Prove its Rules and Procedures," *Business Week*, (October 21, 1961):167.

A committee of brokers led by Gustave L. Levy of Goldman, Sachs initiates an investigation into the Amex's rules, regulations, and procedures. The committee was named by the Amex's Board of Governors in response to the Securities and Exchange Commission's probe which resulted in the expulsion of Gerard and Jerry Re as members. The committee was also named in response to an incipient revolt by Amex members against President Edward T. McCormick.

447. "Wall Street: Attacking the Turks," *Newsweek* (October 30, 1961): 69-70.

When the Securities and Exchange Commission institutes a full-scale investigation of the American Stock Exchange, a "band of dissident members" decides it is time for a change. To avoid open revolt, top administrators name an impartial committee of nine members to review all rules, practices, and procedures of the Exchange. A five day old uneasy truce comes to a sudden halt when, in an unprecedented speech from the

Exchange floor, Amex chairman Joseph F. Reilly launches a scathing attack against trading specialist David S. Jackson, Sr. Jackson serves as leader of the "Young Turks," a group seeking the ouster of president Edward T. McCormick for his part in the Re debacle.

448. "The Market Pattern: Policing the ASE's Rules," *Business Week* (November 4, 1961): 137.

The Amex becomes "the most investigated market on earth." The SEC conducts a full-scale inquiry while a private committee, made up of representatives from many of Wall Street's big brokerages and led by Gustave Levy of Goldman, Sachs, is undertaking a "comprehensive review." Because both investigations are taking place in private, rumors abound with little information on just how widespread infractions have been. Perhaps the professional management of Amex should not take all the blame. Many of the big retail brokerage firms admit to a double standard; while they exercise extreme care in their behavior on the NYSE, they are much less cautious in their dealings on the Amex.

449. "Exchange Urged To Revise Its Set-Up," *New York Times*, 22 December 1961, pp. 31, 37.

The Levy Committee, a nine-man special committee appointed on October 12th by the Amex Board of Governors to review the operations of the Exchange after disclosure of trading irregularities, makes several recommendations regarding rules, policies, and procedures. Recommendations include strengthening the Board of Governors and eliminating standing committees. The report concludes that committees result in a division of authority and an absence of well-defined responsibility; they tend to assume greater powers than exercised by the President or the Board and stifle staff initiative. Policies are developed and presented to the Board in such a manner that the Board is unable to make an informed judgment. Decisions on difficult problems, particularly disciplinary matters, are often delayed.

1962

450. Bedingfield, Robert E., "S.E.C. Finds Many Abuses in the American Exchange," *New York Times*, 6 January 1962, pp. 1, 22.

The SEC tells the Amex to move quickly to end abuses of trading rules by members. A 127-page fact-finding report attacks many of the Amex's administrative practices and procedures, particularly the supervision of stock specialists and floor traders. The report is most critical of the specialist firm of Gilligan, Will & Co., which is the specialist firm handling 13 percent of the 1,000 issues on the Exchange. The report compares the activities of James Gilligan to the Res. The SEC sends copies of the report to the Chairman of the Exchange and to Gustave Levy, chairman of the Exchange's special investigative committee.

451. Bedingfield, Robert E., "American Board Studying Report," *New York Times*, 9 January 1962, pp. 83, 89.

Amex President Joseph F. Reilly announces that the SEC's 127-page study of the Exchange is undergoing a "complete analysis." The Amex will take additional steps where needed to address the severe criticism of its administrative practices and procedures. The study's findings parallel those of the Amex's Levy Committee. Mr. Reilly, at the insistence of the Levy Committee, has withdrawn as a candidate for re-election.

452. "Wall Street: the SEC Moves In," *Time* 72 (January 12, 1962): 69-70.

"To look at the solid building in Manhattan's Trinity Place that houses the American Stock Exchange, it would seem that the old days of the raucous Curb Exchange were far behind. But last week the SEC, after closeting itself for a seven-month study, issued a 127-page report excoriating the practices of the nation's second largest stock exchange, and suggesting that too many vestiges of its past still hang on." In the aftermath of the Re scandal and resignation of President Edward T. McCormick, it is suggested that "the four controllers"--Board Chairman Joseph F. Reilly, Vice Chairman Charles J. Bocklet, Finance Committee Chairman James R. Dyer, and Floor Transactions Manager John J. Mann--were "using their positions to manipulate stock prices for their own profit." The SEC cites "a general deficiency of standards and a fundamental failure of controls."

453. "The Heat Is on the Street," *Business Week* (January 13, 1962): 23-25.

A 127-page report on the Amex is the first installment of the SEC's special investigations of the securities markets to be made public. Its impact is instantly apparent--the Amex announces a series of reform moves, including revision of its constitution. The SEC pictures the Amex as being run along the lines of a private club with a result of "manifold and prolonged abuses" that constitute "a general deficiency of standards and fundamental failure of controls." The report is based on investigations of the "fantastic financial manipulations" of Lowell M. Birrell and the father-son specialist team of Re and Re.

454. "No Free Lunch," *Business Week* (January 13, 1962): 88.

The SEC report on the American Stock Exchange is described as "a black eye for Wall Street as a whole." The Exchange's "shoddy ethical standards" were known to many responsible individuals who turned a blind eye in the club-like atmosphere of the Street. Part of the blame should go also to the SEC which waited too long for Wall Street to do its own policing. The SEC is also investigating the over-the-counter market, the new issues market, and mutual funds.

455. "Report on the Curb: Both the Regulators and the Regulated Have Fallen Short," *Barron's National Business and Financial Weekly* 42 (January 15, 1962): 1.

A 127-page "Staff Report on Organization, Management, and Regulation of Conduct of Members of the American Stock Exchange" is written by the staff of the Securities and Exchange Commission. While the Exchange established an impressive record in dollars and cents, this record came at the expense of its integrity as a marketplace. The Exchange seems guilty as charged, but the reader is cautioned that the SEC was an unwitting accomplice. The "general deficiency of standards and a fundamental failure of controls" noted in the report would not have been possible if the Commission had been doing its job.

456. "American Board Hires Law Firm for Study of Possible Discipline," *New York Times*, 18 January 1962, p. 36.

The Amex announces that its Board of Governors has retained the law firm of White & Case as special counsel. As the result of findings by the SEC, the Amex may take disciplinary action against some members for alleged violations of trading rules.

457. "Big Scandal Exposed on the Little Board," *Life* 52 (January 19, 1962): 40A.

Sixty SEC investigators, supported by a $750,000 special Congressional appropriation, complete a months-long study of the inner workings of the Little Board. Their report cites members for laxity in looking after the public interest and accuses a small group of officials with "self-perpetuating dominance of the exchange of the past 10 years, during which gross abuses of regulations were condoned."

458. "Broad SEC Investigation Coming," *Financial World* 117 (January 24, 1962): 18.

In May 1962, when the SEC expelled two specialists from the American Stock Exchange, the Commission initiated an extensive study of the Exchange and Congress appropriated $750,000 for an investigation of the entire securities industry. Now, the SEC has released a 127-page report. The role of specialists is the subject of one section and is involved in three others. The fifth deals with floor traders. Some observers believe the SEC will recommend elimination of the specialist's dealer function.

459. Hammer, Alexander R., "Exchange Urged to Tighten Rules," *New York Times*, 16 February 1962, pp. 39, 46.

The third and final report of the Levy Committee advises the Amex to get tougher with specialists. The most important recommendations include the elimination of the present standing committee system and the centering of all administrative authority in the paid staff under the president. The Amex is looking for a new president to replace Edward McCormick, who resigned under fire in December. The committee further recommends that the Amex strengthen supervision of the activities of specialists, who are responsible for maintaining an orderly market and preventing wide fluctuations in price; and abolish associate memberships, which have no vote and no proprietary interest in the Exchange, and pay reduced commissions for their trades. The SEC found that specialists, besides financing their own accounts, were also acting as bankers in financing other specialists. They recommend that specialists should be required to obtain necessary capital to carry on normal operations effectively without sharing their profits with other specialists or members; the minimum capital requirement should be increased to $50,000 from the present level of $10,000.

460. Farnsworth, Clyde H., "Wall Street Reform Moving Quickly," *New York Times*, 15 April 1962, sec. III, pp. 1, 16.

Protests are light at the Amex, focusing mainly on new capital requirements and elimination of associate memberships. The Amex now finds itself in almost the same position held by the NYSE before 1938, when a new constitution gave it a salaried president and strong administrative staff. Wall Street fears new restrictive legislation and hopes that a clean house will make legislation less severe. The SEC's primary concerns include: member firms trading for their accounts and abuses resulting from this practice; specialist activities in dealing with the public; broker/dealer activities in the over-the-counter market and rules for unlisted securities; financial public relations activities involving PR houses using their influence to manipulate stock prices; and, the new issues market and underwriters' fees.

461. "American Board Votes New Rules," *New York Times*, 26 June 1962, p. 41.

Members approve an 86-page constitutional amendment which transfers daily operating responsibilities to a president and his staff and designates a Board of Governors as a policy-making unit. Edwin D. Etherington, a partner of Pershing & Co., will take office as president in September.

462. "American Board Disciplines Two," *New York Times*, 27 September 1962, pp. 51, 56.

James P. Gilligan is suspended from membership for three years and fined $5,000; Albert Will is suspended for one year and also fined $5,000. Both are general partners in the firm of Gilligan, Will & Co. Their offenses include violation of short selling rules, failure to learn essential facts about various customers, improper operations as specialists, failure to make proper reports to the Exchange, and abuse of discretionary accounts. Gilligan is the son of James Gilligan, Sr., who was involved in breaches of the 1934 Securities Exchange Act and rules of the Exchange; Gilligan, Sr., retired from the firm in 1961.

1963

463. "Wall Street Forms Liaison Unit To Consult S.E.C. on New Laws," *New York Times*, 18 April 1963, pp. 49, 53.

A seven-member Securities Liaison Group, including the presidents of the NASD, Amex, NYSE, and Midwest Stock Exchange, is formed for the purpose of consulting with the SEC on possible new laws to govern operations of securities markets.

1964

464. "American Board Files New Rules," *New York Times*, 1 July 1964, pp. 45, 47.

An SEC plan to regulate floor trading on the Amex calls for lower capital requirements than those for the New York Stock Exchange--$75,000 on the Amex, and $250,000 on the NYSE.

1966

465. Krefetz, Gerald, "Wall Street: a Walk on the Wild Side," *Nation* 194 (April 7, 1966): 306-311.

"It ain't me!" summarizes the reaction of Wall Street traders to securities investigations. The Street has been rocked by scandals, swindles, and manipulations and hasn't received so much attention from Washington since the early 1930s. A Securities and Exchange Commission report on the American Stock Exchange has become a bestseller almost overnight and is in its second printing. The expelling of Gerard A. Re and his son, Gerard F., in 1961 was the first significant shock in some time. The Res' manipulations date back to 1954 and involve trading in I. Rokeach and Son, Inc., producers of kosher food products. To summarize the SEC charges, the Res acquired stocks in companies illegally, used dummy accounts to manipulate the prices, failed to maintain the required general ledger, corrupted other floor traders, operated companies as if they were "their own private crap game," and rigged the market to the exclusion of legitimate buyers and sellers.

466. Vartan, Vartanig G., "Stock Exchanges Move To Curtail Speculative Tide," *New York Times*, 22 April 1966, pp. 1, 56.

The Amex and NYSE announce that they are raising from $1,000 to $2,000 the minimum cash required for buying on margin. A person buying 100 shares of stock selling at less than $28.50 per share will be required to put up more than 70 percent of the cost of the stock. The Amex's present minimum is 25 percent. The tighter rules for buying on credit are an effort to reduce the speculative wave that has swept the securities market. Amex President Etherington says that wide price swings and high volume point to an unusual degree of speculation on the Amex.

1967

467. "Stock Market: Dead Men Tell No Tales," *Newsweek* 69 (May 8, 1967): 83.

It appears to be the most baffling mystery to strike Wall Street since Anthony (Tino) De Angelis engineered the great salad oil swindle of 1936. Teams of investigators from the American Stock Exchange, the Securities and Exchange Commission, the New York U. S. Attorney's Office, and the Chicago police force are investigating the rigging of eight stocks. It appears that in a bold stock-kiting operation, a group of swindlers has bought sizable blocks of Hercules Galion Products and Rowland Products and spread false rumors of their merger or earnings prospects. Edward N. Siegler Co., a reputable Cleveland brokerage house, goes bankrupt. Syndicate mobster Alan R. Rosenberg, 36, is found curled in the back seat of a leased 1967 Cadillac with his hands manacled behind his back, one bullet in his skull and seven through his chest.

468. "Stock Scandal, '67 Style," *Newsweek* 69 (June 12, 1967): 71.

United States Attorney Robert M. Morgenthau brings charges of a bold stock swindle reminiscent of the notorious "pool" operations of the '20s. A Federal grand jury indicts six businessmen on charges of rigging the price of Pentron Electronics Corp. Pentron chairman Osborn Andreas, "graying and soft spoken, seemed an improbable participant in a major stock swindle." Osborn himself is "something of an esthete. He has written two scholarly books (*Henry James and the Expanding Horizon* in 1948 and *Joseph Conrad, a Study in Non-Conformity* in 1959), once operated a New York art gallery, and has studied concert piano. Morgenthau may have only bared the tip of an iceberg. His investigation reportedly embraces at least seven other Amex and over-the-counter stocks and Wall Street rumors indicate that two Big Board stocks are under scrutiny. Among the Amex issues, Hercules Galion Products and Rowland Products are believed by Morgenthau to have been the target of undisclosed manipulators, some of whom possibly used "prostitutes, blackmailers, and even Mafia elements" in their schemes.

469. Hammer, Alexander R., "Amex Tightens Rules for Listing," *New York Times*, 21 November 1967, pp. 65, 69.

The Amex announces more stringent requirements for listing on the Exchange. Net worth has been increased from a minimum of $1 million to $3 million; earnings, from a minimum of $150,000 to $300,000; and, publicly held shares from a minimum of 250,000 to 300,000. A pre-tax earnings requirement of $500,000 is instituted and a stock must sell at a minimum price of $5 per share for a reasonable period prior to filing. President Ralph Saul says that the upgrade is necessary to keep pace with the expanding national economy and the growth of the Exchange. The new criteria go into effect immediately.

1969

470. Rustin, Richard E., "Two Top Exchanges Adopt Plan on Gripes of Customers; Members Privately Object," *Wall Street Journal*, 22 August 1969, p. 2.

After experiencing an increase in customer complaints based on "back office" or operational problems, the Amex and NYSE approve a new program which addresses complaints that the brokerage house made mistakes involving the sale, purchase, or delivery of securities or made errors involving case items. The program calls for customer service controls to be established at brokerage firms to provide month-to-month comparisons of numbers and causes of complaints. A monthly customer service report must be submitted to the firm's management listing the number of trades processed by each exchange, the number of trade corrections processed, the number of corrected confirmations sent to customers, and the number of such pending confirmations. Firms with high levels of complaints would send reports directly to the exchanges; others would be internal only.

1972

471. Robards, Terry, "Amex Developing Disclosure Plan," *New York Times*, 22 December 1972, pp. 45, 46.

The Amex announces development of a new public disclosure policy in order to give greater publicity to major disciplinary actions involving members and their firms. Intent is to be more responsive to the needs of the public. The NYSE announces a similar proposal.

1973

472. "People and Business," *New York Times*, 13 April 1973, p. 53.

The Amex creates a new division for regulatory and compliance activities. Edwin B. Peterson, senior vice president of the Amex, will have overall responsibility for the division. He was a founder of the compliance division of the Association of Stock Exchange Firms and has served four years as an Amex governor.

1975

473. Gordon vs. New York Stock Exchange, Inc., et al., 422 U.S. 659 (1975).

Richard A. Gordon, individually and on behalf of a class of small investors, files an appeal in the United States Supreme Court against the New York Stock Exchange, the American Stock Exchange, and two member firms of the Exchanges. He claims that the system of fixed commission rates used by the Exchanges for transactions of less than $500,000 violates the Sherman Act. The District Court and the Court of Appeals both concluded that the fixed commission rates were immunized from antitrust attack because of the authority of the Securities and Exchange Commission under the Securities Exchange Act of 1934 to approve or disapprove exchange commission rates. Therefore, the system of fixed commission rates, which is under the active supervision of the SEC, is beyond the reach of the antitrust laws. On June 26, 1975, the Supreme Court affirmed the earlier decisions. Justice Blackmun delivered the opinion for a unanimous court. (95 S. Ct. 2598, 45 L.Ed. 2d 463)

474. Cole, Robert J., "Problems Found in Option Trading," *New York Times*, 2 December 1975, p. 75.

The Amex and Chicago Board Options Exchange have notified the SEC of irregularities in the trading of stock options. The irregularities involve illegal prearranged trades by investors who want to establish losses for tax purposes. Official warnings to members on both exchanges have halted such trading; the Amex has not initiated disciplinary procedures against the violators. The SEC acknowledges that it was aware of the situation and that it will not take action unless corrective measures by the exchanges are ineffective.

1978

475. The People of the State of New York, Plaintiff, v. Arnold Barysh et. al., Defendants, 95 Misc. 2d 616 (1978).

> Defendants, specialists on the American Stock Exchange, were charged with "over-all criminal schemes" by entering fictitious options trades in the transaction journal of the American Stock Exchange in violation of the Martin Act. In June 1978, charges were dismissed "since the prosecutor's inadequate and erroneous charge to the Grand Jury" prevented them from determining any "intent to defraud." (408 N.Y.S.2d 190)

1984

476. "Drexel Fined by Amex," *New York Times*, 5 April 1984, sec. IV, p. 7.

> Drexel Burnham Lambert, Inc., is censured and fined $7,500 by the Amex for "front-running." Drexel placed an options order on its own account when it knew it had customer orders pending to buy 100,000 shares of underlying stock. Drexel pays the fine without admitting or denying the charges.

1986

477. Makin, Claire, "Wall Street's Electronic Cops," *Institutional Investor* 20:2 (February 1986): 69-71.

> It started when the NYSE's computer systems issued a warning that something might not be right on the trading floor. It ended when a *Value Line* secretary and her husband were found by the Securities and Exchange Commission and returned more than $157,000 allegedly made trading on inside information. In an effort to prevent stock market abuse, the major exchanges are building a formidable array of "technological weaponry." They are integrating their surveillance systems under the Intermarket Surveillance Group, which they established in 1981. The Amex's Stock Watch Alert Terminal monitors stocks against their own characteristics and calls out stock symbols while printing a list of "kickouts."

478. "Rules Altered on Specialists," *New York Times*, 31 October 1986, sec. IV, p. 5.

> The SEC approves rules allowing large brokerage firms to operate as specialists on the floors of the NYSE and Amex. The firms are expected to bring added capital to the specialist system, now straining under expanding volume. Brokerage firms have been slow to enter the specialist business because of restrictions on affiliates trading stock or options of any issue for which they act as specialist.

1988

479. "Computers and the Crash II: How the Systems Performed," *Institutional Investor* Volume 2, Financial Technology Forum Supplement (June 1988): 8-10.

Article reprints excerpts from reports prepared by government agencies, the exchanges, and a Presidential commission concerning performance of automated systems during the October 19th crash. The Amex's Post Execution Reporting (PER) System averaged approximately 25,000 trades on October 19th and 20th, and experienced relatively few problems. On October 19th, at 3:49 p.m., the system was shut down for the remainder of the trading day while the computer disk was changed.

1992

480. Michael, Douglas C., "Untenable Status of Corporate Governance Listing Standards under the Securities Exchange Act," *Business Lawyer* 47:4 (August 1992): 1461-1504.

In discussing the Exchanges' system of supervised self-regulation created by the Securities Exchange Act of 1934, Michael provides a history of listing standards. The Amex's first standard, a corporate governance standard, appeared in 1946. Most of the Amex's standards were first set during the comprehensive reform of the Exchange in the 1960s. Those rules have been marginally revised since, but most dramatically in the area of voting rights, where the Exchange maintains distinctive rules while advocating uniformity among exchanges.

481. Pressman, Aaron, "Congress Wants More Info on Amex's Troubled ECM," *Investment Dealers Digest* 58:46 (November 16, 1992): 11.

Congress is asking questions about the Amex's Emerging Company Marketplace (ECM) and has asked to be kept informed of the Exchange's cooperation with an SEC investigation. In addition, the General Accounting Office has begun an inquiry. In October, the Amex announced that an outside counsel found no wrongdoing on the part of Exchange employees or the board of governors. Controversy stems from the listing of PNF Industries. PNF was controlled by Alfred Avasso, who was barred from the Amex in 1986. When the ECM was announced in March 1992, Amex officials stated that they hoped to have 50 companies listed by the end of the year. After delisting PNF and moving two companies to the larger Amex market, the ECM lists only 28 companies.

Chapter 7

ECONOMIC ASPECTS

The price of a seat on the American Stock Exchange often serves as an economic indicator. Traditionally, seat prices rise and fall with both stock prices and market volume, providing as reliable a guide to the health of the market as other measures. The 1929 price of $254,000 remained the record high for many years, finally broken by the $350,000 sale of 1969 and $420,000 of October 1987; the record low is $650 from 1942.

ARTICLES

1957

482. "Turnover Is High on American List," *New York Times*, 2 January 1957, p. 100.

During the last two years, share turnover on the Amex has been double that of any year between 1947 and 1953. The main factor keeping the volume high is new listings; there were 65. This steady growth is reflected in the prices of memberships. In 1942, a seat sold as low as $650. The post-war low was $5,500 in 1949. In 1956, prices ranged from a high of $31,500 to a low of $21,500.

1958

483. "Seat Prices Lower on Both Exchanges," *New York Times*, 6 January 1958, p. 64.

Membership costs in 1958 mirror lower stock prices on the major exchanges. On the Amex, seat prices range from $21,500 to $26,000. This is lower than 1956 prices which ranged from $21,500 to $31,500.

1959

484. "Big Board Seats Rise to $140,000," *New York Times*, 12 January 1959, pp. 81, 86.

As the exchanges experience the heaviest trading levels in several years, seats are at a premium. One seat on the Amex brought $42,000, the highest price paid since 1936. In 1929, a seat on the New York Curb Exchange sold for $254,000. The range of prices for memberships sold in 1958 was from $18,000 on April 10th to $42,000 on December 1st, 12th, and 30th.

1960

485. "High Cost of Seat That Isn't a Seat," *New York Times*, 11 January 1960, p. 72.

A seat is not what the word implies. Brokers really stand during trading, working at trading posts on the exchange floor. A seat is simply a trade term for a membership which gives the holder the right to transact the sale and purchase of securities on the floor of the exchange. In 1959, with trading more than 100,000,000 shares greater than in 1958, demand for seats on the Amex rose substantially. Prices ranged from $44,000 to $65,000, compared to $18,000 to $42,000 in 1958. The Amex has 499 regular members and 386 associate members. An associate member does not have the privilege of trading on the floor, but may trade through a regular member firm at a reduced commission rate.

1962

486. "Memberships Shifted," *New York Times*, 8 January 1962, p. 57.

In 1961, 84 memberships--51 regular memberships and 33 associate memberships-- were transferred. Prices ranged between a high of $60,000 and a low of $51,000. The record price remains the $254,000 paid in 1929; the low, the $650 of 1942. At the close of 1962, there were 499 regular and 411 associate memberships.

1974

487. "American Exchange Calls 'Time Out' on Seats," *New York Times*, 5 May 1974, sec. III, p. 15.

When word began to circulate on Thursday, April 25th, that the SEC was about to give conditional approval of Amex trading in options, the Exchange took the unusual step of suspending seat sales. The quotation for an Amex seat was $29,000 bid, $35,000 asked; the preceding sale was at $32,000 on April 23d. The Exchange feared that inside information might provide an advantage; the suspension prevented anyone from making a killing. Prices are still a long way from the high of $350,000 paid in 1969. The low was $650 in 1942. For security analysts, the book value of a seat is

$30,251--the Exchange's $19.7 million in assets at the end of 1973 divided by its 650 members.

1976

488. "Amex Plans Options Seats," *New York Times*, 25 February 1976, p. 63.

The Amex proposes creation of 200 special memberships for trading stock options. If approved by the SEC, the seats will be offered in March at $15,000. New members will begin floor trading in May.

1984

489. Christman, Eddy, "N.Y. Funds Assail Proposal To Purchase Exchange Seat," *Pensions and Investment Age*, 12 (March 19, 1984): 9.

A New York state legislator proposes that the state purchase seats on both the NYSE and Amex to "save millions of dollars in unnecessary brokerage commissions." Immediate strong criticism comes from the state's three public retirement systems. They feel that current anonymity must be maintained to prevent a decline in prices once the intent to make large sales becomes known. The pension funds pay annual brokerage commissions totalling $20-25 million on the 200 million shares traded. Connecticut has used a public broker at the Philadelphia Stock Exchange for its $2.6 billion retirement systems since 1972.

1987

490. "Prices of Seats Tumbling, Too," *New York Times*, 27 October 1987, sec. IV, p. 10.

Prices of memberships on the NYSE and Amex fall almost as fast as stock prices. On Friday, October 16th, as the Dow Industrials fall 508 points, prices in four seat sales slide from the $420,000 record set a week previously to $386,000. An options membership sold for $345,000 on October 16th; by the 27th, the price was $186,000.

1989

491. Jaffe, Thomas, ed., "Streetwalker: American Anomaly," *Forbes* (August 7, 1989): 164.

Looking at the Exchange's recent equity trading records, one might think the Exchange is booming. The Amex index hits an all-time high for the ninth time since June 1989, closing at a record 369 on July 18th. On October 16, 1987, just before the crash, an Amex seat sold for $410,000; on the day the index reached its post crash low, a seat sold for $175,000. The last seat auctioned, on May 24th, brought just $181,000. The columnist believes that seat value, not the Amex's 60 percent gain, may prove to be a better indicator of Wall Street's malaise.

1993

492. Raghaven, Anita, "Stock Boom Fails To Spur Bull Market in Seats," *Wall Street Journal*, 24 March 1993, sec. C, pp. 1, 20.

Trading is higher than ever before, but seat prices on the NYSE are still far below the $1 million high set in the 1987 bull market. Cost cutting throughout the industry, plus mergers among brokerage firms have reduced personnel on the trading floor and lessened the demand for seats. During the 1980s, seat prices tended to parallel the trend of stock prices and trading volume. In February, an Amex seat sold for $98,000, well below the all-time high of $420,000 in 1987.

493. The *New York Times* (NYT) and *Wall Street Journal* (WSJ) have consistently reported seat prices during the history of the Exchange. These reports are summarized in the following table.

Sale Price	Publication	Date	Sec:Page:Col
$ 5,000	NYT	Nov. 2, 1921	---:26: 2
7,000	NYT	Mar. 12, 1924	---:28: 4
10,000	NYT	Jan. 15, 1925	---:23: 4
20,000	NYT	Oct. 22, 1925	---:24: 2
31,000	NYT	May 21, 1927	---:27: 2
33,000	NYT	May 22, 1927	---:16: 3
30,000	NYT	Sep. 3, 1927	---:25: 6
32,000	NYT	Sep. 15, 1927	---:45: 3
33,000	NYT	Sep. 30, 1927	---:39: 1
34,000	NYT	Nov. 15, 1927	---:44: 7
34,500	NYT	Nov. 22, 1927	---:48: 2
35,000	NYT	Nov. 23, 1927	---:41: 4
40,000	NYT	Nov. 24, 1927	---:25: 6
55,000	NYT	Nov. 30, 1927	---:31: 2
60,000	NYT	Nov. 30, 1927	---:31: 2
65,000	NYT	Dec. 1, 1927	---:45: 3
65,000	NYT	Dec. 7, 1927	---:49: 3
67,000	NYT	Dec. 8, 1927	---:37: 4
65,000	NYT	Dec. 22, 1927	---:37: 6
67,000	NYT	Dec. 22, 1927	---:37: 6
60,000	NYT	Jan. 28, 1928	---:24: 2
60,000	NYT	Feb. 17, 1928	---:27: 2

60,000	NYT	Mar. 27, 1928	---:37: 5
65,000	NYT	Mar. 28, 1928	---:42: 3
66,000	NYT	Apr. 13, 1928	---:36: 5
70,000	NYT	Apr. 14, 1928	---:31: 1
70,000	NYT	Apr. 18, 1928	---:37: 4
80,000	NYT	Apr. 21, 1928	---:26: 2
80,000	NYT	Apr. 25, 1928	---:44: 2
85,000	NYT	Apr. 25, 1928	---:44: 2
90,000	NYT	Apr. 26, 1928	---:43: 3
90,000	NYT	Apr. 27, 1928	---:40: 5
95,000	NYT	May 1, 1928	---:46: 4
95,000	NYT	May 2, 1928	---:34: 2
95,000	NYT	June 2, 1928	---:24: 6
97,000	NYT	June 8, 1928	---:27: 4
98,000	NYT	Sep. 13, 1928	---:40: 8
103,000	NYT	Oct. 21, 1928	II:12: 8
110,000	NYT	Oct. 25, 1928	---:41: 2
120,000	NYT	Oct. 25, 1928	---:41: 2
125,000	NYT	Oct. 26, 1928	---:40: 3
125,000	NYT	Oct. 31, 1928	---:42: 2
135,000	NYT	Nov. 10, 1928	---:29: 7
140,000	NYT	Nov. 11, 1928	---: 7: 7
150,000	NYT	Nov. 15, 1928	---:41: 1
165,000	NYT	Nov. 29, 1928	---:43: 2
150,000	NYT	Jan. 6, 1929	II: 9: 5
175,000	NYT	Jan. 11, 1929	---:36: 7
175,000	NYT	Feb. 6, 1929	---:42: 6
180,000	NYT	Feb. 9, 1929	---:29: 3
185,000	NYT	Feb. 12, 1929	---:37: 4
187,000	NYT	Feb. 16, 1929	---:26: 7
170,000	NYT	Mar. 9, 1929	---:32: 7
165,000	NYT	June 20, 1929	---:38: 6
170,000	NYT	June 29, 1929	---:27: 5
195,000	NYT	July 16, 1929	---:31: 3
200,000	NYT	July 17, 1929	---:41: 2
235,000	NYT	July 21, 1929	II: 9: 5
240,000	NYT	Sep. 18, 1929	---:45: 2
250,000	NYT	Sep. 22, 1929	II:16: 2
250,000	NYT	Oct. 10, 1929	---:53: 1
200,000	NYT	Dec. 6, 1929	---:42: 2
160,000	NYT	Feb. 14, 1930	---:38: 2
185,000	NYT	Mar. 7, 1930	---:38: 1
198,000	NYT	Apr. 3, 1930	---:46: 2

225,000	NYT	Apr. 5, 1930	---:32: 2
150,000	NYT	Aug. 5, 1930	---:34: 2
140,000	NYT	Sep. 24, 1930	---:29: 2
110,000	NYT	Sep. 24, 1930	---:29: 2
105,000	NYT	Sep. 26, 1930	---:30: 2
85,000	NYT	Oct. 19, 1930	II:11: 5
78,000	NYT	Oct. 31, 1930	---:37: 2
92,000	NYT	Nov. 25, 1930	---:39: 3
100,000	NYT	Nov. 26, 1930	---:34: 2
105,000	NYT	Nov. 29, 1930	---:28: 2
92,000	NYT	Dec. 9, 1930	---:39: 2
95,000	NYT	Jan. 1, 1931	---:53: 1
85,000	NYT	Jan. 1, 1931	---:53: 1
100,000	NYT	Jan. 31, 1931	---:29: 2
104,000	NYT	Jan. 31, 1931	---:29: 2
120,000	NYT	Feb. 15, 1931	II:19: 1
137,500	NYT	Feb. 28, 1931	---:29: 5
120,000	NYT	Apr. 1, 1931	---:47: 2
92,000	NYT	May 27, 1931	---:45: 5
80,000	NYT	June 3, 1931	---:40: 3
82,500	NYT	June 27, 1931	---:27: 6
77,500	NYT	Aug. 7, 1931	---:27: 2
77,000	NYT	Aug. 16, 1931	II: 7: 7
65,000	NYT	Sep. 10, 1931	---:38: 4
61,500	NYT	Sep. 11, 1931	---:30: 2
60,000	NYT	Sep. 11, 1931	---:30: 2
57,000	NYT	Sep. 11, 1931	---:30: 2
54,000	NYT	Sep. 22, 1931	---:40: 2
51,000	NYT	Sep. 22, 1931	---:40: 2
40,000	NYT	Oct. 6, 1931	---:44: 2
42,000	NYT	Dec. 12, 1931	---:32: 1
41,500	NYT	Dec. 15, 1931	---:45: 1
38,000	NYT	Dec. 18, 1931	---:40: 6
40,000	NYT	Jan. 9, 1932	---:26: 1
41,000	NYT	Jan. 28, 1932	---:34: 2
38,000	NYT	Feb. 6, 1932	---:29: 2
36,000	NYT	Feb. 11, 1932	---:34: 2
35,000	NYT	Feb. 12, 1932	---:35: 2
40,000	NYT	Feb. 19, 1932	---:27: 3
38,500	NYT	Feb. 24, 1932	---:29: 7
30,500	NYT	Mar. 25, 1932	---:31: 1
22,000	NYT	Apr. 5, 1932	---:18: 7
21,000	NYT	Apr. 26, 1932	---:34: 2

18,500	NYT	Apr. 30, 1932	---:25: 7
19,000	NYT	May 28, 1932	---:23: 2
16,500	NYT	June 3, 1932	---:33: 2
19,500	NYT	June 10, 1932	---:34: 2
17,500	NYT	June 18, 1932	---:23: 2
16,500	NYT	July 12, 1932	---:31: 2
18,000	NYT	July 24, 1932	IV: 6: 4
20,000	NYT	Aug. 4, 1932	---:32: 2
36,000	NYT	Aug. 16, 1932	---:30: 1
55,000	NYT	Sep. 3, 1932	---:21: 1
75,000	NYT	Sep. 7, 1932	---:25: 7
40,000	NYT	Oct. 11, 1932	---:38: 3
38,500	NYT	Oct. 12, 1932	---:37: 1
37,500	NYT	Oct. 12, 1932	---:37: 1
35,000	NYT	Oct. 14, 1932	---:33: 2
30,000	NYT	Oct. 25, 1932	---:33: 2
32,000	NYT	Nov. 12, 1932	---:26: 2
29,000	NYT	Nov. 27, 1932	IV: 8: 2
30,000	NYT	Dec. 20, 1932	---:32: 2
30,000	NYT	Jan. 18, 1933	---:32: 2
25,000	NYT	Feb. 22, 1933	---:33: 6
35,000	NYT	Mar. 14, 1933	---:27: 2
39,000	NYT	Mar. 17, 1933	---:27: 6
30,000	NYT	Apr. 16, 1933	II:11: 6
30,000	NYT	Apr. 20, 1933	---:33: 5
30,000	NYT	Apr. 28, 1933	---:32: 2
40,000	NYT	May 4, 1933	---:25: 3
40,000	NYT	May 21, 1933	II:13: 2
32,000	NYT	May 27, 1933	---:19: 2
42,000	NYT	June 3, 1933	---:17: 8
43,000	NYT	June 3, 1933	---:17: 8
45,000	NYT	June 4, 1933	---: 9: 5
49,000	NYT	June 4, 1933	II: 9: 5
50,000	NYT	June 16, 1933	---:30: 2
50,000	NYT	June 17, 1933	---:17: 2
50,000	NYT	July 23, 1933	II:11: 2
35,000	NYT	Aug. 31, 1933	---:30: 2
35,000	NYT	Sep. 13, 1933	---:27: 7
25,000	NYT	Oct. 18, 1933	---:36: 2
30,000	NYT	Nov. 10, 1933	---:36: 2
25,000	NYT	Dec. 2, 1933	---:23: 2
26,000	NYT	Dec. 3, 1933	II:11: 6
25,000	NYT	Dec. 5, 1933	---:40: 2

31,000	NYT	Jan. 7, 1934	II:12: 8
40,000	NYT	Jan. 16, 1934	---:29: 3
40,000	NYT	Jan. 17, 1934	---:33: 1
17,500	NYT	Mar. 22, 1934	---:31: 7
26,500	NYT	June 24, 1934	II:12: 6
30,000	NYT	July 3, 1934	---:32: 2
30,000	NYT	July 4, 1934	---:29: 2
18,500	NYT	Aug. 10, 1934	---:32: 2
20,000	NYT	Sep. 8, 1934	---:23: 8
18,000	NYT	Sep. 14, 1934	---:40: 2
17,000	NYT	Sep. 22, 1934	---:26:20
20,000	NYT	Oct. 11, 1934	---:40: 1
17,500	NYT	Oct. 24, 1934	---:36: 2
20,000	NYT	Dec. 7, 1934	---:41: 1
21,500	NYT	Dec. 20, 1934	---:42: 2
21,000	NYT	Jan. 3, 1935	---:38: 1
22,000	NYT	Jan. 20, 1935	II:14: 2
23,000	NYT	Jan. 29, 1935	---:34: 2
12,000	NYT	Mar. 16, 1935	---:21: 7
13,000	NYT	Mar. 16, 1935	---:21: 7
22,000	NYT	May 28, 1935	---:41: 7
25,000	NYT	July 10, 1935	---:34: 2
27,500	NYT	July 12, 1935	---:32: 1
22,500	NYT	Sep. 6, 1935	---:30: 2
32,500	NYT	Sep. 17, 1935	---:38: 2
32,500	NYT	Sep. 20, 1935	---:36: 2
33,000	NYT	Nov. 10, 1935	III: 6: 2
30,000	NYT	Dec. 4, 1935	---:38: 1
38,000	NYT	Jan. 18, 1936	---:26: 2
40,000	NYT	Jan. 19, 1936	III: 8: 4
40,000	NYT	Jan. 29, 1936	---:33: 6
47,000	NYT	Feb. 14, 1936	---:25: 1
48,000	NYT	Feb. 18, 1936	---:40: 2
36,000	NYT	Apr. 30, 1936	---:34: 2
26,000	NYT	May 15, 1936	---:43: 2
30,000	NYT	July 16, 1936	---:27: 6
30,000	NYT	Aug. 12, 1936	---:27: 8
30,000	NYT	Aug. 18, 1936	---:27: 8
30,000	NYT	Sep. 12, 1936	---:25: 2
32,000	NYT	Nov. 10, 1936	---:37: 5
33,000	NYT	Dec. 13, 1936	III: 6: 2
33,000	NYT	Dec. 16, 1936	---:47: 4
33,000	NYT	Dec. 19, 1936	---:35: 1

34,000	NYT	Dec. 20, 1936	III: 5: 1
33,000	NYT	Feb. 5, 1937	---:29: 5
32,500	NYT	Mar. 18, 1937	---:42: 2
32,500	NYT	Mar. 19, 1937	---:39: 4
29,000	NYT	Apr. 9, 1937	---:36: 2
22,500	NYT	May 29, 1937	---:23: 4
22,000	NYT	May 29, 1937	---:23: 4
19,800	NYT	June 25, 1937	---:36: 2
19,000	NYT	July 20, 1937	---:36: 6
23,000	NYT	Aug. 1, 1937	III: 6: 7
17,500	NYT	Dec. 23, 1937	---:37: 1
15,500	NYT	Jan. 7, 1938	---:32: 3
15,500	NYT	Jan. 8, 1938	---:21: 5
17,000	NYT	Jan. 13, 1938	---:34: 7
17,500	NYT	Jan. 14, 1938	---:32: 8
16,000	NYT	Jan. 29, 1938	---:27: 2
15,000	NYT	Feb. 1, 1938	---:25: 7
12,000	NYT	Mar. 2, 1938	---:35: 6
10,000	NYT	Apr. 1, 1938	---:32: 2
8,000	NYT	Apr. 8, 1938	---:29: 6
9,500	NYT	May 27, 1938	---:25: 5
9,500	NYT	May 29, 1938	III :1: 3
13,000	NYT	July 20, 1938	---:25: 8
15,000	NYT	July 22, 1938	---:25: 2
12,500	NYT	Aug. 3, 1938	---:30: 5
10,000	NYT	Mar. 10, 1939	---:35: 5
9,000	NYT	Apr. 12, 1939	---:35: 2
8,000	NYT	May 3, 1939	---:42: 1
8,000	NYT	May 11, 1939	---:44: 5
7,000	NYT	Aug. 26, 1939	---:25: 4
8,500	NYT	Sep. 9, 1939	---:21: 4
9,500	NYT	Sep. 9, 1939	---:21: 4
8,500	NYT	Dec. 15, 1939	---:44: 1
7,000	NYT	Feb. 29, 1940	---:32: 8
7,250	NYT	Mar. 30, 1940	---:27: 5
7,000	NYT	Apr. 21, 1940	III: 6: 7
6,900	NYT	June 26, 1940	---:35: 3
2,600	NYT	Jan. 3, 1941	---:23: 6
2,500	NYT	Jan. 3, 1941	---:23: 6
2,500	NYT	Jan. 30, 1941	---:29: 7
2,500	NYT	Feb. 4, 1941	---:31: 3
1,200	NYT	Mar. 5, 1941	---:34: 3
1,100	NYT	Mar. 27, 1941	---:33: 6

1,000	NYT	Apr. 25, 1941	---:32: 8
1,000	NYT	May 14, 1941	---:35: 4
1,000	NYT	June 19, 1941	---:37: 6
1,000	NYT	July 16, 1941	---:27: 3
1,000	NYT	July 24, 1941	---:29: 6
1,100	NYT	Nov. 18, 1941	---:43: 8
1,000	NYT	Dec. 10, 1941	---:44: 2
1,000	NYT	Dec. 30, 1941	---:31: 8
1,000	NYT	Feb. 12, 1942	---:34: 5
900	NYT	June 23, 1942	---:30: 4
850	NYT	July 12, 1942	III: 4: 2
800	NYT	July 23, 1942	---:27: 6
838	NYT	Aug. 4, 1942	---:27: 2
846	NYT	Aug. 5, 1942	---:28: 6
800	NYT	Aug. 6, 1942	---:30: 7
800	NYT	Aug. 22, 1942	---:22: 3
750	NYT	Sep. 11, 1942	---:35: 2
650	NYT	Sep. 24, 1942	---:31: 1
650	NYT	Sep. 26, 1942	---:26: 2
750	NYT	Oct. 6, 1942	---:32: 1
787	NYT	Oct. 6, 1942	---:32: 1
1,200	NYT	Nov. 5, 1942	---:40: 2
1,500	NYT	Nov. 11, 1942	---:36: 2
1,700	NYT	Dec. 1, 1942	---:36: 2
1,600	NYT	Jan. 14, 1943	---:34: 2
1,800	NYT	Jan. 19, 1943	---:31: 1
2,950	NYT	Jan. 28, 1943	---:28: 8
2,500	NYT	Jan. 31, 1943	III: 7: 4
2,500	NYT	Feb. 19, 1943	---:32: 5
7,500	NYT	Apr. 4, 1943	III: 7: 3
7,500	NYT	May 5, 1943	---:33: 8
8,500	NYT	May 28, 1943	---:35: 8
7,400	NYT	June 6, 1943	III: 7: 5
6,700	NYT	June 18, 1943	---:31: 6
6,800	NYT	Sep. 10, 1943	---:33: 4
7,000	NYT	Oct. 27, 1943	---:35: 4
6,800	NYT	Nov. 6, 1943	---:22: 3
6,800	NYT	Nov. 18, 1943	---:39: 2
6,700	NYT	Nov. 30, 1943	---:36: 1
6,300	NYT	Dec. 1, 1943	---:31: 8
7,500	NYT	Jan. 4, 1944	---:26: 4
7,500	NYT	Jan. 8, 1944	---:18: 2
8,000	NYT	Jan. 20, 1944	---:28: 5

8,000	NYT	Feb. 5, 1944	---:20: 8
9,000	NYT	Feb. 11, 1944	---:27: 2
10,000	NYT	Mar. 26, 1944	III: 6: 5
12,000	NYT	Mar. 28, 1944	---:25: 2
13,000	NYT	July 11, 1944	---:24: 3
14,000	NYT	July 29, 1944	---:19: 8
13,500	NYT	Aug. 26, 1944	---:18: 3
14,000	NYT	Aug. 26, 1944	---:18: 3
15,000	NYT	Sep. 26, 1944	---:28: 7
14,000	NYT	Nov. 29, 1944	---:29: 1
15,000	NYT	Jan. 12, 1945	---:23: 5
16,000	NYT	Jan. 14, 1945	III: 4: 5
16,000	NYT	Feb. 7, 1945	---:29: 1
12,000	NYT	Mar. 24, 1945	---:27: 2
13,000	NYT	May 25, 1945	---:24: 7
14,500	NYT	June 30, 1945	---:22: 7
13,000	NYT	Aug. 10, 1945	---:26: 8
15,000	NYT	Sep. 15, 1945	---:24: 8
15,000	NYT	Sep. 28, 1945	---:30: 2
17,500	NYT	Oct. 6, 1945	---:22: 4
19,000	NYT	Oct. 16, 1945	---:29: 1
25,000	NYT	Oct. 26, 1945	---:28: 5
30,000	NYT	Nov. 1, 1945	---:32: 4
30,000	NYT	Dec. 7, 1945	---:33: 2
32,000	NYT	Dec. 7, 1945	---:33: 2
32,000	NYT	Dec. 16, 1945	III: 3: 5
36,000	NYT	May 2, 1946	---:36: 3
37,500	NYT	June 1, 1946	---:23: 2
27,500	NYT	Aug. 17, 1946	---:19: 7
19,000	NYT	Oct. 16, 1946	---:44: 8
25,000	NYT	Jan. 30, 1947	---:35: 3
18,500	NYT	Mar. 16, 1947	III: 3: 3
18,000	NYT	Apr. 16, 1947	---:40: 8
18,000	NYT	May 13, 1947	---:35: 3
19,500	NYT	July 10, 1947	---:35: 8
20,000	NYT	July 10, 1947	---:35: 8
15,000	NYT	Aug. 19, 1947	---:35: 4
13,000	NYT	Sep. 6, 1947	---:21: 8
15,000	NYT	Oct. 24, 1947	---:35 :5
15,000	NYT	Dec. 4, 1947	---:54: 7
16,000	NYT	Dec. 13, 1947	---:26: 4
13,000	NYT	Sep. 6, 1947	---:21: 8
15,000	NYT	Jan. 15, 1948	---:36: 3

17,000	NYT	Feb. 18, 1948	---:41: 8
20,000	NYT	May 18, 1948	---:33: 5
23,000	NYT	May 19, 1948	---:41: 4
15,500	NYT	Nov. 27, 1948	---:23: 7
7,600	NYT	June 10, 1949	---:44: 1
7,500	NYT	June 11, 1949	---:22: 5
7,500	NYT	July 7, 1949	---:40: 2
5,500	NYT	July 21, 1949	---:34: 2
8,000	NYT	Oct. 19, 1949	---:49: 1
7,500	NYT	Nov. 17, 1949	---:47: 8
10,000	NYT	Feb. 2, 1950	---:41: 4
10,000	NYT	Feb. 18, 1950	---:18: 7
3,900	NYT	May 8, 1950	---:29: 5
4,200	NYT	May 26, 1950	---:39: 2
3,600	NYT	Aug. 31, 1950	---:37: 1
3,850	NYT	Sep. 14, 1950	---:52: 3
4,500	NYT	Nov. 8, 1950	---:47: 4
4,700	NYT	Nov. 17, 1950	---:46: 4
5,000	NYT	Nov. 22, 1950	---:43: 7
5,500	NYT	Dec. 16, 1950	---:25: 2
10,500	NYT	Feb. 10, 1951	---:22: 3
10,000	NYT	Mar. 16, 1951	---:46: 8
10,500	NYT	May 11, 1951	---:43: 4
10,500	NYT	May 15, 1951	---:63: 4
10,500	NYT	June 19, 1951	---:46: 5
9,500	NYT	Sep. 22, 1951	---:22: 1
11,000	NYT	Sep. 29, 1951	---:24: 4
9,500	NYT	Oct. 12, 1951	---:44: 2
11,000	NYT	Oct. 17, 1951	---:48: 4
14,000	NYT	Nov. 6, 1951	---:46: 8
14,500	NYT	Nov. 6, 1951	---:46: 8
15,000	NYT	Nov. 9, 1951	---:35: 8
14,500	NYT	Nov. 29, 1951	---:53: 2
13,500	NYT	Jan. 25, 1952	---:32: 8
13,000	NYT	Mar. 21, 1952	---:38: 3
14,000	NYT	Apr. 1, 1952	---:47: 5
13,000	NYT	May 1, 1952	---:47: 1
13,000	NYT	July 24, 1952	---:36: 4
13,000	NYT	Aug. 21, 1952	---:28: 7
12,500	NYT	Sep. 30, 1952	---:50: 4
12,000	NYT	Oct. 31, 1952	---:42: 7
13,000	NYT	Nov. 4, 1952	---:39: 6
13,000	NYT	Nov. 11, 1952	---:42: 8

14,000	NYT	Dec. 12, 1952	---:48: 3
14,500	NYT	Jan. 7, 1953	---:38: 6
14,500	NYT	Jan. 9, 1953	---:29: 4
15,000	NYT	Feb. 27, 1953	---:34: 6
15,000	NYT	May 1, 1953	---:35: 8
13,000	NYT	May 29, 1953	---:29: 1
12,000	NYT	Aug. 29, 1953	---:21: 5
10,500	NYT	Nov. 11, 1953	---:47: 3
10,000	NYT	Dec. 10, 1953	---:77: 6
10,000	NYT	Jan. 5, 1954	---:33: 3
11,500	NYT	Mar. 26, 1954	---:35: 8
12,000	NYT	Apr. 3, 1954	---:25: 4
13,000	NYT	Apr. 24, 1954	---:32: 5
13,000	NYT	Oct. 8, 1954	---:39: 4
16,000	NYT	Nov. 17, 1954	---:47: 6
17,000	NYT	Nov. 30, 1954	---:45: 5
19,000	NYT	Dec. 23, 1954	---:27: 4
18,000	NYT	Dec. 28, 1954	---:33: 6
18,000	NYT	Jan. 21, 1955	---:31: 6
19,000	NYT	Jan. 25, 1955	---:33: 2
20,000	NYT	Jan. 29, 1955	---:19: 5
21,000	NYT	Mar. 30, 1955	---:41: 6
22,000	NYT	Apr. 20, 1955	---:47: 7
21,000	NYT	Apr. 22, 1955	---:35: 6
20,500	NYT	June 28, 1955	---:35: 6
17,500	NYT	Nov. 11, 1955	---:38: 3
18,000	NYT	Nov. 12, 1955	---:26: 3
19,500	NYT	Dec. 28, 1955	---:34: 3
20,500	NYT	Dec. 29, 1955	---:28: 2
21,500	NYT	Feb. 29, 1956	---:71: 1
31,500	NYT	Sep. 19, 1956	---:71: 1
28,000	NYT	Dec. 12, 1956	---:62: 3
26,000	NYT	Jan. 9, 1957	---:42: 3
25,000	NYT	Mar. 5, 1957	---:42: 3
24,000	NYT	May 11, 1957	---:28: 3
25,000	NYT	June 5, 1957	---:50: 3
23,000	NYT	Aug. 30, 1957	---:24: 3
22,500	NYT	Sept. 5, 1957	---:40: 2
22,000	NYT	Nov. 30, 1957	---:25: 2
20,000	NYT	Jan. 17, 1958	---:32: 3
20,000	NYT	Feb. 21, 1958	---:32: 3
20,000	NYT	Mar. 13, 1958	---:42: 2
18,000	NYT	Apr. 11, 1958	---:34: 3

18,500	NYT	Apr. 19, 1958	---:25: 2
21,000	NYT	May 17, 1958	---:24: 3
24,000	NYT	June 18, 1958	---:53: 2
24,000	NYT	July 24, 1958	---:34: 2
28,500	NYT	Sep. 27, 1958	---:32: 3
30,000	NYT	Sep. 27, 1958	---:32: 3
32,000	NYT	Oct. 14, 1958	---:60: 3
42,000	NYT	Dec. 2, 1958	---:54: 3
42,000	NYT	Dec. 31, 1958	---:30: 3
44,000	NYT	Mar. 18, 1959	---:53: 6
47,500	NYT	May 7, 1959	---:48: 2
48,000	NYT	May 9, 1959	---:26: 3
50,000	NYT	May 15, 1959	---:42: 3
53,000	NYT	May 19, 1959	---:42: 6
55,000	NYT	May 28, 1959	---:42: 2
60,000	NYT	May 28, 1959	---:42: 2
60,000	NYT	July 31, 1959	---:28: 3
60,000	NYT	Aug. 1, 1959	---:22: 3
65,000	NYT	Aug. 27, 1959	---:38: 2
58,000	NYT	Sep. 16, 1959	---:56: 3
58,000	NYT	Dec. 19, 1959	---:35: 4
60,000	NYT	Dec. 30, 1959	---:28: 8
60,000	NYT	Jan. 23, 1960	---:32: 5
53,000	NYT	Apr. 26, 1960	---:51: 4
55,000	NYT	May 5, 1960	---:52: 4
55,000	NYT	May 17, 1960	---:56: 5
55,000	NYT	June 3, 1960	---:43: 1
54,000	NYT	June 24, 1960	---:33: 3
54,000	NYT	July 15, 1960	---:34: 4
52,000	NYT	July 28, 1960	---:43: 3
52,000	NYT	Aug. 3, 1960	---:42: 8
52,000	NYT	Aug. 5, 1960	---:27: 5
51,000	NYT	Nov. 5, 1960	---:36: 2
57,000	NYT	Feb. 28, 1961	---:50: 3
65,000	NYT	Nov. 29, 1961	---:63: 1
58,000	NYT	Mar. 4, 1961	---:35: 5
64,000	NYT	Mar. 11, 1961	---:26: 3
70,000	NYT	Mar. 18, 1961	---:28: 3
80,000	NYT	Mar. 28, 1961	---:48: 3
78,000	NYT	Mar. 28, 1961	---:48: 3
79,000	NYT	Mar. 28, 1961	---:48: 3
75,000	NYT	May 11, 1961	---:61: 1
70,000	NYT	May 20, 1961	---:30: 4

67,500	NYT	June 1, 1961	---:58: 4
65,000	NYT	July 14, 1961	---:31: 1
75,000	NYT	Sep. 2, 1961	---:20: 5
46,000	NYT	May 29, 1962	---:38: 3
40,000	NYT	June 14, 1962	---:47: 6
50,000	NYT	July 28, 1962	---:29: 5
53,000	NYT	Aug. 24, 1962	---:35: 8
50,000	NYT	Sep. 6, 1962	---:47: 3
52,500	NYT	Sep. 22, 1962	---:33: 3
50,000	NYT	Oct. 2, 1962	---:52: 5
50,000	NYT	Dec. 4, 1962	---:61: 4
55,000	NYT	Apr. 18, 1963	---:57: 1
57,000	NYT	May 30, 1963	---:27: 1
57,000	NYT	June 8, 1963	---: 8: 1
57,000	NYT	June 26, 1963	---:57: 6
58,000	NYT	July 3, 1963	---:30: 3
60,000	NYT	July 6, 1963	---:26: 5
65,000	NYT	July 10, 1963	---:44: 3
65,000	NYT	July 19, 1963	---:37: 6
59,000	NYT	Aug. 6, 1963	---:40: 4
59,000	NYT	Sep. 19, 1963	---:36: 3
60,000	NYT	Oct. 3, 1963	---:52: 3
60,000	NYT	Oct. 12, 1963	---:34: 6
61,500	NYT	Oct. 17, 1963	---:54: 5
63,500	NYT	Nov. 1, 1963	---:51: 7
65,000	NYT	Nov. 21, 1963	---:56: 2
66,000	NYT	Nov. 21, 1963	---:56: 2
66,000	NYT	Nov. 22, 1963	---:59: 3
52,000	NYT	Mar. 17, 1964	---:54: 4
60,000	NYT	June 20, 1964	---:36: 2
60,000	NYT	Oct. 8, 1964	---:69: 1
55,000	NYT	Feb. 27, 1965	---:30: 3
58,000	NYT	Apr. 16, 1965	---:43: 7
58,000	NYT	July 28, 1965	---:51: 2
58,000	NYT	Aug. 5, 1965	---:46: 6
59,000	NYT	Aug. 31, 1965	---:48: 6
88,000	NYT	Jan. 27, 1966	---:44: 2
92,000	NYT	Jan. 27, 1966	---:44: 2
95,000	NYT	Feb. 1, 1966	---:46: 3
98,000	NYT	Feb. 18, 1966	---:46: 3
98,000	NYT	Apr. 2, 1966	---:39: 8
104,000	NYT	Apr. 19, 1966	---:56: 3
120,000	NYT	Apr. 29, 1966	---: 2: 3

70,000	NYT	Oct. 7, 1966	---:60: 8
150,000	WSJ	Mar. 18, 1967	---:13: 3
160,000	NYT	June 7, 1967	---:69: 2
210,000	NYT	Dec. 6, 1967	---:69: 2
250,000	NYT	Jan. 21, 1968	III: 1: 1
260,000	NYT	Jan. 23, 1968	---:51: 3
260,000	NYT	Jan. 25. 1968	---:60: 3
275,000	NYT	Oct. 15, 1968	---:65: 4
277,000	NYT	Oct. 24, 1968	---:72: 3
300,000	NYT	Dec. 4, 1968	---:69: 4
315,000	NYT	Dec. 5, 1968	---:72: 1
335,000	NYT	Dec. 20, 1968	---:84: 2
330,000	NYT	Mar. 6, 1969	---:65: 4
315,000	NYT	Apr. 22, 1969	---:67: 1
350,000	NYT	June 3, 1969	---:75: 2
310,000	NYT	June 18, 1969	---:64: 4
280,000	NYT	July 2, 1969	---:49: 6
200,000	NYT	Aug. 19, 1969	---:64: 6
220,000	NYT	Sep. 3, 1969	---:69: 2
150,000	NYT	Dec. 9, 1969	---:93: 8
180,000	WSJ	Jan. 7, 1970	---:32: 3
180,000	WSJ	Jan. 8, 1970	---:19: 6
185,000	WSJ	Jan. 15, 1970	---: 3: 5
180,000	WSJ	Jan. 15, 1970	---: 3: 5
170,000	WSJ	Jan. 21, 1970	---:26: 4
160,000	WSJ	Mar. 16, 1970	---:23: 3
150,000	WSJ	Mar. 23, 1970	---: 8: 5
120,000	WSJ	Apr. 29, 1970	---:15: 3
115,000	WSJ	Apr. 30, 1970	---:17: 2
105,000	WSJ	May 20, 1970	---: 3: 4
100,000	WSJ	May 21, 1970	---:29: 2
105,000	WSJ	June 16, 1970	---:34: 5
100,000	WSJ	June 17, 1970	---: 7: 4
110,000	WSJ	June 23, 1970	---:34: 5
80,000	WSJ	July 9, 1970	---:26: 4
100,000	WSJ	July 23, 1970	---:23: 4
90,000	WSJ	Aug. 5, 1970	---:25: 6
80,000	WSJ	Aug. 13, 1970	---:20: 4
80,000	WSJ	Aug. 14, 1970	---:18: 2
70,000	NYT	Aug. 23, 1970	III: 6: 1
100,000	WSJ	Sep. 22, 1970	---:15: 1
125,000	WSJ	Oct. 5, 1970	---:18: 3
95,000	WSJ	Dec. 2, 1970	---: 8: 4

115,000	WSJ	Dec. 15, 1970	---: 3: 6
115,000	WSJ	Dec. 24, 1970	---:16: 6
130,000	NYT	May 25, 1971	---:64: 4
80,000	NYT	Oct. 7, 1971	---:73: 4
65,000	NYT	Nov. 30, 1971	---:71: 3
130,000	WSJ	Mar. 21, 1972	---:34: 5
120,000	WSJ	Mar. 23, 1972	---:26: 4
110,000	WSJ	May 22, 1972	---:14: 6
88,000	WSJ	July 14, 1972	---:17: 1
85,000	WSJ	Sep. 22, 1972	---:25: 6
100,000	WSJ	Dec. 14, 1972	---: 2: 2
90,000	WSJ	Dec. 29, 1972	---:19: 2
38,000	NYT	Apr. 28, 1973	---:42: 2
28,000	NYT	May 22, 1973	---:53: 5
37,500	NYT	June 8, 1973	---:53: 4
41,000	NYT	June 13, 1973	---:65: 2
27,000	NYT	July 3, 1973	---:36: 1
29,000	NYT	July 6, 1973	---:31: 1
40,000	NYT	Aug. 16, 1973	---:58: 4
35,000	NYT	Aug. 21, 1973	---:44: 4
40,000	NYT	Sept. 8, 1973	---:42: 4
37,000	NYT	Dec. 4, 1973	---:67: 8
36,000	NYT	Dec. 4, 1973	---:67: 8
40,000	NYT	Dec. 11, 1973	---:71: 7
37,500	NYT	Dec. 28, 1973	---:41: 8
31,000	NYT	Mar. 2, 1974	---:45: 1
34,000	NYT	May 23, 1974	---:60: 2
30,000	NYT	June 13, 1974	---:71: 4
39,000	NYT	Sep. 10, 1974	---:64: 2
35,000	NYT	Sep. 13, 1974	---:50: 4
38,500	NYT	Oct. 19, 1974	---:43: 8
38,500	NYT	Oct. 20, 1974	III:15: 6
40,000	NYT	Oct. 20, 1974	III:15: 6
40,000	NYT	Oct. 22, 1974	---:59: 1
45,000	NYT	Nov. 1, 1974	---:57: 8
48,000	NYT	Nov. 1, 1974	---:57: 8
50,000	NYT	Nov. 1, 1974	---:57: 8
52,000	NYT	Nov. 1, 1974	---:57: 8
60,000	NYT	Nov. 14, 1974	---:77: 1
55,000	NYT	Nov. 28, 1974	---:54: 2
53,000	NYT	Nov. 28, 1974	---:54: 2
50,000	NYT	Feb. 14, 1975	---:53: 1
35,000	NYT	Mar. 25, 1975	---:53: 3

34,000	NYT	May 14, 1975	---:66: 4
50,000	NYT	May 20, 1975	---:63: 4
50,000	NYT	May 31, 1975	---:36: 8
55,000	NYT	June 3, 1975	---:42: 1
58,000	NYT	June 19, 1975	---:59: 1
58,000	NYT	June 20, 1975	---:53: 1
60,000	NYT	July 1, 1975	---:42: 4
48,000	NYT	Sep. 24, 1975	---:65: 6
40,000	NYT	Sep. 26, 1975	---:53: 8
38,000	NYT	Oct. 15, 1975	---:73: 4
40,000	NYT	Nov. 26, 1975	---:41: 3
41,000	NYT	Nov. 26, 1975	---:41: 3
50,000	NYT	Dec. 2, 1975	---:59: 6
44,000	NYT	Dec. 30, 1975	---:36: 5
44,000	NYT	Jan. 3, 1976	---:33: 4
47,000	NYT	Feb. 4, 1976	---:55: 3
59,000	NYT	Feb. 24, 1976	---:46: 3
60,000	NYT	Feb. 24, 1976	---:46: 3
58,000	NYT	June 15, 1976	---:64: 4
50,000	NYT	July 17, 1976	---:34: 6
44,000	NYT	Nov. 9, 1976	---:57: 3
49,000	NYT	Feb. 19, 1977	---:36: 6
50,000	NYT	Feb. 19, 1977	---:36: 6
52,000	NYT	Feb. 19, 1977	---:36: 6
50,000	WSJ	Mar. 9, 1977	---:40: 4
37,000	WSJ	May 21, 1977	---:11: 1
30,000	WSJ	Oct. 14, 1977	---: 2: 3
27,000	WSJ	Oct. 19, 1977	---: 2: 3
21,000	WSJ	Oct. 26, 1977	---: 6: 3
30,000	WSJ	Nov. 22, 1977	---:48: 5
25,500	WSJ	Nov. 25, 1977	---:17: 6
28,000	WSJ	Feb. 6, 1978	---:20: 4
28,000	WSJ	Mar. 16, 1978	---:24: 2
28,000	WSJ	Mar. 28, 1978	---:21: 2
26,500	WSJ	Apr. 7, 1978	---:26: 6
28,000	WSJ	Apr. 17, 1978	---:31: 1
11,500	WSJ	Apr. 18, 1978	---:45: 2
27,000	WSJ	May 1, 1978	---:33: 6
28,000	WSJ	May 2, 1978	---:14: 3
28,000	WSJ	May 5, 1978	---:24: 6
33,000	WSJ	June 2, 1978	---:31: 6
35,000	WSJ	June 20, 1978	---:41: 6
35,000	WSJ	July 25, 1978	---:43: 5

40,000	WSJ	Aug. 23, 1978	---:43: 2
52,000	WSJ	Sep. 5, 1978	---:15: 4
62,500	WSJ	Sep. 29, 1978	---:43: 4
57,500	WSJ	Oct. 23, 1978	---:40: 6
49,000	WSJ	Oct. 31, 1978	---:43: 6
52,000	WSJ	Nov. 17, 1978	---:43: 6
44,000	WSJ	Dec. 18, 1978	---:38: 6
40,000	WSJ	Dec. 21, 1978	---:10: 4
195,000	NYT	Aug. 9, 1979	IV:13: 2
210,000	NYT	Aug. 10, 1979	IV: 4: 2
120,000	NYT	Jan. 24, 1980	IV: 5: 2
120,000	NYT	Jan. 27, 1980	III:19: 1
180,000	NYT	Sep. 5, 1980	IV: 5: 4
245,000	NYT	Nov. 20, 1980	IV: 4: 5
250,000	NYT	Nov. 20, 1980	IV: 4: 5
252,000	NYT	Nov. 20, 1980	IV: 4: 5
220,000	NYT	May 8, 1981	---:35: 6
183,000	WSJ	July 7, 1982	---:38: 5
220,000	WSJ	Sep. 22, 1982	---:46: 1
325,000	WSJ	Jan. 10, 1982	---:39: 4
308,000	WSJ	Mar. 2, 1983	---:50: 6
290,000	WSJ	Apr. 18, 1983	---:38: 6
285,000	WSJ	July 26, 1983	---:54: 6
261,000	WSJ	Nov. 9, 1983	---:57: 6
230,000	WSJ	Apr. 11, 1984	---:47: 5
150,000	WSJ	July 2, 1984	---:31: 3
175,000	WSJ	Oct. 25, 1984	---:45: 5
165,000	WSJ	Nov. 12, 1984	---:35: 3
148,000	WSJ	Jan. 23, 1985	---:55: 2
145,000	WSJ	Feb. 22, 1985	---:56: 6
150,000	WSJ	Feb. 22, 1985	---:56: 6
145,500	WSJ	Apr. 5, 1985	---:32: 6
380,000	WSJ	Apr. 10, 1987	---:36: 6
400,000	NYT	May 28, 1987	IV: 5: 2
400,000	WSJ	May 28, 1987	---:61: 3
235,000	WSJ	Aug. 5, 1988	---:20: 6
207,500	WSJ	Oct. 31, 1988	C:10: 6
180,000	WSJ	July 31, 1989	C:14: 5
165,000	WSJ	Sep. 18, 1989	C: 6: 6
165,000	WSJ	Oct. 30, 1989	C: 9: 6
160,000	WSJ	Oct. 31, 1989	C:10: 6
155,000	WSJ	Nov. 3, 1989	C: 9: 6
155,000	WSJ	Nov. 13, 1989	C:13: 1

84,000	WSJ	Nov. 20, 1990	C:10: 1
107,000	WSJ	Feb. 20, 1991	C:19: 3
100,000	WSJ	May 30, 1991	C:10: 6
82,000	WSJ	Oct. 17, 1991	C:10: 6
82,000	WSJ	Nov. 18, 1991	C:15: 2
90,000	WSJ	Feb. 21, 1992	---: 9:l6
105,000	WSJ	Oct. 1, 1992	C:17: 6
110,000	WSJ	Dec. 28, 1992	C: 2: 1
98,000	WSJ	Feb. 16, 1993	C:13: 1
132,000	WSJ	June 18, 1993	C:10: 6
150,000	WSJ	Aug. 18, 1993	C: 2: 4

APPENDIX A

HIGHLIGHTS OF ANNUAL REPORTS

New York Curb Exchange, Report of the President, 1929
James S. Kenny; William S. Muller, President

Report provides a glowing, rosy report of "general industry in the United States" reaching a "high peak of prosperity." The year was notable for the amount and variety of new stock issues which were successfully floated. All previous trading records were surpassed and the magnitude of dealings on the Exchange during the year, aggregating 475,000,000 shares, was impressive when compared with the volume for the first year the Exchange was housed in 1921, 15,500,000 shares. The Exchange did 7,096,000 shares in one day, October 19, 1929, or almost one-half the volume for the whole year of 1921. Sixty five percent of the total active stocks, slightly more than 1,300 issues, paid dividends. Approximately 3,000 tickers were in operation and the western terminus of the ticker circuit was extended from Chicago to the west coast. The galleries were visited by over 25,000 visitors. Memberships were transferred for prices ranging from $150,000 to the $254,000 paid on September 24, 1929.

Report of the President, New York Curb Exchange, 1930
James A. Corcoran; William S. Muller, President

The year 1930 will go down in the annals of financial history as a period in which "prices on all security markets experienced drastic declines." The report looks back at "the sharp industrial recession in the second half of 1929 and the still more widely advertised decline in security values in the fall of that year." Statistics show that 1,470 stocks were in the dividend paying class. Memberships transferred at prices ranging from a high of $225,000, down to $70,000, and back up to $95,000 by the end of the year.

Report of the President, New York Curb Exchange, 1931
Howard C. Sykes, President

"While fundamentals of business are bad, they are not at all as precarious as the current state of the public mind would have us believe." While "the heavy shrinkage in prices of securities and in corporate earnings power caused a reduction of dividend rates," 1,488 of a total of 2,400 issues traded did pay dividends. Approximately 140 foreign issues were added to the trading list in the form of certificates of deposit issued by American banking institutions. Rules were promulgated for companies dealing in investment trusts. Memberships were transferred at prices ranging from $137,500 down to $40,000. A new addition to the Exchange building was completed.

Report of the President, New York Curb Exchange, 1932-1933
Howard C. Sykes, President

Although progress was made in the past year, "the process of reconstruction still has a considerable way to go before economic conditions will be restored to normal." During the past three years, the Exchange passed first through an unexpected and unprecedented shock, then a period of consternation and dismay, and now has come to conquer its fears and work its way out. Maintenance of the gold standard and currency stability are hailed as "fortunately we escaped this undemocratic eventuality" of government price controls. Of the 2,200 stocks trading on the Exchange, only 741 issued dividends. Memberships transferred at prices ranging from $41,000, down to $16,500, up to $55,000, and ended the year at $29,000.

New York Curb Exchange, Report of the President, 1933-34
Howard C. Sykes, President

In 1933, 574 stocks paid dividends. In January 1934, there were 711 tickers operating in 37 cities. Membership was 423; seat prices ranged from $30,000 to $50,000, down from the high of $254,000 paid September 23, 1929. Total sales for 1933 were 100,916,602 shares with June being the largest trading month.

New York Curb Exchange, Report of the President, 1934-35
E. Burd Grubb, President

Four thousand stories about the Exchange were clipped from 50 newspapers scattered throughout the country. The report notes establishment of the Securities and Exchange Commission and far-reaching new security legislation enacted by the Federal government. Forty two percent of listings, 492 stocks, paid dividends. The President's address to the meeting of the Board of Governors in October 1934 stressed the "magnitude of the task dealing with the preparation of our application for registration as a national securities exchange, which involved twenty-five pages of a closely printed matter, presenting 105 technical questions which took some very deep thinking to answer." Total sales were 60,050,695 shares with February the largest trading month. Total sales topped one billion dollars. Membership of the Exchange, as of December 1, 1934, was 500 regular members and 396 associates.

New York Curb Exchange, Report of the President, 1935-36
Fred C. Moffatt, President

A short report indicates that memberships transferred at prices ranging from $12,000 to $33,000. Total sales were 75,747,764 shares with November the largest trading month. Increased interest in sports among the membership of the Exchange was revealed in spring and fall golf tournaments.

New York Curb Exchange, Report of the President, 1936-37
Fred C. Moffatt, President

There was a substantial increase in the number of stocks and bonds listed. More than 200 tickers were added to the system bringing the total to 1,100. There were 12,000 visitors to the gallery. Memberships were transferred at prices ranging from $26,000 to $48,000. Regular membership remained limited at 550 with associates increasing to 399. Only 645 issues, or 58 percent of the 1,120 stocks listed, paid dividends. The volume of stock transactions which amounted to 134,845,196 shares was the heaviest in six years, comparing with 75,747,764 shares in 1935 and 60,050,695 in 1934. The New York Curb Exchange Athletic Association won a high place in amateur sports with its hockey team capturing the Metropolitan Amateur Hockey League title and the track team continuing to gain national recognition.

New York Curb Exchange, Report of the President, 1937-38
Fred C. Moffatt, President

Decreased public interest in securities during the year 1937 was responsible for the reduction in the number of tickers printing New York Curb Exchange prices. As of December 31, 1937, 880 tickers were operating in 45 cities compared with 1,100 tickers operating in 48 cities at the close of 1936 and 986 tickers in 35 cities at the end of 1935. At the end of 1937, 773 common stocks listed 694,258,012 shares at an average price of $11.46. Total sales for the year were 104,178,804 shares with the largest trading month January and largest day October 19th when 1.6 million shares traded. Memberships sold between $19,000 and $35,000. As of December 31, 1937, the membership of the Exchange was 500 regular members and 393 associates.

New York Curb Exchange, President's Report, 1946-47
Edwin Posner, President

The Exchange completed 25 years as an indoor securities market in a "most gratifying year" with "a number of signs of healthy growth." Membership was 499 with 270 associates; 30 memberships transferred at prices ranging from $19,000 to $37,500. Securities on the Exchange list at the close of 1946 had a total market value of $14,499,407,851. Trading reached 137,309,392 shares. In conclusion, Posner announced the appointment of Francis Adams Truslow as president of the Exchange.

New York Curb Exchange, President's Report, 1947-48
Francis Adams Truslow, President

The report for 1947 describes a year of "international uncertainty in which the smoldering difference in points of view and objectives between the Western nations and Russia flared" and "not a year in which people were encouraged to look to the future with confidence." Volume of transactions fell to 53 percent of the 1946 volume. Memberships remained at 499 with 276 associates; they were transferred at an average price of $17,500. At the end of the year, 950 security issues included 836 stocks and 114 bonds, with an aggregate value of $13,202,653,987. During the year, the ticker system declined from 748 tickers in 81 cities in 23 states and the District of Columbia to 630 tickers located in 64 cities, but still covering most of the "important sections of the country;" 387 of the tickers were located in New York City. Commencing January 1, 1947, the approximately 300 employees of the Exchange were covered by hospitalization insurance and each received a Christmas bonus of one week's salary.

New York Curb Exchange, President's Report, 1948-49
Francis Adams Truslow, President

The year 1948 "reflected little change from the pattern established" in 1947. Average value of a share was $18 and 75 million shares were traded. At the end of the year, 929 security issues were listed including 819 stocks and 110 bonds. Trading totaled 75,016,108 shares, making 1948 the third most active trading year of the decade, exceeded only by 1945 and 1946. Total market value of common stocks was $2,097,259,035. The average price of a share was $8.06 for common stock and $30.48 for preferred.

New York Curb Exchange, President's Report, 1949-1950
Francis Adams Truslow, President

"Business was released in late 1945 from the controls of war." During 1946, 1947 and 1948 it expanded enormously. The record reveals that 1949 was a "pivotal year" for business and for finance. Net working capital increased and dividend payments grew both in dollar amount and in their relationship to earnings (48.5 percent of net earnings were disbursed). The average stock price rose from $18.05 at the end of 1948 to $19.53 at the close of 1949. The Exchange membership voted an increase in commission rates, the first change in Exchange commissions since 1942. The aggregate market value of all securities was $13,222,556,357. A total of 901 security issues were available for trading; 797 were stocks and 104 bonds. Stock transactions totaled 66,201,828 shares, a decrease of nearly nine million compared to 1948. The ticker service extended to 564 tickers in operation in 55 cities. Midway through the year, the Exchange adopted an employee retirement plan under which employees would contribute two percent of their base pay; all eligible employees elected to participate. This marked the thirtieth year of the Curb indoors. It was "one more year of proof of the strength that an institution can gain when there is hard work and harmonious cooperation between all the human beings who own and serve it."

New York Curb Exchange, President's Report, 1950-51
Francis Adams Truslow, President

The single, overshadowing event of the year 1950 was the attack by communist forces of North Korea, supplied by Russia and later openly joined by Red China, on the territory of South Korea. War and inflation became overriding factors in the economy. The volume of transactions on the floor of the Exchange was 63 percent greater in 1950 than in 1949. The average price per share increased from $19.53 to $22.71. Applications for listing of new or additional issues of securities rose sharply during the year. The aggregate value of all securities dealt in on the Exchange was $14,832,133,008; 856 security issues available for trading included 767 stocks and 89 bonds. Stock transactions on the Exchange totaled 107,792,340 shares. Business machines were installed. Expansion of the ticker system moved into the south and west; six new states and forty new cities were added comprising 716 tickers located in 101 cities in 27 states and the District of Columbia. Associate membership increased to 189 with member firms maintaining offices in 396 cities and the District of Columbia. In addition, Exchange member firms had offices in eight foreign countries. The number of Exchange employees grew to 293; in April, a contract was made between the Exchange and the United Financial Employees Union (AF of L). For the third time, the Exchange took part in the Hemispheric Conference of Stock Exchanges held in Santos, Brazil.

President's Report, New York Curb Exchange, 1951-1952
Edward T. McCormick, President

Market value of all securities traded on the Exchange amounted to $17,361,237,336 at the close of 1951, an increase of 17 percent over the previous year. Among the 860 issues traded were 777 stocks and 83 bonds. Trading volume totaled 111,629,218 shares, an increase of 3.6 percent. Regular memberships remained at 499; associates rose to 307, a peak since 1940. The ticker system continued to grow and service was inaugurated in Toronto.

President's Report, American Stock Exchange, 1952-1953
Edward T. McCormick, President

The year 1952 is reported as one of important decision and change for the Exchange. McCormick notes that "in this eventful year I should like to single out two noteworthy events." In the first of these, Saturday trading became a thing of the past and longer trading sessions recognized the important role of Western investors. The second notable decision, by overwhelming vote on October 30, 1952, was the birth of the

American Stock Exchange, set for January 5, 1953. At the close of 1953, 808 stocks and 84 bond issues were listed. The market value of the traded securities totaled $17,683,603,396. The average price of all stocks was $21.49. Four stocks of Canadian origin were approved for listing. Stock trading volume totaled 106,237,657 shares, a five percent decrease below the five-year high established in the previous year. Across the United States and Canada, 828 tickers operated in 135 cities.

American Stock Exchange, President's Report, 1953-1954
Edward T. McCormick, President

The year 1953 marked the most prosperous twelve months in American business history. In marked contrast, security markets operated at a low volume and small profit level. Traded securities, with a market worth of $16.1 billion, included 808 stocks and 84 bonds. Over 175 foreign securities representing 21 countries were traded. The 794 issues traded included 844,744,650 outstanding shares with an average price of $18.11. Stock trading volume was 102,378,937 shares, a decline of four percent from 1952; the dollar volume was $1,125,699,042. ASE member firms maintained 1,760 offices in 444 United States and foreign cities; 796 tickers were in operation, 396 of them in New York City. Associate memberships reached a 15 year peak of 314. Seat prices ranged from $10,100 to $14,500.

President's Report, American Stock Exchange, 1954-55
Edward T. McCormick, President

Capped by twenty-three one million share days, 1954 trading volume climbed to 162,948,716 shares, an increase of 59 percent over the previous year. Dollarwise, stock trading volume totaled $1,872,548,600. At the year's end, 911.2 million shares were available for trading. The market value of all stocks totaled $23 billion, including 684 common and 124 preferred issues. Listing over 139 equities from 11 foreign countries, the Exchange became the nation's foremost market for foreign stocks. Associate memberships reached a sixteen year peak of 318; member firm offices grew to 1,835. Strong evidence of prosperity was found when 300 common stocks, 49 percent of common issues, were listed on a "Common Stock Honor Roll," a list of corporations that paid dividends for 10 to 106 consecutive years.

President's Report, American Stock Exchange, 1955-1956
Edward T. McCormick, President

The 1955 economy is described as "bounding." Regular memberships sold for up to $22,000, their best level since 1948. The year 1955 saw the establishment of new highs in the accepted averages and trading volume of 228,955,915 shares, an increase of 40 percent over 1954. Trading was marked by 75 one million or more share days and business reached its highest peak since 1929. Stock trading volume totaled $2,593,455,627. The Exchange continued as the leading market for foreign stocks with 149 stock issues representing 13 foreign countries. The system passed the 1,000 ticker mark for the first time since 1937; locations in 173 cities represented 33 states, the District of Columbia, and the Canadian Provinces of Ontario and Quebec. *American Stock Exchange Investor*, the Exchange's first venture in the magazine field, made a June debut. A new 16 MM Technicolor motion picture, *Behind the Ticker Tape*, was "greeted with critical acclaim."

American Stock Exchange, President's Report, 1956/1957
Edward T. McCormick, President

"Nineteen hundred and fifty-six was viewed with mixed emotions by most Americans who saw prosperity at home and strife abroad." Trading volume was 228,231,047 shares, almost equal to 1955's. Stock trading volume totaled $2,695,908,925. The Board of Governors approved a total of 70 new stock issues aggregating 101,940,438 shares, a high mark that goes back almost a quarter of a century for comparison. The list of securities available for trading comprised 863 common and preferred stock issues with a combined market value of $31,788,974,252. A program was launched to provide, for the first time, an instantaneous coast to coast automated quotation operation. Associate memberships reached an 18 year peak of 355. Regular memberships sold up to a ten year high of $31,500 and sales averaged $26,450.

American Stock Exchange, President's Report, 1957/1958
Edward T. McCormick, President

The mixed feelings with which most Americans viewed the business situation during 1957 were reflected on the trading floor, where share turnover ran six percent behind the 1956 pace. At year end, the list of securities included 862 common and preferred stock issues totaling 1,375,038,202 shares with a combined market value of $25,545,237,684. Regular memberships sold at a high of $28,000 and a low of $21,500, averaging $24,333, second only to 1956 during the past ten years. Associate memberships climbed to 361. The Exchange maintained its position as the top ranking market for foreign stocks with 133 Canadian and 39 other stock issues from eleven foreign countries. Geographical distribution of tickers had changed remarkably since 1950. The increase out of town was 396 tickers or 166 percent, against a gain of 126 tickers or 34 percent in New York City. There were more tickers outside of New York City than there were in the entire network in 1950.

American Stock Exchange, President's Report, 1958/1959
Edward T. McCormick, President

The year 1958 marked the second most active twelve months in the Exchange's history. The volume of 240,340,524 shares traded was 12 percent ahead of 1957. The number of tickers increased to 1,234. A woman, Mrs. Mary G. Roebling, a noted banker, was appointed a Public Governor and hailed as the first woman in history to serve as a member of a stock exchange board. Memberships sold at a 22 year high of $42,000. Associate memberships rose to 371, a 20 year peak.

American Stock Exchange, President's Report, 1959/1960
Edward T. McCormick, President

In "the most prosperous twelve months in our nation's history," every business indicator pressed to a new high in a massive expression of economic strength. Summarizing the decade, McCormick reports that "the 'Fabulous Fifties' moved into high gear right from the opening gong and, continuing to gather steam in the face of the nation's industrial growth and the ever-increasing public awareness of securities as an investment medium, generated our most active and productive decade for all time." Trading volume averaged under 120 million shares annually during the first half of the Fifties, crossed the 200 million mark in 1955 and averaged close to 260 million shares annually for the second half of the decade. In 1959, trading volume was at 374,058,546 shares, a 56 percent increase over the previous year, the second most active twelve month period in the history of the Exchange. Regular Exchange membership prices enjoyed a flourishing decade, rising from a 1949 low of $5,500 to a 1959 high of $65,000, a record for the past 28 years. A new, high speed ticker tapped out a fast 500 character per minute greeting to highlight the market opening for the year. The Visitors' Gallery welcomed 110,000 people, twenty times the 1950 total.

American Stock Exchange, President's Report, 1960-1961
Edward T. McCormick, President

McCormick notes that "at the outset, the year was greeted with high hopes by many forecasters. They were wrong." Exchange seat sales fluctuated from a low of $51,000 to a high of $60,000. Although there was a trading decline of 88 million shares from the previous year, 1960, with its turnover of 286 million shares, was the third most active year in the history of the Exchange. The year included observation of the fiftieth anniversary of the formal association which stems from March 16, 1911; the fortieth anniversary of indoor dealings which opened on June 27, 1921; and, the thirtieth anniversary of the opening of the present American Stock Exchange building on September 14, 1931. On January 10, 1961, the Exchange announced purchase of a revolutionary communications facility and data processor to provide instantaneous, automatic electronic reports on open-high-low-last-bid-asked-volume to the moment and size, as contrasted with the present manually posted, operator-reported, bid-asked-last sale procedure. Reporting at the rate of 72,000 inquiries per hour on up to 2,000 issues, the system will serve at least 750 member firm subscribers who will never hear a busy signal.

American Stock Exchange, President's Report for 1961/1962
Edwin Posner, Chairman, Board of Governors

Posner reports that "for both members and management 1961 was one of the most difficult years in the long history of this institution. It is a great tribute to the members that their problems became opportunities." Sales of regular memberships ranged between a low of $52,000 in January and a high of $80,000 in March, a thirty-one year record. A program to expand floor facilities, reactivate trading posts, provide new equipment, and establish additional communication installations was a vital factor in the Exchange's ability to handle trading volume which reached an all-time record of 488,831,037 shares. New issues approved for listing were the largest in number and shares since 1937--113 stock issues aggregating 145 million shares. Revised listing and de-listing standards were approved by the Board of Governors. Pacing the record volume of shares traded was the increase in the number of stock tickers to 2,186.

American Stock Exchange Annual Report for 1963
Edwin D. Etherington, President

The report looks back to 1962, a year in which "the Exchange weighed the implications of a government critique of its management structure and past operations. At the same time, the Board adopted in principle the recommendations of an industry committee appointed to suggest changes in the organization and standards of the Exchange." In 1963, the pace of trading activity accelerated as the year progressed, reversing the trend of 1962. First half volume of 145,396,373 shares was down 14.8 percent while volume for the second half was up 24 percent. The dollar volume of shares traded jumped dramatically to $4,755,285,746, an increase of more than 30 percent. Share volume increased despite a decline in transactions in Canadian and other foreign issues from 18.1 percent of total trading in 1962 to 14.9 per cent in 1963. On Friday, November 22nd, after the tragic news flashed that President Kennedy had been shot, the Exchange took the rare step of ending a session before the regular 3:30 p.m. closing. When trading resumed on Tuesday, November 26th, a heavy influx of buy orders reversed the previous Friday's downward trend and produced the second highest trading day of the year. The November 26th total of 2,316,100 shares was exceeded only on the final day of the year when 2,796,420 shares changed hands. The Exchange extended its national reach when a membership expansion program, the first in 43 years, approved the sale of 151 new regular memberships.

American Stock Exchange Annual Report 1964
Edwin D. Etherington, President

Highlights of the year included: 374.1 million shares traded in the Exchange's third most active year with dollar volume up 24.5 percent to $5.9 billion; regular membership at an all-time high of 598; 87 stock issues added. The Exchange responded to the SEC's "Special Study," which called for abolition of floor trading unless the Exchanges demonstrated usefulness to the public. A highlight of the year was the introduction of Am-Quote, a unique telephone quotation service featuring an electronic voice which provided subscribers with market information on all American Exchange stocks and could handle 72,000 inquiries an hour.

American Stock Exchange Annual Report for 1965
Edwin D. Etherington, President

Highlights of 1965 include 534.2 million shares traded in a record year; dollar volume up 28.8 percent to $7.6 billion; regular membership at a peak of 650; seat prices up to $80,000; 87 issues admitted to trading. As Etherington notes, "a surge in market activity during the fourth quarter climaxed a year of unprecedented share and dollar volume." The Exchange had its first half-billion share year as 534,221,999 shares were traded. The figure was 42.8 percent higher than in 1964 and 9.3 percent above the previous record set in 1961. The dollar value of stocks traded was $7.6 billion, 28.8 percent higher than in 1964 and 11.7 percent more than the 1961 high of $6.8 billion. The pattern of trading was punctuated by extremes. Daily share volume ranged from a low of 792,710 shares on July 22nd to a high of 4,963,495 on December 8th. The average market value of all outstanding shares at year-end was $17.95, up from $16.02 at the end of 1964. More than 750,000 copies of Exchange publications were distributed. A survey of the nation's largest dailies revealed that 160 newspapers in 111 cities carried the Amex stock quotation table in full.

American Stock Exchange Annual Report 1966
Ralph S. Saul, President

Share and dollar volume again reached record levels. Stock trading totaled 690,762,585 shares, up 29 percent from the previous high reached in 1965. Share volume averaged nearly 2.8 million daily, compared with 2.1 million in 1965. Dollar volume of all securities traded increased 64 percent to $14,807,069,570. A new monthly record was set, with 99,584,121 shares traded during April. Seventy-eight memberships were transferred, four at the 35-year high price of $120,000. The first complete set of market indexes published by a stock exchange was introduced in June. The American Stock Exchange Index System consisted of three separate indicators: an hourly Price Level Index, a daily Breadth of Market Index, and a monthly Price/Earnings Index.

1967 Annual Report, American Stock Exchange
Ralph S. Saul, President

Trading activity in 1967 rose to record levels for the third successive year. Volume totaled more than one billion shares, up 65.8 percent from 1966 and more than double 1965. Average daily volume was 4.5 million shares, compared with 2.7 million in

1966. Other peaks were reached during October: dollar volume of $23,491,311,698 up 63.1 percent, new daily high, new weekly high, and new monthly high. The Price Level Index also recorded an historic high, closing the year at $24.52, a gain of $10.83 over 1966. As volume on the exchanges and over-the-counter markets gained momentum, concern grew regarding the amount of paperwork accumulating in back offices. In a coordinated effort, the NYSE and the Amex were closed for nine business days during August. The Exchange adopted a number of measures to handle increased clearing activity. It expanded day and night staffs, extended hours, temporarily installed a fourth IBM 1401 computer, and simplified procedures for reporting by firms to the Clearing Corporation. A program was completed to boost ticker transmission speed from 500 to 900 characters per minute. In April, the Exchange announced its cooperation with the Securities and Exchange Commission and the United States Attorney's Office in separate investigations of trading in a small group of stocks which may have been influenced by alleged manipulative activities. Two indictments were later returned by a grand jury in the southern district of New York. Value of memberships rose steadily; four seats were sold in December at $230,000 each, nearly double the 1966 high closing price of $120,000.

1968 Annual Report, American Stock Exchange
Ralph S. Saul, President

> Saul reports that "in 1968 few things were done in moderation. It was a record year, one remembered for the pace of trading, the issues faced, the weight of new dilemmas." In February, the American and New York exchanges announced a broad, multi-level program looking toward fundamental changes in the way securities and related paperwork are processed. Trading volume on the Exchange again exceeded one billion shares, setting a record level of activity for the fourth consecutive year. A total of 1,435,765,734 shares was traded, a gain of 25.4 percent over 1967; daily volume averaged 6.4 million shares. Dollar volume of shares traded rose 51 percent to a record $35,479,186,174. Trading records included new daily, weekly, and monthly highs. The largest share transaction was for 506,200 shares of Brazilian Light & Power Co., Ltd., valued at $7,086,800. The Exchange's Price Level Index closed the year at $32.72, up $8.20 from the 1967 close. The Exchange continued to place emphasis on the backlog of paperwork and other operational problems resulting from record market activity. In January, it shortened the trading day by 90 minutes. The Board subsequently approved Wednesday closings. Wednesday trading was resumed at the end of the year, but all trading days were reduced from five-and-a-half to four hours (10 AM to 2 PM).

AMEX 1969: American Stock Exchange 1969 Annual Report
Ralph S. Saul, President

> A total of 1,240,742,012 shares changed hands compared with 1,435,765,734 in 1968 and 1,145,090,300 in 1967. Daily volume averaged five million shares, compared

with 6.4 million the previous year and 4.5 million in 1967. This was based on 253 trading days in 1969 and 226 in 1968, when Wednesday closings were instituted on an interim basis to help alleviate member firms' operational problems resulting from record market activity. Dollar volume of shares traded totaled $31,036,896,363, compared with $35,479,186,174 in 1968. The largest share transaction was for 508,000 National General (N) warrants valued at $4,953,000. The largest block transaction in terms of dollar volume came to $14,476,800 for 301,600 shares of Kane-Miller common stock. The Exchange Price Change Index closed at 26.27, down 6.45 from the 1968 close. The closing Price/Earnings median ratio also declined, from 26.30 in 1968 to 16.95. The Clearing Corporation processed a total of 1,320,037,351 Exchange shares valued at $30,288,493,033. Average daily Amex share volume processed was 5,280,150 (down 24 percent from 1968), with 11,801,799 shares handled on the Exchange's record trading day, December 31st. On several occasions the Exchange expressed concern for the future viability of the public market, for the protection of individual stockholders, and for the continued adequacy of existing securities laws. The Board adopted, in November, constitutional amendments to strengthen the Exchange's powers in disciplinary procedures. These established, for the first time, the Exchange's authority over its affiliated member organizations as well as its members. In addition, they increased the dollar amount of fines that could be imposed--from a maximum of $10,000 to levies of $25,000 and $100,000 in any single proceeding against a member or member organization respectively. Price for Amex seats ranged from $150,000 on December 30th, to an all-time high of $350,000 on June 26th. The previous record was $315,000 in 1968. The Board approved more shares (431,287,987) for original listing in 1969 than in any recent previous year; the former high was 245,952,207 shares listed in 1968.

American Stock Exchange Annual Report for the year ending December thirty-first
Nineteen Hundred and Seventy
Ralph S. Saul, President

Total trading volume for the year reached 843,116,260 shares compared with 1,240,742,012 in 1969, the first time in four years that Amex volume fell below the one billion share level. Average daily turnover was 3.3. million shares, down 32.7 percent from the previous year's 5.0 million daily average. Dollar volume of shares traded came to $14,536,527,827, another four-year low. The largest share transaction was for 364,000 shares of Braniff Airways (A) stock valued at $3,640,000. The largest block transaction in terms of dollar value came to $11,692,200 for 149,900 shares of Mohawk Data Sciences common stock. The Exchange's Price Change Index closed at 22.75, down 3.52 from the 1969 close. The closing Price/Earnings median ratio stood at 14.27, a decline of 2.68 from the previous year. The Amex played an active role in one of the industry's major goals for the year: establishment of a comprehensive industry-government plan to protect investors in the event of brokerage house failure. The goal became a reality on December 30, 1970, when President Nixon signed into law legislation establishing the Securities Investor Protection

Corporation Act of 1970. In another innovation, the Exchange participated with major elements of the securities and banking industries as a member of the Banking and Securities Industry Committee (BASIC), established in March, 1970. Among its first actions, BASIC recommended, and the Amex Board approved, a three-step timetable for the mandatory use of CUSIP (Committee on Uniform Securities Identification Procedures) numbers on all stock certificates and bonds. A transaction revenue study released during the year revealed that member firms in the three Middle Atlantic States of New York, Pennsylvania and New Jersey accounted for more than 50.5 percent of public trading volume on the Amex. The North Central States ranked second with 13.5 percent, followed by the Pacific States with 12.2 percent. The study also revealed that individual investors accounted for 75.2 percent of Amex public volume; institutional investors, the remaining 24.8 percent. The figures confirmed a recent trend in Amex trading: a decrease in individual trading--down from 84.3 percent in 1967.

American Stock Exchange 1971 Annual Report
Paul Kolton, President

In one of the major industry developments of the year, the Amex and NYSE Boards of Governors announced plans in November to consolidate the communications, clearing and automation facilities of their respective exchanges into a jointly owned subsidiary known as the Securities Industry Automation Corporation (SIAC). The Amex incorporated on October 1, 1971 and became officially known as the American Stock Exchange, Inc. There were major changes during the year on all levels of Amex leadership. Ralph S. Saul, president of the Exchange since November, 1966, resigned and was replaced on May 20, 1971 by Paul Kolton, who had served as Executive Vice President of the Exchange since 1962. In announcing Mr. Kolton's election, Board Chairman Frank C. Graham, Jr., noted that this was the first time the presidency of a major exchange had been assumed by a professional staff member. New stock and warrant issues listed on the Amex reached 162 at year-end, second only to 1969's record high of 187. The total number of shares approved for original listing in 1971, 317,559,228, was also the second highest in recent Amex history. In October, the Amex Board adopted new standards regarding minimum size and earnings requirements for original listing of real estate investment trusts (REITs) and special standards dealing with possible conflicts of interest that could result from relationships between REITs and their advisors. The Amex broadened its West Coast services by establishing an Exchange office in California. During June, the Exchange marked its 50th anniversary indoors and published a 50th anniversary edition of the Amex Databook, a statistical profile which featured tabulations going back to 1921, when records on Exchange trading activity were compiled for the first time. Trading volume for the year totaled 1,070,924,002 shares, up 27 percent compared with 1970, the fourth time in five years that Exchange volume exceeded one billion shares. Average daily turnover came to 4.2 million shares compared to 3.3 million shares the previous year. Dollar volume of shares traded was $19,316,088,366 for the year compared with $14,536,527,827 for 1970, an increase of 32.9 percent. The largest share transaction was for 622,900 National General Corp. warrants valued at $2,256,925. The largest block transaction in terms of dollars was for 565,600 shares of The Offshore Company valued at $17,109,400. The Exchange's Price Change Index closed at 25.59 up 2.84 from the 1970 close. The closing Price/Earnings Median ratio stood at 16.76, an increase of 2.49 from the previous year's P/E ratio.

American Stock Exchange, Inc., 1972 Annual Report
Paul Kolton, Chairman of the Board

Trading volume for the year totaled 1,117,989,153 shares, up 4.39 percent compared with 1971, the fifth time in six years that Exchange volume exceeded one billion shares. Average daily turnover came to 4.5 million shares compared with 4.2 million the previous year. Dollar volume of shares traded was $21,366,935,317 for 1972 compared with $18,606,042,201 for 1971, an increase of 14.8 percent. The largest share transaction was for 539,900 shares of Braniff Airways, Inc. Special Class A Stock valued at $9,043,325. The largest block transaction in terms of dollars was for 209,900 shares of New Process Co. common stock valued at $9,078,175. The Exchange's Price Change Index closed at 26.36, up .77 from the 1971 close. The closing Median Price/Earnings ratio stood at 13.85, a decrease of 2.91 from the previous year's. During 1972, the Exchange transferred its electronic data processing, communications, clearing and other operations functions to the Securities Industry Automation Corporation (SIAC), a jointly owned subsidiary of the American and New York Stock Exchanges. The Exchange reorganized its governing structure late in 1972 to provide equal representation on the Board between securities industry and public members, ten from each sector. The first overall revision of the industry's commission rate structure since 1958 became effective April 3rd following approval by the boards and memberships of the American and New York Stock exchanges and review by the Securities and Exchange Commission. The Amex added the second highest total of original listings in recent history when the Board approved 179 new stock and warrant issues for admission. This brought the total number of securities traded on the Exchange to 1,419, up from 1,328 in 1971; the year ended with a market value of $55.65 billion compared with $49.05 billion the previous year.

American Stock Exchange, Inc., 1973 Annual Report
Paul Kolton, Chairman of the Board

The year 1973 was most difficult. Volume, prices, listings, and income were down significantly. The report quotes from a late fall article in *Barron's*: "Weep not for the Amex. Thanks to a revamped management team, aggressive marketing, and hard-nosed cost cutting, the nation's second largest stock exchange is alive and well and busily planning for the better days that hopefully lie ahead." Trading volume for the year totaled 759,840,245 shares, down 32 percent from 1972. Average daily turnover came to 3.0 million shares in 1973, compared with 4.5 million the previous year.

Dollar volume of shares traded was $10,847,748,956, against $21,366,935,317 for 1972. The largest trade in dollar value was 714,000 shares of Vetco Offshore Industries, Inc. common stock, valued at $16,779,000. The largest share transaction was 1,021,400 shares of McCulloch Oil Corp. common stock, valued at $5,107,000. During the year, the Exchange introduced a Market Value Index, replacing the Price Change Index. The new index closed at 90.33, down from the base of 100.00 set at the end of August. The closing 1973 median Price/Earnings Ratio was 6.49, down from 13.85 at the previous year's close. A plan to trade options in a pilot project was developed and awaited an SEC decision. Also under consideration were more listings of quality foreign issues and trading in mortgage futures and other financial instruments. The Board approved an affirmative action employment plan aimed at increasing employment opportunities for women and minority groups at the Amex.

American Stock Exchange, Inc., 1974 Annual Report
Paul Kolton, Chairman of the Board

Trading volume for the year totaled 482,173,297 shares, down 37 percent from 1973. Average daily turnover came to 1.9 million shares in 1974, compared with 3.0 million the previous year. Dollar volume of shares traded was $5,223,492,869, against $10,847,748,956 for 1973. The largest trade in 1974, in both dollar value and number of shares, was 278,000 shares of Imperial Oil, Ltd., Class A common stock, valued at $8,340,000. The Exchange's Market Value Index closed at 50.32 compared with 90.33 at 1973 year-end. In the first two months of options trading on the Amex, beginning on January 13, 1975, a total of 251,766 contracts representing 25,176,600 underlying shares changed hands. This was a daily average of 5,855 contracts, covering 585,500 shares. The options trading program received major priority during the year. In a coordinated effort with the Chicago Board Options Exchange, the Amex formed the Options Clearing Corporation (OCC), a jointly owned subsidiary, which became the issuer and obligor of all exchange-traded options. The many months of planning and testing culminated on January 13, 1975 with the opening of call options trading on the Amex in the stocks of six leading U.S. corporations. Fourteen more classes of options were phased in the following week. During the early months of 1974, the Exchange's Planning Division began studying the feasibility of developing a market for trading U.S. government securities in odd-lots of $1,000 to $99,000, principal amount. Trading started in seven U.S. Treasury bond and note issues on a pilot basis on January 31, 1975. The total was expected to increase to approximately 60 by mid-1975. Products related to the options market were receiving particular attention. Among the opportunities being studied for future development at the Amex were other forms of options trading, further expansion of the market in fixed income securities, a market related to gold and silver commodities, and mortgage futures. Among the Exchange's new listings for 1974 was a $20 million, 15-year convertible debenture issued by Mitsui & Co., Ltd. believed to be the first foreign offering in the U.S. public debt market since the introduction, in 1963, of the Interest Equalization Tax, which was eliminated in 1974. The Amex approved transfer of 106 regular memberships; 45 were seat sales ranging from $27,000 on March 19th to $72,000 on December 18th.

American Stock Exchange, Inc., Annual Report 1975
Paul Kolton, Chairman of the Board

For the American Stock Exchange, 1975 proved to be a markedly different year from the two that preceded it. As the economy turned, equity trading volume rose and the Amex Market Value Index retraced much of the ground lost in 1974. A proposal to merge the Amex Clearing Corporation with NYSE and NASD counterparts was approved by the Amex Board. Options listings increased to 44 underlying stocks. A plan for trading put options was forwarded to the SEC. Stock trading volume totaled 540,934,210 shares in 1975, up 12.2 percent from 482,173,297 in 1974. Average daily turnover was 2.1 million shares, compared with 1.9 million the previous year. Dollar volume of shares traded amounted to $5,776,621,977. The Exchange's Market Value Index closed at 83.48, up from 60.32 at 1974 year end. In the first year of options trading, beginning January 13th, a total of 3,482,258 contracts, representing 348,225,800 underlying shares, changed hands. Trading in U.S. Government notes and bonds, which began on January 31st, came to $44,269,000 in principal amount. The daily average rose to $360,000 in December from $154,000 in February. Seat sale prices recovered from their early 1975 decline; the Exchange approved the transfer of 100 regular memberships with seat prices ranging from $34,000 to $72,000. The Securities Industry Automation Corporation (SIAC), jointly owned by the Amex and NYSE, put into operation several programs to increase efficiencies in trading and processing securities while reducing costs substantially. Key developments included the Amex Market Data System.

American Stock Exchange, Inc., 1976 Annual Report
Paul Kolton, Chairman of the Board

The year 1976 was one of continuing change in the securities industry, and the American Stock Exchange responded by extending its markets and services. Trading volume rose in all Amex market segments--stocks, call options, corporate bonds, and odd-lot U.S. government securities. New stock listings also increased, reversing a three-year downtrend, and the number of call options authorized for trading by the Securities and Exchange Commission was raised. Plans were carried forward for the introduction of more investment products--put options, options on debt securities, and options on gold and silver bullion. Stock trading volume rose to 648,297,321 shares in 1976 from 540,934,210 the year before, an increase of 19.8 percent. Average daily turnover was 1.6 million shares, compared with 2.1 million in 1975. Dollar volume of shares traded amounted to $7,573,927,602 against $5,776,621,977 in 1975. The Exchange's Market Value Index closed at 109.84, up from 83.48 at 1975 year end. Options contracts traded in 1976 totaled 8,828,456, representing 882,845,600 underlying shares. Trading in U.S. government securities came to $97,516,000 in principal amount, against $44,401,000 the previous year. The Amex Board of Governors took an historic step in July by voting to recommend Constitutional changes that opened the way for direct trading competition between the Amex and the New York Stock Exchange. Dual trading began on August 23rd, when Varo, Inc., an Amex-listed stock, began trading on the New York Stock Exchange. In an important step in the clearing and settlement area, the SEC approved, in January 1977, the merger of the NASD's National Clearing Corporation, the NYSE's Stock Clearing Corporation, and the American Stock Exchange Clearing Corporation into a single entity, the National Securities Clearing Corporation (NSCC). The merger was expected to save users more than $12 million annually in operating costs. The Exchange announced that it was developing plans to provide two major new markets-- for options on gold and silver bullion and for options on debt securities. The Exchange approved the transfer of 101 regular memberships; 38 were seat sales ranging in price from $40,000 to $68,000.

American Stock Exchange, Annual Report, 1977
Arthur Levitt, Jr., Chairman of the Board

Looking forward, the new chairman notes the philosophy of the Exchange: "The year 1978 will be a crucial one, not only because critical decisions on the National Market System will be made, but because it will be our responsibility to see that the individual investor is truly served by the changes and that he believes this to be the case. Our listed companies, mostly medium-sized and relatively new to public ownership, also have an important stake in these developments. The Amex provides a public following for these emerging, growth companies." During 1977, the Amex outpaced other stock markets as the Exchange's Market Value Index increased 16.4 percent, while the Dow Jones Industrial Average fell 17.3 percent, the NYSE Composite declined 9.3 percent, and the NASDAQ Industrial Index rose 7.3 percent. Paul Kolton announced his retirement in July. On November 10th, the Amex Board elected Arthur Levitt, Jr., as new chairman and chief executive officer. Amex products included nearly 1,200 stock issues, call options on 64 of America's leading corporate stock issues, nearly 200 corporate bond issues with a combined market value of nearly $4 billion, and nearly 300 government issues. Being formed was the Amex Commodities Exchange (ACE), a contract market for trading futures on Government National Mortgage Association (GNMA) securities. The Amex continued to be the major market for foreign issues with approximately one of every 20 stock issues the security of a foreign corporation.

American Stock Exchange, 1978 Annual Report
Arthur Levitt, Jr., Chairman of the Board

The year 1978 was an exciting one for the Amex. Stock trading volume rose for the fourth consecutive year, reaching nearly one billion shares. The Amex Market Value Index gained nearly 18 percent, with every industry category sharing in the advance.

Volume in options contracts rose more than 40 percent from 1977, and the Amex portion of public business in dually listed options with other exchanges climbed to more than 80 percent. On January 3, 1978, Arthur Levitt, Jr., became Amex Chairman. The Amex Commodities Exchange (ACE) began trading in GNMA (Government National Mortgage Association) futures on September 12th.

American Stock Exchange, Annual Report, 1979: Perspectives on the Listed Auction Market
Arthur Levitt, Jr., Chairman of the Board

The year 1979 was strong for the American Stock Exchange. Stock volume exceeded one billion shares for the first time since 1972. The Amex Market Value Index advanced 64 percent, closing the year at 247.07 and recording the largest advance of any major index during 1979. Completing its fifth year of operation, the Amex options marketplace saw annual volume climb to a record 17.4 million contracts, almost five times greater than in 1975.

American Stock Exchange, Annual Report, 1980
Arthur Levitt, Jr., Chairman of the Board

As the Exchange entered a new decade, the annual report provided a 280 year history of securities markets, 1700-1980. Equity volume rose 48 percent in 1980 as more than 1.6 billion shares changed hands, topping the previous annual high of 1.4 billion shares recorded in 1958. Trading in the Amex options market was up 66 percent. The 19.0 million contracts represented options to purchase and sell approximately 2.90 billion underlying shares. The Amex Market Value Index broke through the 300 mark for the first time, while posting new records 51 times during the year. The Amex options market increased the number of classes traded to 80 call classes and 80 put classes and became the first listed options exchange to trade puts on all securities underlying its call classes. An Amex seat sold at $270,000 in early December, highest since 1969. An options seat sold at an all-time high of $160,000 in mid-December. The Amex listed 120.7 million common shares of Texaco Canada, Inc., the largest number of shares ever approved by the Exchange for an original listing.

1981 Annual Report, American Stock Exchange
Arthur Levitt, Jr., Chairman of the Board

Stock trading at the Amex exceeded the billion share mark for the third consecutive year with 1,343,400,220 shares traded, compared with 1,626,072,625 in 1980 and 1,100,263,500 in 1979. Amex options trading totaled an all-time high of 34,859,475 contracts in 1981, up 20 percent from the 9,048,323 contracts of 1980 and double the level in 1979. The Amex had the best financial performance in its history as both revenues and net income topped all previous records. Construction began on a $7 million building program to increase floor capacity by nearly 40 percent; the adjoining office building was purchased to provide administrative space. During 1981, the

Amex listed the highest number of new issues in nine years. The American Gold Coin Exchange (AGCE), a new Amex subsidiary, began a pilot trading program in the Canadian Maple Leaf on January 21, 1982. On February 10th, the Exchange added four other gold bullion coins: the Austrian 100 Corona, South African Krugerrand, and Mexican 50 Peso and One-Ounce coins. During the year, the Exchange filed applications to trade options on U.S. Treasury bills, bonds and notes and on Certificates of Deposit issued by "top-tier" U.S. banks. By year's end, the SEC had approved the Treasury options proposals and the Certificate of Deposit application was still pending. Equity and options trading set single-day trading records on January 7, 1981 with stock volume of 15,763,245 shares and options volume of 246,607 contracts.

American Stock Exchange, Annual Report, 1982
Arthur Levitt, Jr., Chairman of the Board

Stock trading on the Amex in 1982 exceeded the billion share mark for the fourth consecutive year with 1,337,725,430 shares traded, compared with 1,343,400,200 shares traded in 1981. Options trading totaled an all-time high of 38,766,996 contracts in 1982, up 11.2 percent from the 34,859,475 contracts of 1981, and 33.5 percent higher than the 1980 level. The Amex opened trading in interest rate options on various Treasury notes and bills. The American Gold Coin Exchange, a new Amex subsidiary, traded more than 51,000 gold bullion coins. After a slow start at the beginning of the year, Amex equity volume rose dramatically, ending with a total volume of 1.3 billion shares traded, the fourth consecutive year in a row that the Exchange topped the one billion mark. With this volume came a rise in the Market Value Index. The report includes a ten year statistical summary.

American Stock Exchange, Annual Report, 1983
Arthur Levitt, Jr., Chairman of the Board

The year 1983 is described as "extraordinary." For the first time, on December 14th, stock volume passed the two-billion share mark, surpassing previous weekly, monthly, and annual figures. Total options volume also topped the previous record, set in 1982, with 38,967,725 contracts traded. The year witnessed heavy institutional activity reflected in blocks of 10,000 or more shares. Some 20,629 such blocks were traded in 1983, compared with 12,330 in 1982. These block share transactions represented 24 percent of total stock volume, climbing sharply from less than 10 percent of volume five years previously. The Amex Market Value Index outperformed all other leading indices, setting new records 45 times during the year and closing up 31 percent from the previous year's close. This was a banner year for Amex stocks. Nearly one third of all common stocks on the Amex appreciated at least 50 percent in value; 12 percent of stocks at least doubled in value during the year. The Amex Market Value Index outperformed every other major index for the year; it gained 31 percent, closing at 223.01. This compared with increases by Value Line of 22.3 percent, the Dow Jones

Industrial Average of 20.3 percent, the NASDAQ Composite of 19.9 percent, the New York Stock Exchange Composite of 17.5 percent, and the Standard & Poor's 500 of 17.3 percent. In 1983, the Amex added four new index options to its existing options program, beginning with the listing of options in the Major Market Index (XMI) on April 29th. The Major Market Index is based on the stock prices of 20 "blue chip" companies representing a broad cross section of leading American industrial corporations. On July 8th, a distinctively different index option was introduced--the Amex Market Value Index option (XAM), which tracks the collective performance of the over 800 companies traded on the Amex. In September, the Amex became the first exchange to introduce "narrow-based" options on specific industry groups. These new products included options on the Computer Technology Index (XCI) and the Oil and Gas Index (XOI). Wendy Rolfe, a student at the Parsons School of Design, won a poster competition of impressions of the Amex; her winning design was on the cover of the annual report which contained reproductions of all entries. The Rolfe design became the official poster of the Exchange.

American Stock Exchange, Annual Report, 1984
Arthur Levitt, Jr., Chairman of the Board

Completing its first decade of trading, the Amex options market continued its rapid growth, paced by the Major Market Index option, which attracted nearly 15 percent of total options volume. For options trading as a whole, average daily volume was the highest ever, peaking on August 3rd with a new one-day record as 380,544 contracts changed hands. The year also saw institutional activity continue to climb as blocks of 10,000 or more shares accounted for 31 percent of total volume. There was additional positive news on new common stock listings as the number of companies joining the Exchange during the year rose to 63, a 47 percent increase over 1983. The Exchange negotiated an agreement with the Chicago Board of Trade, licensing that marketplace to trade a future on the Major Market Index, and established an electronic trading link with the Toronto Stock Exchange. Another major development in the options area was the formation of the Amex Commodities Corporation, a wholly owned subsidiary of the American Stock Exchange. The new market's premier product was a cash-settled option on gold bullion, as opposed to options on gold futures. During the year, the Amex became the first stock exchange to transmit live television broadcasts via satellite across the country. Cable News Network (CNN) broadcast its *Market Update* live daily from the Amex trading floor.

Report: On Being American. American Stock Exchange, Annual Report, 1985
Arthur Levitt, Jr., Chairman of the Board

Kenneth R. Leibler is named president and chief operating officer. Among the trading records set in 1985 were: February 6th, the highest daily volume ever--19 million shares; December 9-13th, the highest weekly volume ever--76 million shares; the highest number of blocks traded in one year--29,094; record equity volume for a single year--over 2.1 billion shares (this was a dramatic 36 percent increase over 1984 and surpassed the previous record set in 1983); December 16th, the highest daily options volume--407,000 contracts; December 9-13th, the highest weekly options volume--1.7 million contracts; December, the highest monthly options volume--5.6 million contracts. Investors were particularly attracted to the Major Market Index option; volume in the three-year-old product more than doubled. The Amex initiated a program to expand XMI option trading in European markets. As the year closed, the market value of the Amex list stood at a new high of $87 billion.

American Stock Exchange, Annual Report, 1986
Arthur Levitt, Jr., Chairman of the Board

Record volume in both equities and options, a significant expansion of the market communications network, and an increase in new listings made 1986 a banner year. The report notes a share volume of 2,978,611,984 and daily average share volume of 11,773,170. The number of listed companies/stock issues reached 796,957. Aggregate market value of the 7,437,339,000 outstanding shares was $96,440,275,166.

American Stock Exchange, Annual Report, 1987
Arthur Levitt, Jr., Chairman of the Board

In the aftermath of the October market shock, the Exchange was left with formidable challenges in preparing for levels of volume that might have seemed unimaginable a few months earlier; establishing more effective communication links among markets; and, reexamining trading regulations and procedures to ensure that they made sense in the new post-October world. January 2nd, the first trading day of 1987, was a slow post-holiday Friday so the question remained whether, after end-of-the-year profit taking, the bull market would resume its four year reign. The answer came quickly. On the next trading day, stock volume slumped 75 percent. However, by the end of the week, it had more than doubled, while options volume had almost tripled. By the end of January, the Amex had set seven volume and index records. Options on the Major Market Index were offered on the floor of the European Options Exchange (EOE) in Amsterdam marking the first time that a U.S. index option was available for trading before the markets opened in New York. On October 5th, the Exchange filed an application with the SEC to trade an international market index which would create the first broad worldwide index with real time pricing of the component securities during the U.S. trading day. On October 19th, like a tidal wave, trading started in the Far East, swept across Europe, and then crashed onto U.S. markets. On October 19th and 20th, volume soared three times higher than the year's previous average. The specialists intervened, increasing their participation in trades some sixfold, providing an opportunity for calm to reassert itself. Reported share volume was 3,505,954,875 with a daily average share volume of 13,857,529. Over 850 companies listed 8,253,485,077 total shares with an aggregate market value of $99,171,058,732.

Speaking Out on Real Issues
American Stock Exchange, 1988 Annual Report

Statistics included a reported share volume of 2,515,025,340; daily average share trading volume of 9,940,812; and 895 listed companies with 1,100 stock issues. The Amex restated its commitment to encouraging the individual's active involvement in the market. The small investor suffered extensive losses in the 1987 Market Break. The events during and immediately following Black Monday severely challenged the small investor's belief that the market was a hospitable--or, indeed, even a fair--place for his or her investment dollars. Statistics oversimplified the situation. Institutional investors represented about 70 percent of total market volume. But this figure obscured the fact that the individual continued to play a central role in certain markets. The small investor represented approximately 60 percent of equity volume. The individual was, without question, the financial backbone of the mid-sized growth companies that predominated on the Amex's trading floor. Over the past decade, the Amex Market Value Index, a broad-based measure of market growth, increased almost 15 percent per year, a rate that was considerably higher than inflation. The Index's 17.4 percent increase in 1988 supported the view that the market continued to be one of the best places to invest money.

Focus on the Future: American Stock Exchange, 1989 Annual Report
James R. Jones, Chairman of the Board

James R. Jones, who assumed the chairmanship in November 1989, began his first report by stating two goals: to merit the confidence of the public investor and to make a substantial contribution to the growth of listed companies. Globalization was key. Equity volume was up sharply. The Market Value Index closed with a gain of 23.5 percent. Options volume on the Amex in 1989 was 10.8 percent ahead of the previous year's. Some 49.9 million contracts changed hands, compared with 17.5 million at the start of the decade. In 1989, the Amex had its fifteenth consecutive year of profitability, with net income exceeding $4 million. Application was made to the SEC to begin trading two important new products: options based on an index of 50 foreign stocks actively traded in the United States and options on a Japanese index, based on 200 major companies traded on the Tokyo Stock Exchange.

American Stock Exchange, 1990 Annual Report
James R. Jones, Chairman and Chief Executive Officer

Jones solidly established his tenure at the Exchange as having a global vision solidly rooted in advanced technology. The past decade provided the Exchange with a reputation as an aggressive, innovative force on the world market scene. On December 28, 1989, the final listing of the year was a foreign company-- Electrochemical Industries (Frutarom) Ltd. of Israel. Six days later, the first listing of 1990 was again for a foreign company--Elan Corporation of Ireland. A week later, the

Exchange listed a new product illustrating globalization--put warrants issued by the Kingdom of Denmark, underwritten by America's Goldman Sachs, and based on the Nikkei Stock Average of leading Japanese companies. The Amex's mix of equities and options made it the nation's best balanced market. Several new products were on the way--basket instruments, international products, and futures in areas such as fixed-income securities. In 1989, the Amex had a reported share volume of 3,125,107,840, up from 2,515,025,340 in 1988 and a daily share volume of 12,401,222, up from 9,940,812 in 1988. The Amex share of the equity options market stood at 29.31 percent with an 11.19 percent share of the index options market. Shares outstanding totaled 8,816,726,864, slightly more than 1988, with an aggregate market value of $130,795,337,552.

American Quality: American Stock Exchange, 1991 Annual Report
James R. Jones, Chairman and Chief Executive Officer

Jones noted that, since his election as Chairman in late 1989, the Amex had been "proactive, not reactive," with dramatic results. New financial products attracted investors worldwide. The drive toward globalization included alliances with Reuters Holdings PLC and with the Chicago Board Options Exchange to establish an after-hours trading market for equities, options and derivatives. New product strategy included the advent of trading warrants on the Financial Times-Stock Exchange 100 Share Index of leading companies trading in London; on France's blue-chip index, the CAC 40, while the Paris Bourse began trading warrants on the Major Market Index; and, an exclusive license with the European Options Exchange in Amsterdam to trade option and equity derivative products on a new nine-nation European index. Close communication with customers resulted in two developments in 1991. An unmet need for trading in emerging growth companies generated the Emerging Company Marketplace, launched on March 18, 1992. In response to a trend looking for participation in larger, mid-size stocks, the Amex obtained an exclusive license from Standard & Poor's Corporation to trade options on the S&P MidCap 400 Index beginning February 13, 1992. This continuing responsiveness to customer needs was apparent in the performance of the Amex Market Value Index, which closed out 1991 at 395.05, a 28.2 percent increase. The year 1990 saw a reported share volume of 3,328,918,215, a daily average share volume of 13,157,780, an Amex 30.69 percent share of the equity options market, and a 7.58 percent share of the index options market. The Amex Market Value Index reached 308.11. Total shares outstanding numbered 9,767,749,621 with an aggregate market value of $102,301,457,254.

American Stock Exchange: Setting a Higher Standard. American Stock Exchange, 1992 Annual Report
James R. Jones, Chief Executive Officer

In addition to achieving a number of all-time highs in 1992, the Amex emphasized innovation and planning. The Emerging Company Marketplace provided the first new marketplace in 20 years. Several derivative products were introduced including options based on the Standard & Poor's MidCap 400 Index. The Exchange reported all-time annual and monthly equity volume records and the Market Value Index reached a new high of 418.99. Trading volume was 3,595,789,405 shares, passing the former record of 1987. Total shares outstanding numbered 10,177,908,769 with an aggregate market value of $109,354,448,986. The Exchange's theme for 1992 was "The Business behind the Business." Highlights of the year included establishing strategic alliances and information-sharing agreements with stock exchanges in Argentina, Chile, Brazil, Spain, Hong Kong, and Malaysia; enhancing market quality and liquidity by expanding the number of issues trading in 1/16 increments; and, kicking off a new television campaign highlighting the support available to listed companies. With the market for the year 2000 in focus, the Exchange examined an increasingly competitive environment and acknowledged the importance of public trust. These issues were addressed in a comment letter to the Securities and Exchange Commission for their *Market 2000*, the first comprehensive review of securities markets in 20 years. The Exchange "urged the SEC to closely scrutinize all securities markets with this overriding thought: Public investors benefit from fair competition within a framework that promotes equal and rigorous investor protection standards across all marketplaces."

Fair trade. Fair practice. Fair play. (1993)
Jules L. Winters, Chief Operating Officer

The American Stock Exchange records one of its best years in history with record breaking performances in the Amex Market Value Index and trading volume. The marketplace proved especially attractive in the housing, construction, and land development industry. The Market Value Index celebrated its 20th anniversary by gaining 19.5 percent and outpacing all other major U. S. indicators. The Exchange continued to build on its strengths--the core equity business, technology, and derivative products. There were 133 new listings, the highest number since 1987. Amex Asia was formed to develop opportunities in the Pacific Rim. In technology, Electronic Display Books were installed at all specialist posts; wireless hand-held terminals were tested; XTOPS, an advanced options pricing system was introduced; and Intra-Day Comparison (IDC) connected advanced order-processing systems. New derivative products included Standard & Poor's Depositary Receipts (SPDRs), Amex Hong Kong 30 Index Put and Call Warrants, and options on Morgan Stanley's Cyclical and Consumer Indexes. Additional Amex-listed derivative products included the North American Telecommunications Index (XTC) Options; FLEXible Exchange Index Options, U. S. Dollar Increase Warrants; Equity-Linked Term Notes (ELKS and YEELDS), FT-SE Eurotrack 200 Index Call Warrants, Stock Index Return Securities on the S&P MidCap 400 Index; Bankers Trust Convertible Capital Securities; Deutsche Mark and Japanese Yen Currency Warrants; Quarterly Expiration Index Options, and Long-term Equity AnticiPation Securities (LEAPS). A major print and television advertising campaign used the theme "Fair trade. Fair practice. Fair play."

Appendix B

PUBLICATIONS BY AND ABOUT THE AMERICAN STOCK EXCHANGE

This appendix provides a sample of the variety of topics covered by the American Stock Exchange; it is not meant to capture and list all publications issued by the Amex. Also included are unannotated guides to, and publications of, the Exchange by other publishers. (Lists of publications available from the Amex and ordering information may be obtained from: American Stock Exchange Publications Department, 86 Trinity Place, New York, NY 10006-1881, phone 212-306-1386.)

PUBLICATIONS BY THE AMEX

Brochures, Pamphlets, and Monographs

ACE: Amex Commodities Exchange, Inc.: the First Six Months. N.d.

ACE Update. 1979.

Advantages for Munis. July 1993.

American Gold Coin Exchange. [1985]

American Stock Exchange Guide. Institutional Services. N.d.

American Stock Exchange Index System. June 17, 1966.

American Stock Exchange Market Data. N.d.

American Stock Exchange's Options on the International Market Index. December 1988.

American Stock Exchange's Options on the Japan Index: Meeting the Changing Needs of the World's Investors. August 1990.

American Stock Exchange's Options on the XII, the Institutional Index. August 1986.

American Way. [June 1993]

Amex: Tale of the Tape (photo essay). [April 1993]

Amex: We Extend Your Reach. N.d.

Amex Advantage: Building Blocks for the Future. August 1993.

Amex Advantage: Listing on the American Stock Exchange. December 1989.

Amex Clerks. December 1986, May 1989.

Amex Clubs: An Innovative Forum for Presenting Your Company's Story to the Investment Community. Market Research Dept. Corporate Services Series. August 1979.

Amex Commodities Corporation By-Laws and Rules. February 1985.

Amex Derivative Securities: Options on the Pharmaceutical Index: Opportunities in a High-Performing Global Industry. June 1992.

Amex Derivative Securities: Options on the EuroTop 100 Index: the European Stock Market in One Market. October 1992.

Amex in Brief. [1969]

Amex Options: Underlying Stock Price Information, Quarterly Price Ranges 1976-1980, Dividend Payment Schedule. 1980.

Amex Options Alert. 1991.

Amex Options Calculator. N.d.

Amex Options Rules. January 1986.

Amex Public Transaction Study. [1967]

Application of U.S. Securities Laws to Canadian Companies. October 1986.

Arbitration Procedures for Resolution of Small Claims. N.d.

Auction or Dealer Market: When and Why? Market Research Dept. Listed Company Performance Series. Analysis No. 211. December 1979.

Banner Year: the Story Behind a Great Year at the American Stock Exchange. February 1989.

Buying a Put To Protect a Profit in Stock. N.d.

Buying Options for Profit Opportunities. February 1986.

Buying Stocks and Puts Simultaneously. N.d.

Call Options: Versatile Investment Tools. November 1984.

Capped Options on XMI and XII for More Investor Control. 1991.

Centralized Gold Coin Market on an Exchange Trading Floor . . . To Service Your Gold Coin Needs. September 1983.

Changes in Institutional Support after Listing. 1987.

Changes in Market Maker Participation in NASDAQ Stocks following the Crash of October 1987. 1987.

Characteristics and Risks of Standardized Options. 1987.

Communicating with Your Specialist; a Guide for the Listed Company. October 1986.

Comparative Market Quality on October 19-20 of the Seven Most Active Amex and NASDAQ/NMS Stocks. 1987.

Complete Options Index. [1980]

Corporate Bonds on the Amex. April 1990.

Covered Call Writing. N.d.

Customer Disclosure Statement. February 1982.

Evening at the American Stock Exchange for the Benefit of the U.S. Olympic Team. 1980.

Floor Transaction Handbook. 1967, 1971.

Gold Coin News. 1963.

Guide to Listed Options: Terms and Characteristics, Trading Strategies, Puts/Calls, Tax Planning, Supervising Customer Accounts, Margin Requirements. 1981.

Handling Options Transactions for Public Customers. (Prepared jointly by the Amex, Chicago Board Options Exchange, Midwest Stock Exchange, National Association of Securities Dealers, New York Stock Exchange, Pacific Stock Exchange, and Philadelphia Stock Exchange.) March 1980.

How To Read the American Stock Exchange Ticker. N.d.

In the Public Eye: a Comparative Survey of Stock Table Coverage in U.S. Daily Newspapers.
Market Research Dept. Research Series. Analysis No. 123. June 1979.

Increasing Your Income with Options. December 1987.

Industrial Classification of Stocks Dealt in on the New York Curb Exchange as of June 27, 1939. (New York Curb Exchange.)

Installation Guide for Management Planning and Control Manual for Brokerage Organizations. April 1970.

Institutional Services. January 1986.

Institutional Trading Program. May 1985, March 1986.

Interest Rate Options: Study Guide. September 1984.

Introducing Puts. N.d.

Investor Relations Services for the Listed Company. August 1985, December 1985.

Journey through a Stock Exchange (comic book; for primary and secondary school audiences). 1969.

LEAPS: Long-Term Equity Anticipation Securities: Opportunities for the Longer Term. April 1992.

Listing Day at the American Stock Exchange. Market Research Dept. Corporate Services Series. June 1979, September 1980.

Listing Foreign Securities. March 1987.

Listing on the American Stock Exchange: Some Questions and Answers. N.d.

Major Market Index Options. February 1987.

Market for Millions. 1969.

Nerve Center (Spanish, French, German, Italian, Japanese). N.d.

Odd-Lot Differentials of Stock Dealt in on the New York Curb Exchange. (New York Curb Exchange Partners Association.) May 3, 1937.

100 Most Active Issues on the Amex. 1972.

Options at the American Stock Exchange 1975-1985. January 1985.

Options on the Airline Index. November 1985.

Options on the Amex Market Value Index. March 1984.

Options on the Major Market Index. February 1987.

Options on the Oil Index. February 1987.

Options on the S&P MidCap Index: The New Benchmark for Today's Investor. January 1992.

Options on the XMI: the Way to "Trade" the Market. October 1991.

Options on U.S. Treasury Bills. January 1986.

Options on U.S. Treasury Notes. March 1986.

Plan for the Re-Organization of the New York Curb Exchange Adopted by the Board of Governors. October 4, 1938.

Post-Crash Survey of Chief Executive Officers of Amex and NASDAQ Companies. 1987.

Post-Crash Survey of Member Firm Equity and OTC Traders. 1987.

Pre-Offering Price Stability. [1987]

Protecting Your Investments with Options. February 1986.

Put Options: Versatile Investment Tools. November 1984.

Quotation Spread by Selected Price Category. 1987.

Reaching the U.S. Investor: Listing on the American Stock Exchange. August 1985.

Requirements and Procedures for Additional Listings. July 1980.

Requirements and Procedures for Original Listing. August 1984.

Requirements for Original Listing. September 1986.

Research Coverage by Security Analysts. [1987].

Re-Source: A Guide to an American Stock Exchange Listing. 1986, November 1988, September 1989.

Selecting the Appropriate Specialist Unit for Newly Listed Securities. N.d.

Selling Puts. N.d.

Shareownership Change after Listing. [1987].

Solutions for Visibility. [July 1993].

Specialist on the Amex. May 1974, June 1977.

Specialist Participation on the Amex during the October 1987 Crash. 1987.

Spreading Strategies. 1975.

Stock Index Options: Institutional Index Options. September 19, 1988; December 24, 1990.

Stock Index Options: International Market Index Options. December 8, 1988.

Stock Index Options: Japan Index Options. September 21, 1990

Stock Index Options: Major Market Index Options (XMI). N.d.

Stock Index Options: Oil Index Options (XOI). N.d.

Stock Index Options: Options on the EuroTop 100 Index. October 6, 1992.

Stock Index Options: Treasury Bill Options, Puts, and Calls. N.d.

Stock on the Amex. 1971, 1972.

Stock Options Strategy Sheet
   Buying Major Market Index (XMI) Puts and Calls. June 1986.
   Combination Writing (Selling) Using Major Market Index Options (XMI). October
      1986.
   Selling (Writing) Major Market Index (XMI) Puts and Calls for Income. June 1986.
   Buying Major Market Index (XMI) Puts for Portfolio Protection. June 1986.

Stock Splits: the Pros and Cons. N.d.

Stock Watch. December 1989.

Summary of Listed Options. September 1986.

Summary of Listed Stock Options. February 1984.

Tax Planning for Listed Options. 1980.

Trading Government Issues on the Amex: 25 Questions and Answers. June 1977.

Trading Halts. August 1976.

Trading Liquidity . . . a Major Benefit of an Amex Listing. Market Research Dept. Listed Company Performance Series. Analysis No. 209. September 1979.

Types of Orders and Offers Defined and Explained. November 1970.

Versatile Option. N.d.

Visit the Amex: Visitors Gallery Trading Floor. N.d.

Why Your Company Should List on the American Stock Exchange. N.d.

Your Specialist: a Guide for the Chief Executive Officer. December 1978.

Conferences

Amex Options and Derivatives Colloquium 13. March 25-26, 1993.

CEO Leadership Institute. October 4-9, 1987; October 2-6, 1988.

China Conference (Beijing). December 10-13, 1981.

Environmental Conference, 2nd Annual (New York). April 17, 1991.

Financing in the International Markets (Mexico City). November 19, 1991.

Global Markets of the 1990s: 4th Annual Options and Futures Colloquium. December 3-4, 1990.

Health Care Conference (New York). June 5-6, 1991.

International Options Colloquium. (Cosponsored with the Belgian Futures and Options Exchange.) December 7-8, 1992.

New Realities: a Briefing for CEOs and Financial Professionals (New York). (Cosponsored with Donaldson, Lufkin, Jenrette; PaineWebber, and The Wall Street Journal.) June 11, 1991.

Oil & Gas Symposium, 4th Annual. The Canadian Energy Industry: On the Move, (Calgary, Alberta). November 1-2, 1983.

Oil & Gas Symposium, 5th Annual. The Canadian Energy Industry: a Forward Perspective, (Calgary, Alberta). October 30-31, 1984.

Oil & Gas Symposium, 6th Annual. The Canadian Energy Industry: an Evaluation and Update, (Toronto, Ontario). October 22-23, 1985.

Options & Derivatives: a Legal Perspective (New York). October 3-4, 1991.

Options & Derivatives Colloquium XIII. March 25-26, 1993.

Options Colloquium VII (New York University). March 26-27, 1987.

Options Colloquium XI (New York University). March 21-22, 1991.

Options Industry Conference, 8th Annual (Palm Beach Gardens, Florida). April 25-27, 1990.

Options Legal Forum (New York). October 17-18, 1985.

Options Traders Conference III: the Yearly Meeting of Options Industry Professionals (Kiamesha Lake, New York). June 12-14, 1985.

Reaching the World from Israel: Opportunities for Global Investing (New York). November 20, 1990.

U.S. Perspectives. Washington: a Decade of Insights. November 7-9, 1988.

U.S. Perspectives 1981: Views from Washington and Wall Street. October 25-27, 1981.

U.S. Perspectives II. October 20-22, 1982.

U.S. Perspectives V. October 14-16, 1985.

Washington. Growth Companies: Opportunity and Challenge. June 4-5, 1979.

Washington III. The Reagan Plan: a Progress Report (Washington, D.C.) June 22-23, 1981.

Washington VII: a New American Revolution (Washington, D.C.) June 9-11, 1985.

Washington VIII: Confronting the Issues (Washington, D.C.) June 8-10, 1986.

Media and Software

Amex Access (IBM PC Compact Disc). [1988]

Amex Options Seminar System (158 slides, 3 audio cassettes, 2 scripts, and 3 flip charts). August 1984.
>   Part 1.   *Increasing Your Income with Options.*
>   Part 2.   *Protecting Your Investments with Options.*
>   Part 3.   *Buying Options for Profit Opportunities.*

Hear it Here (radio broadcast). N.d.

Index Options Videos. N.d.
>   *XMI: the Investor's Advantage.*
>   *Buying XMI: Options on the Major Market Index.*
>   *Writing XMI: Options on the Major Market Index.*

Investor and the Marketplace (color film). N.d.

Live . . . from the American Stock Exchange Trading Floor. N.d.

Stock Watch: Private Eye on the Public Interest (motion picture). N.d.

Reports

American Stock Exchange: Quality of Market Report 1983. Listed Company Advisory Committee. 1984.

Amex Pilot Program for Trading Options (prepared for the Securities and Exchange Commission). January 1974.

Amex Report. Equity Performance on the American Stock Exchange. Institutional Services. 1986.

Auction Market for Options: Economic Impact, Functions, Users, Structure, Regulations (prepared for the Securities and Exchange Commission in response to SEC Release No. 10490, November 14, 1973). January 18, 1974.

Census of Amex Shareholders. 1970, 1971.

Hasbrouck, Joel and Robert A. Schwartz, (Graduate School of Business Administration, New York University). *The Liquidity of Alternative Market Centers: a Comparison of the New York Stock Exchange, the American Stock Exchange, and the NASDAQ National Market System.* American Stock Exchange Transactions Data Research Project, Report No. 1. January 1986.

Marsh, Terry (Sloan School of Management, Massachusetts Institute of Technology and Hoover Institution, Stanford University) and Kevin Rock (Graduate School of Business Administration, Harvard University). *Exchange Listing and Liquidity: a Comparison of the American Stock Exchange with the NASDAQ National Market System.* American Stock Exchange Transactions Data Research Project, Report No. 2. January 1986.

Performance on the Amex: a Report on the Quality of Markets. Listed Company Advisory Committee. 1983.

Report to the Board of Governors on the Organization and Administration of the New York Curb Exchange. Special Committee on Organization and Administration. August 31, 1938.

Research & Forecasts, Inc. *The Amex Indicator: Opinion and Forecast: a Continuing Study of Attitudes Expressed by the Chief Executive Officers of Companies Listed on the American Stock Exchange.* Sponsored by the American Stock Exchange, December 1980.

Year End Statistical Report. 1984, 1986, 1987.

<u>Serials</u>

American Insight. [1987-   ]

American Investor. [1956-   ]

American Investor Yearbook (a compilation of articles from *American Investor*). 1967-

American Quarterly. 1987-

Amex Action (newsletter for employees). 1981-

Amex Daily Circular. N.d.

Amex Databook. 1968-

Amex Derivative Securities (newsletter for member firms). 1983-

Amex Facts. 1980-

Amex Indices. [1984-   ]

Amex Insights. 1989-

Amex Journal. January 1982-

Amex Options (information circular). 1986-

Amex Statistical Review (annual; continued by Amex Fact Book). 1981-1982.

Amex Stats. [1977-1985]

Amex Weekly Bulletin. N.d.

Company Guide: Rules and Policies Applicable to Companies with Securities Listed on the American Stock Exchange (loose-leaf). [1988-   ]

Fact Book (annual). 1985-

Floor Focus. [September 1980-   ]

Listed Company. [1987-   ]

New Listing Annual. 1971-

Open Interests. Amex Options. 1986-

Stocks, Bonds, Options, & Derivatives Symbol Book (quarterly). Dividends and Rulings Dept. [1993-   ]

PUBLICATIONS ABOUT THE AMEX

<u>Monographs</u>

American Stock Exchange. *American Stock Exchange Directory.* Chicago: Commerce Clearing House, 1974.

Amex Options: Momentum. (Supplement to *Euromoney* sponsored by the American Stock Exchange). London: Euromoney Publications, September 1986.

Amex Options Rules: Rules Principally Applicable to Trading of Option Contracts. Chicago: Commerce Clearing House, 1976.

Amex: Proposals for the American Stock Exchange: Expansion in Lower Manhattan. New

York: City of New York, Department of City Planning, [1977]

AP's Guide to Stock Abbreviations: AMEX. New York: Associated Press, Business News Dept., 1985.

Conferences

Currie, Gord. *American Stock Exchange: 11th Annual Canadian Oil and Gas Symposium, November 7-8, 1990.* [Toronto]: RBC Dominion Securities, 1990.

Media and Software

Little, Jeffrey B. *American Investor: the Official Simulation of the American Stock Exchange.* [U.S.]: Blue Chip Software, 1962.

Zahorchak, Michael G. *Why Dual Listing on NYSE and American Stock Exchange: Advantages and Disadvantages.* Hollywood, CA: Convention Seminar Cassettes, 1977.

Serials

American Stock Exchange Guide: Official Organ of the American Stock Exchange: Directory, Constitution and Rules, American Stock Exchange Clearing Corporation Requirements (loose-leaf). Chicago: Commerce Clearing House, [1960-   ]

American Stock Exchange, Inc., Constitution and Rules: Revised to . . . Chicago: Commerce Clearing House, [1973-   ]

American Stock Exchange, Inc., Stocks & Bonds. New York: Francis Emory Fitch, Inc., [1988-   ]

Amex Commodities Exchange Guide. Chicago: Commerce Clearing House, 1978-   .

Daily Graphs. American/OTC Stock Exchange. Los Angeles: William O'Neil & Co., Week ending September 4, 1987-   .

Daily Stock Price Record. American Stock Exchange. New York: Standard & Poor's Corp., July/September 1972-   .

Financial World's Amex Special Situations Newsletter. New York: Financial World Partners, 1986-   .

Appendix C

GLOSSARY

Amcode: a computerized trading, quotation, order-handling and price-reporting system developed by the Amex. When established in 1972, it was expected to be the central national securities market of the future. Using Amcode, specialists on all of the nation's exchanges would be linked electronically and the price quotations of each would be visible on a TV screen.

American Depositary Receipt (ADR): a negotiable receipt issued by an American Depositary, or trust company, certifying that a stated number of shares of a company domiciled in some other country have been deposited with the depositary's overseas branch or custodian.

American Stock Exchange Index: see Amex Market Value Index.

American Stock Exchange Network (AMNET): local area network (LAN) proposed by the Amex in the early 1980s in response to increases in trading levels on the floor. The LAN design was chosen because it promised a significant reduction in the number of dedicated lines and modems and helped to reduce future wiring and installation costs.

Amex Commodities Exchange: exchange established in 1978 to trade futures contracts in Treasury securities and other financial instruments. The Exchange found that it could not compete with the Chicago commodity exchanges, which had been trading futures contracts for several years. Amex chose to merge with the New York Futures Exchange (NYFE) over the New York Commodity Exchange, because they perceived that the NYFE would be the more successful in finding new issues for the Amex.

Amex Market Value Index: index introduced in 1973 made up of all of the more than 800 issues which trade on the Amex and priced daily. Options on the index were introduced in 1983.

Amex Options Switching System (AMOS): computerized order-routing system, developed in 1978, which transmits incoming options orders to appropriate trading posts. If the orders are executed, AMOS reports the executions to the Exchange member initiating the order.

Arbitrage: buying a security in one market and selling the same security simultaneously in another market, taking advantage of the price differential between the two markets.

Auto-Ex (Automated Execution System): an extension of the AMOS order-routing system which provides automatic and instant execution of market orders.

Autoper: a touch sensitive screen display introduced in 1983, enabling brokers in branch offices anywhere in the world to buy and sell stocks on the Amex and receive return reports within seconds. In addition to increasing order execution speed, the system improved transaction accuracy.

Average: an aggregate measure of stock prices.

Basket: short-lived securities based on the S&P 500 stock index or other indexes, giving the investor the equivalent portion of the stocks in those indexes. Each stock is represented in the basket in the same proportion as it is represented in the index. Baskets have elements of mutual funds, futures and stocks; the Chicago Mercantile Exchange and the CBOE have argued that the SEC does not have jurisdiction over their trading, because they are actually futures.

Bear market: a time of declining stock market prices.

Beta: the measure of a stock's relative volatility, compared with the rest of the stock market. The S&P 500 has a beta of 1; a stock with a beta higher than 1 is riskier than the S&P 500 because its price can be expected to rise and fall more quickly.

Bid/ask: the price offered by the buyer for the purchase of a stock, and the price asked by a seller for the sale of a stock. The difference between the bid price and asked price is called the spread.

Biotechnology Index (BTK): index designed to measure the performance of a cross section of companies in the biotechnology industry. The Index is equal dollar weighted, meaning that each of its component stocks is represented in approximately equal dollar value. The Amex introduced options on this index in 1992.

Blue chip stocks: securities of major companies which are household names, known for their price stability in good and bad times.

Bond: a long-term, interest-bearing debt instrument issued by a corporation or a government, which promises to pay specific sums of interest at designated times and to pay back principal in a lump sum at maturity.

Book value: the value of an outstanding share of stock, determined by dividing net assets by the number of outstanding shares. Net assets are based on total assets minus intangible assets minus current liabilities minus long-term liabilities minus the liquidation value of any preferred stock.

BOUND (Buy-Write Option Unitary Derivative): long-term, option-like securities giving investors the equivalent of selling a call option on their common stock. Investors participate in stock price gains, up to a preset amount, while receiving the equivalent of dividends on the underlying stock.

Breadth of Market Index: a daily report developed by the Amex in 1966 which shows the extent to which the day's price changes were spread across the market.

Broker: a person or firm acting as an intermediary between a buyer and a seller.

Bull market: a time of advancing stock market prices.

Call: an option to buy a certain security at a specified price within a specified period of time. Usually a call is purchased by one who thinks the price of the underlying stock will rise above the call price during the life of the call.

Centaur: computer system under the direction of SIAC which would automate communications, trading, reporting and clearing operations by 1978. Centaur was based on earlier systems, including Amex's Amcode, but was not meant to replace the trading floor.

Chicago Board of Trade (CBT): the world's largest grain exchange, where spot or futures contracts are completed in a variety of agricultural products, including corn and soybeans; also trades futures and futures options in silver, Treasury bonds, and Treasury notes.

Chicago Board Options Exchange (CBOE): an exchange set up by the Chicago Board of Trade for the open market trading of certain stock options, including index options of the S&P 100 Index and S&P 500 Index.

Chicago Mercantile Exchange (CME): national marketplace founded in 1919 for trading in cash and futures contracts for commodity items, including live cattle, potatoes, and lumber. The CME is the leading exchange for the trading of international currency futures and options in the U.S.

Clearing: the physical transfer of securities and monies in the completion of a trade.

Commodities Futures Trading Commission (CFTC): the regulating agency established in 1974 by the U.S. Congress for all futures contracts traded in organized contract markets. It is responsible for matters of information and disclosure, fair trading practices, registration of firms and individuals, and the protection of customer funds, record keeping, and the maintenance of orderly futures and options markets.

Composite tape: the stock price reporting system that includes trading from all organized exchanges and the over-the-counter market.

Computer Technology Index (XCI): index designed to measure the performance of a cross section of companies in the computer industry. The Amex introduced options on the index in 1983.

CUSIP (Committee on Uniform Security Identification Procedures): committee assigned to develop a system for alphabetically and numerically identifying securities to speed their handling.

The CUSIP number consists of a base number of six digits known as the issuer number, with a two-character suffix known as the issue number.

Dealer: a person or organization that buys assets for and sells assets from its own portfolio.

Derivative: a financial instrument whose value is based on another security. For example, an option is a derivative instrument based on an underlying stock, stock index, or future.

Disclosure: requirements of the SEC and stock exchanges for companies to provide all information on its financial condition, positive and negative, which might influence any investment decision. The Amex also requires immediate disclosure by a company of any activities or conditions that are likely to have a significant effect on the price of its securities.

Dividend: payment from a company's profits distributed to its stockholders.

Dual Trading: trading of the same security on more than one exchange.

Earnings per share: a corporation's net income after taxes divided by the number of shares of common stock that are outstanding.

Emerging Company Marketplace: a stock market under the Amex having lower listing requirements to lure new business to the Amex. It opened in 1992 with 25 listed companies, taken out of the OTC market and brought to the Amex's auction market. An immediate advantage was the reduction in the cost of trading the companies' stock, because it was traded directly to investors instead of via middlemen. This benefit had been limited to large and mid-sized companies.

Equity: stock, either common or preferred.

EUROTOP 100 INDEX (EUR): index that measures the collective performance of the most actively traded stocks on Europe's major stock exchanges and is designed to reflect the European stock market as a whole. The Amex introduced options on the index in 1992.

EXYSYS: a rule-based expert system used in connection with the Market Expert Surveillance System (MESS), which evaluates insider trading data using approximately 160 rules. The result is one of two weighted responses: "open an investigation" or "do not open an investigation." A major advantage is that the same set of rules is applied for each case.

Flexible Exchange Options (FLEX): derivatives developed by the Chicago Board Options Exchange in 1992 which allow investors to pick and choose expiration, strike and exercise style for S&P 100 and 500 options.

Floor trader: a representative of a member of the stock exchange who executes trades by being physically present on the floor of the exchange.

Futures: short for futures contract, which is an agreement to deliver or take delivery of, a commodity at a specified future time and price. The contract is transferable and can be traded like a security. In recent years contracts have been extended to financial instruments, currencies, and indexes.

Government National Mortgage Association (GNMA): a government-owned corporation which purchases mortgages from private lenders, such as banks and savings and loans, packages them into securities called Ginnie Maes, and sells the certificates to investors. Because Ginnie Maes' monthly payments consist of principal and earned interest collected on mortgages, they are considered to be a high-yielding alternative for conservative investors.

Hand signals: a system used by brokers during the early days of the Amex to communicate executions and quotations to their clerks.

Hong Kong Index: index based on stocks traded on the Hong Kong Stock Exchange.

Index: a statistical component that measures changes in the economy or in financial markets, expressed in percentage changes from the previous month, day, or from a base year. The S&P 500 Index is a broad-based measurement of changes in stock market conditions based on the average performance of 500 widely held common stocks, weighted to reflect differences in the number of outstanding shares.

Index fund: a mutual fund whose investment objective is to equal the composite performance of a large group of publicly traded common stocks, like the S&P 500 Composite Stock Index.

Index options: options contracts based on a stock index instead of an individual security. When they are exercised, settlements are made in cash rather than delivery of shares.

Index participation: equity index based on the S&P 500 Stock Index or other indexes in which each stock is represented in the same proportion as it is represented in the index. Also called a "basket."

Insider trading: buying or selling of securities by officers, large shareholders or other key members of a corporation. Under SEC rules, such transactions must be reported within ten days after the close of the month during which the transaction took place.

Instinet: a proprietary trading system owned by Reuters Holdings PLC, which, in 1985, offered foreign investors access to the Amex trading floor. The system allowed immediate two-way communication between foreign investors and the Amex floor specialist.

Institutional Index (XII): index introduced in 1986 which measures the change in the aggregate market value of the 75 major stocks currently held in the highest dollar amounts in institutional portfolios having a market value of more than $100 million in investment funds.

Institutional investor: an organization, such as a bank trust department or an insurance company, which invests substantial sums of money.

Intermarket Trading System (I.T.S): telecommunications link for the NYSE, Amex, Philadelphia, Boston, and Pacific Stock Exchanges allowing traders at any of the five to determine the best available price whenever a customer wants to buy or sell stock.

Issue: a particular class of an organization's securities.

Japan Index (JPN): index introduced in 1990 measuring the aggregate performance of 210 common stocks traded on the Tokyo Stock Exchange. This is a modified price weighted index and closely mirrors the Japanese blue chip stock market. The Amex also introduced short term and long term options on this index in 1990.

Long Term Equity AnticiPation Securities (LEAPS): long term options introduced by the Amex in 1990 and having expirations up to three years out. LEAPS give the investor the right to benefit from the appreciation of a stock or index, above and beyond a preset price.

Liquidity: the characteristic of a stock with enough units outstanding to allow large transactions with only a minor price adjustment; the quality of an asset that allows it to be converted quickly to cash without significant loss in value.

LT-20 Index: index valued at 1/20th of the Major Market Index. The Amex's options on the LT-20 Index are designed to provide a longer-term, more affordable way to trade options on the U.S. stock market.

Major Market Index (XMI): an equity weighted price index introduced in 1983 in which price changes correspond to the aggregate changes in prices of its 20 component blue chip stocks.

Margin account: a brokerage account in which an investor can buy or sell securities on credit. An investor can sometimes borrow up to 50 percent or more of the investment value. When the investment value of margined securities falls below prescribed minimums, a margin call goes out, and the investor must deposit additional money or securities.

Market Expert Surveillance System (MESS): expert system developed for the Amex to assist in initial screening of insider trading referrals. Once the system is activated, trading data is retrieved from Amex records and downloaded into a Lotus spreadsheet program. An analyst uses the spreadsheet to calculate a number of statistics and graph price and volume data. Finally, EXYSYS, a rule-based expert system shell for a personal computer, evaluates data using approximately 160 rules. The result is one of two weighted responses: "open an investigation" or "do not open an investigation." A major advantage of the system is that the same set of rules is applied for each case.

Market maker: one who maintains firm bid and ask prices in a given security or a currency on a continuous basis. The dealer is called a market maker on the over-the-counter market and a specialist on the exchanges.

Market Value Index: see Amex Market Value Index.

Member: a brokerage firm which has at least one seat, or membership, on a major stock exchange. A member firm enjoys such rights and privileges as voting on exchange policy, along with such obligations as the commitment to settle disputes with customers through exchange arbitration procedures.

MidCap 400: Amex index which includes such stocks as Sun Microsystems and U.S. Surgical Corp., popular as an investment representing the sector of the market between the big stocks of the S&P 500 and small stocks.

Monthly Short Interest Ratio: total monthly short sales divided by average daily trading volume. The ratio is a predictor of major market turning points, especially at market bottoms when ratio levels reach 2.0 or better.

Nikkei Stock Average: index of 25 major Japanese stocks. The Amex began trading warrants tied to the Nikkei Stock Average in 1990.

Nikkei 225 Stock Index: the Tokyo equivalent of the S&P 500 Index. The Amex developed the Japan Index to take advantage of fluctuations in the Tokyo market.

Odd lot: a quantity of securities less than a standard trading unit (100 shares).

Odd lot dealer: a member firm of an exchange that buys and sells odd lots of stock (1-99 shares for 100 share units). Customers are commission brokers trading on behalf of their customers.

Oil and Gas Index: see Oil Index.

Oil Index: an index of 30 stocks traded on the Amex. Included are Exxon, Standard of Indiana, and Shell and Standard of Ohio. The Amex began trading options on the Index in 1983.

Option: the privilege or right, but not the obligation to buy (call option) or sell (put option) 100 shares of the underlying stock at a preset price during a preset period of time.

Option Intermarket Communication Linkage: electronic link developed in 1991 by the Amex, the NYSE, the Chicago Board Options Exchange, the Philadelphia Stock Exchange, and the Pacific Stock Exchange under the recommendation of the SEC in order to keep prices the same across all markets.

Over-the-Counter: a market for securities which are not listed or traded on a securities exchange. Trades are made through a phone and computer network connecting dealers in stocks and bonds rather than on the floor of an exchange.

Par value: face value of an instrument (stock or bond).

P/E ratio: current market value of a stock divided by the firm's earnings per share.

Pharmaceutical Index: index designed to represent a cross section of companies involved in various phases of the pharmaceutical industry. In 1992, the Amex introduced options on the index.

Post: the physical location on a stock exchange's trading floor where particular securities are bought and sold by a specialist.

Post Execution Reporting System (PER): computerized order routing system which transmits incoming equity orders to the appropriate trading post. If the orders are executed, PER reports the executions to the exchange member initiating the order.

Price Earnings Index: an index developed by the Amex in the 1960s which indicates the current price level of all common stocks traded on the Amex relative to their current corporate earnings.

Price Level Indicator: a stock market indicator introduced by the Amex in 1966 which reflects daily the average price of the Exchange's common stocks and warrants.

Preserved Rights to Income and Maximum Equity (PRIME): hybrid options contract.

Prudent Man Rule: investment standard reflecting what would be bought or sold by a prudent person of discretion and intelligence who is seeking a reasonable income and preservation of capital.

Put: an option to sell a certain security at a specified price within a specified period of time. A put is usually purchased by one who thinks the price of the underlying stock will fall during the life of the put.

Quick Quote: a computerized touch sensitive screen system developed by Fluke Manufacturing of Everett, Washington, which updates bid and ask prices. Quick Trade updates last-sale prices, and Rapid Quote updates bid/ask prices in multiple options series, simultaneously.

Quotron: a machine providing realtime stock price quotes to brokers.

Rule 144a: SEC legislation designed to encourage capital raising and trading in the private placement market. Only several hundred institutional investors and several dozen investment banks qualify as participants.

Seat: membership on a securities or commodities exchange. Firms owning seats on an exchange are called member firms; firms not owning seats are called non-member firms. Non-member firms must have their orders for listed stocks processed through a member of the exchange where the stocks are listed. Seat prices are set by supply and demand.

Special Claim on Residual Equity (SCORE): hybrid options contract giving its holder the right to all the appreciation on an underlying security above a specified price but not of the dividend income from the stock.

Securities Telecommunications Organization (SECTOR): a member-firm communications network, sponsored by the New York and American Stock Exchanges. The network was initiated under SIAC to offer savings of at least $20 million to member firms in the first five years.

Short interest: the total number of shares of stock that have been sold short and have not yet been purchased for return to lenders.

Short sale: the sale of a security not owned by the seller. An investor "borrows" stock certificates for delivery at the time of short sale. If the seller can buy that stock later at a lower price, a profit results; if the price rises, a loss results.

Securities Industry Automation Corp. (SIAC): a jointly owned subsidiary of the New York and American Stock Exchanges first operational in mid-1972. SIAC began with a budget of $37.6 million and a staff of 1,100 persons, from both clearing corporations. SIAC is owned 2/3 by the NYSE and 1/3 by the Amex.

SITUS: a system for trading privately placed stocks and bonds launched by the Amex, in a joint venture with Reuters Holdings PLC and the NYSE, in an effort to share in the expected boom in the $170 billion private placement market under Rule 144a passed in April by the SEC and to unseat NASD's new electronic Portal system. Companies are exempted from normal disclosure requirements.

Specialist: a broker-dealer member of a stock exchange who has a duty to maintain a fair and orderly market in the stocks in which he/she is registered as a specialist and to act as a broker's broker. The specialist must put the customer's interest above his/her own and must, at times, buy counter to the market in order to equalize supply and demand.

Standard & Poor's 500 Stock Index Depositary Receipt (SPDR): pronounced "Spider," this instrument allows investors to track the performance of the S&P 500 Index. The "Spider" is traded like common stock but looks like an index fund; it gives the investor an interest in a trust holding shares of the stocks in the S&P 500. It promises to match investment returns of the S&P 500 without the high management fees and trading costs of trading the underlying stock.

Spread: the difference between the bid and ask price. The spread narrows or widens according to the supply and demand of the security being traded.

Stock: equity ownership in a corporation, represented by shares that are a claim on the corporation's earnings and assets.

Stock return: same as rate of return; used to measure the total of dividends or interest on the investment plus any increase in price. For example, if a stock is purchased at $25 per share and one year later its price is $28 and $2 in dividends were paid, the total return, if the stock were sold, would be $5 per share, or 20 percent of the original purchase price.

Stock split: a division of outstanding shares of a corporation into a greater or lesser number. The individual shareholder's equity remains the same. In a two-for-one split of a $100 stock, a shareholder owning 100 shares would be given 200 shares, each worth $50. In a reverse two-for-one split, the same shareholder would be given 50 shares, each worth $200.

Stock Watch Alert Terminal (SWAT): the Amex's monitoring device which calls out stock symbols and prints a list of "kickouts."

Ticker: a trade by trade report in chronological order of trades executed, giving stock symbol, price and volume, within minutes of the transaction. Now, the "ticker tape" is an electronic display.

Trader: anyone who buys and sells securities for his or her own account as a dealer or principal rather than as a broker or agent. Also, generally, anyone who buys and sells securities for a profit.

Trading Floor: the physical area where stocks and bonds are bought and sold on a stock exchange.

Transportation Index: an index of 20 stocks introduced in 1984 to measure changes in the aggregate market value of leading corporations in the transportation industry.

Unlisted Stock: securities not listed on an organized exchange but traded as an accommodation to its members; same as over-the-counter stock.

Volatility Index: a contract under development by the Amex in 1992, which would trade against an underlying index of stock volatility.

Warrant: a security issued by a company which gives the holder the right to buy a specified number of its own stock shares at a specified price within a specified period of time.

Yield: percentage rate of return on a stock determined by dividing the annual dividend by the current price.

TITLE INDEX

(References are to record numbers within the body of the text or to titles within Appendix B.)

NAME INDEX

(Index includes personal names of both authors and subjects.
References are to record numbers.)

SUBJECT INDEX

(All references are to record numbers.)